THE ORIGINALITY OF
ST MATTHEW

THE ORIGINALITY OF ST MATTHEW

A Critique of
The Two-Document Hypothesis

BY

B. C. BUTLER
Abbot of Downside

CAMBRIDGE
AT THE UNIVERSITY PRESS
1951

CAMBRIDGE UNIVERSITY PRESS
Cambridge, New York, Melbourne, Madrid, Cape Town,
Singapore, São Paulo, Delhi, Tokyo, Mexico City

Cambridge University Press
The Edinburgh Building, Cambridge CB2 8RU, UK

Published in the United States of America by Cambridge University Press, New York

www.cambridge.org
Information on this title: www.cambridge.org/9780521233033

© Cambridge University Press 1951

First published 1951
First paperback edition 2011

A catalogue record for this publication is available from the British Library

ISBN 978-0-521-23303-3 Paperback

PREFACE

At the end of the first quarter of the present century the Two-Document hypothesis, the theory, that is to say, that our First and Third Gospels depend on the Second Gospel and on a conjectural source of which Q has become the usual designation, was regarded in many scholarly circles as no longer requiring proof, criticism or defence. It was on the way to becoming, if it had not already become, less a hypothesis than a dogma.

But criticism does not stand still. Wellhausen's work on the editorial aspect of St Mark's Gospel was the prelude to the rise of the school of Form Criticism, which contemptuously rejected the supposition that that Gospel is virtually a mere transcript of the oral teaching of an eyewitness. On the other side of the Atlantic the eminent Professor J. H. Ropes admitted that the grounds on which Q's existence is inferred by modern scholars are 'far less secure than is commonly represented or supposed', and that the theory that St Luke's Gospel draws its Q passages from St Matthew's 'has never been shown to be impossible'.

The investigation recorded in the following pages was not, in the main, carried out with direct reference to the Form Critics. Yet it is hoped that what it has in fact achieved is to make possible a synthesis of all that is objectively sound in the work of that modern school with the elements of truth discovered by the documentary critics of the generations preceding them. If the outcome of the investigation may be said to contradict the conclusions of the older critics, it will I hope be agreed that this has been the result of a faithful application of their methods.

In the following pages 'Matthew', 'Mark', etc., mean respectively the several Gospels, and their authors are referred to as 'St Matthew', etc. 'Triple tradition' means those sections in which all three Synoptic Gospels are parallel, excepting only those where Mark is not the connecting-link between Matthew and Luke. 'Marcan passage' means a passage in Matthew or Luke directly (as is usually maintained) connected with a parallel passage in Mark; these passages constitute the 'Marcan tradition', a more inclusive term than 'Triple tradition'. By 'Q passages' I mean such parts of Matthew and Luke as are parallel with one another but are not parts of the Marcan tradition. These terms are all used for convenience and without prejudice. I have regularly used A. Huck's *Synopse der drei Ersten Evangelien*, 6th edition (Tübingen, 1922). This edition has an advantage over the 9th (English) edition inasmuch as when a passage is printed out of sequence this fact is regularly indicated in it by a difference of type.

I am grateful to the editor of the *Harvard Theological Review* for permission to embody the substance (and to a large extent the wording) of my *St Luke's Debt to St Matthew*, which was published in that periodical in October 1939 (vol. XXXII).

I also express my thanks to the University Press, and my appreciation of the accurate care that has been expended on a difficult manuscript.

B. C. BUTLER

DOWNSIDE ABBEY
February, 1951

CONTENTS

CHAPTER I

THE Q HYPOTHESIS TESTED

About two hundred verses of Matthew have parallels in Luke but no parallels in Mark. What is the explanation of this fact? Those who believe that Mark is the earliest of the extant Gospels and was used extensively by St Matthew and St Luke as a source for their 'Marcan' material usually put forward the Q hypothesis to explain these non-Marcan agreements. It is suggested that both evangelists derived these verses from a written source, no longer extant, to which the title Q is conventionally assigned. This source, if it ever existed, must have been in the Greek language, as many of the verbal parallels in the Q passages are too close to be explicable as independent translations of a Semitic original.

It is a fundamental principle of critical method that *sources and their relations are not to be multiplied unnecessarily*. This principle lies behind Turner's magisterial comment with reference to another aspect of the Synoptic problem: 'The hypothesis that Matthew and Luke had before them not our St Mark but an earlier document very like it...is obviously a less simple hypothesis than that their source was just the Mark we know: and so far it would always have been to my mind less probable. I have an incurable preference for simple solutions of literary problems.'[1] We therefore approach the examination of the Q hypothesis with the sense that, as against direct derivation of Luke's Q passages from Matthew (or *vice versa*), the burden of proof is upon the theory that invents a conjectural document and substitutes two processes of derivation for one. The present chapter will draw attention to four or five Q passages where direct derivation of Luke from Matthew is a far more satisfactory critical

[1] *The Study of the New Testament 1883 and 1920*, p. 38, by C. H. Turner (Clarendon Press, 1926). Turner also quotes Sanday, *Oxford Studies in the Synoptic Problem*, p. 26: 'The suggestions made in this essay are all very simple. It is just their simplicity which has had the chief attraction for me.' I venture to adapt these words with reference to the subject-matter of the present chapter: the simplicity of the theory of direct utilization of one Gospel in another gives it an initial advantage over the theory of the influence of an unknown document.

But reality is complex

hypothesis than their common derivation from a third document. I assume the dependence of Luke on Mark in the Marcan tradition.[1]

(1) *The Parable of the Mustard-seed*

Mark iv. 30–2	Matt. xiii. 31–3	Luke xiii. 18–21
καὶ ἔλεγεν· πῶς ὁμοιώσωμεν τὴν βασιλείαν τοῦ θεοῦ, ἢ ἐν τίνι αὐτὴν παραβολῇ θῶμεν; 31. ὡς κόκκῳ σινάπεως, ὃς ὅταν σπαρῇ ἐπὶ τῆς γῆς, μικρότερον ὂν πάντων τῶν σπερμάτων τῶν ἐπὶ τῆς γῆς, 32. καὶ ὅταν σπαρῇ, ἀναβαίνει καὶ γίνεται μεῖζον πάντων τῶν λαχάνων, καὶ ποιεῖ κλάδους μεγάλους, ὥστε δύνασθαι ὑπὸ τὴν σκιὰν αὐτοῦ τὰ πετεινὰ τοῦ οὐρανοῦ κατασκηνοῦν.	ἄλλην παραβολὴν παρέθηκεν αὐτοῖς λέγων· ὁμοία ἐστὶν ἡ βασιλεία τῶν οὐρανῶν κόκκῳ σινάπεως, ὃν λαβὼν ἄνθρωπος ἔσπειρεν ἐν τῷ ἀγρῷ αὐτοῦ· 32. ὃ μικρότερον μέν ἐστιν πάντων τῶν σπερμάτων, ὅταν δὲ αὐξηθῇ, μεῖζον τῶν λαχάνων ἐστὶν καὶ γίνεται δένδρον, ὥστε ἐλθεῖν τὰ πετεινὰ τοῦ οὐρανοῦ καὶ κατασκηνοῦν ἐν τοῖς κλάδοις αὐτοῦ. 33. ἄλλην παραβολὴν ἐλάλησεν αὐτοῖς· ὁμοία ἐστὶν ἡ βασιλεία τῶν οὐρανῶν ζύμῃ, ἣν λαβοῦσα γυνὴ ἐνέκρυψεν εἰς ἀλεύρου σάτα τρία, ἕως οὗ ἐζυμώθη ὅλον.	Ἔλεγεν οὖν· τίνι ὁμοία ἐστὶν ἡ βασιλεία τοῦ θεοῦ, καὶ τίνι ὁμοιώσω αὐτήν; 19. ὁμοία ἐστὶν κόκκῳ σινάπεως, ὃν λαβὼν ἄνθρωπος ἔβαλεν εἰς κῆπον ἑαυτοῦ, καὶ ηὔξησεν καὶ ἐγένετο εἰς δένδρον, καὶ τὰ πετεινὰ τοῦ οὐρανοῦ κατεσκήνωσεν ἐν τοῖς κλάδοις αὐτοῦ. 20. καὶ πάλιν εἶπεν· τίνι ὁμοιώσω τὴν βασιλείαν τοῦ θεοῦ; 21. ὁμοία ἐστὶν ζύμῃ, ἣν λαβοῦσα γυνὴ ἔκρυψεν εἰς ἀλεύρου σάτα τρία, ἕως οὗ ἐζυμώθη ὅλον.

(Full underlining shows Matthew's agreements with Luke against Mark, dotted underlining with Mark against Luke.)

[1] It may be as well to draw attention here to the particular application of critical principles which is invoked throughout this chapter. It is the same application that is paramount in the study of the Marcan tradition:

Where three documents, A, B and C, give substantially the same information; and when numerous agreements are found between all three, together with a notable quantity of agreements between A and B 'against' C, and between B and C 'against' A, but with no significant agreements between A and C 'against' B, then the critical presumption is that A and B are directly connected, and also B and C; but that A and C are only indirectly connected by virtue of the direct connexion of each with B. The natural solutions, in other words, of the critical problem presented by these data are three in number, and only three:

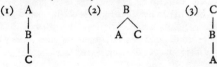

The Lucan passage is from a non-Marcan context, and it is a recognized feature of St Luke's use of Mark that he keeps passages borrowed from Mark in the context in which he found them. As Streeter says: 'Luke... hardly ever departs from Mark's order, and only in trifling ways. On the other hand, whenever Luke substitutes for an item in Mark a parallel version from another source, he always gives it *in a different context* from the item in Mark which it replaces.'[1] Hence Luke's agreement with Mark against Matthew, in introducing the Mustard-seed parable with a double question, is to be explained as reminiscence rather than as normal literary utilization. Similarly, it was perhaps by reminiscence of Mark iv. 26 that St Luke wrote ἔβαλεν in this passage.[2]

Clearly then this is not a straightforward instance of the Marcan tradition. Beside the non-Marcan context of Luke's passage we have to take note of the fact that there are, along with agreements of all three Gospels, significant agreements of Matthew and Mark against Luke, and of Matthew and Luke against Mark, but *a relative absence of agreements of Mark and Luke against Matthew.* Furthermore, both Matthew and Luke, but not Mark, append immediately to the Mustard-seed parable its twin, the parable of the Leaven.[3]

In such cases I call B the 'intermediary', 'connecting-link' or 'middle term' between A and C.

It should be noted that the data are not satisfied by the following 'solution':

Thisis not a solution, because it does not explain the agreements between *all three* documents, which are part of the assumed data; the so-called 'solution' does not explain why A and C ever agree together at all. In the Marcan tradition these considerations lead to the conclusion that Mark is the connecting-link between Matthew and Luke.

[1] *The Four Gospels,* p. 162. To those who use Huck's *Synopsis* it is perhaps worth while to point out that, by an exception, the sequence of Luke is there inverted at one point, Luke vi. 12–16 being printed after Luke vi. 17–19.

[2] I use the word 'reminiscence' to indicate that Luke, in writing one passage, shows that he has knowledge of another passage, whether in his own works or in a source, although he is not using the passage in question as his primary source at the moment. These reminiscences would form an interesting study in themselves. Cf. Luke i. 69, 70 with Acts iv. 24, 25; Luke ix. 61, 62 with xiv. 33–5; xii. 14 with Acts vii. 27. St Luke has pondered his various materials and is full of echoes, intentional or unintentional.

[3] For other twin-parables, cf. the Hidden Treasure and the Pearl of Great Price, the Tares and the Net, the Lost Sheep and the Lost Drachma.

Streeter's explanation [1] of the data here is that the parables of the Mustard-seed and of the Leaven formed part of Q, in which they occurred in immediate juxtaposition. Mark's version of the former is probably independent of Q, the parable being thus one of several items in which Mark and Q 'overlapped'. Luke, he suggests, has taken the two parables from Q, and as he has them in a non-Marcan context and with practically no agreements with Mark against Matthew we may presume that he has given them in relatively pure Q form. Matthew, on the other hand, who gives them in the same context as Mark's context for the Mustard-seed, has 'conflated' the Q and Marcan versions of the Mustard-seed parable. 'We see that practically every word in Matthew is drawn from one or other of his two sources. [But the differences between the Marcan and Lucan (i.e. the Q) version of the parable are *entirely unimportant. They in no way affect the general sense, and no one antecedently would have expected that Matthew would take the trouble to combine the two versions'* (my italics). We note, in fact, that Matt. xiii. 31 a is narrative, derived presumably from Mark v. 30 (discourse); v. 31 b is Q with one word (ἔσπειρεν) inserted from Mark; v. 32 a is Mark except αὐξηθῇ and καὶ γίνεται δένδρον (both from Q); v. 32 b is Q except ὥστε c. inf. (from Mark); v. 33 is Q. [And while composing this patchwork by invisible mending, Matthew has (a) straightened out the false concords in Mark vv. 31, 32; (b) created the climax from seed through herb to tree by taking 'herb' from Mark and 'tree' from Luke—his rhetoric is thus more effective than that of either of his sources.]

Such a mode of procedure on St Matthew's part is not indeed impossible.[2] But it is so improbable, and the success which has attended it is so extremely improbable, that one may be forgiven for asking whether there is no other more satisfactory explanation of the data. And a reference to the phenomena in the genuine triple Marcan tradition and to the generally accepted explanation of them

---

[1] *The Four Gospels*, pp. 246 ff.

[2] A distant parallel will be found in the Oxateuchist's conflation of a section of *Ap. Constitutions* VIII with phrases from the Prologue to *The Apostolic Tradition* of Hippolytus. See Dom R. H. Connolly in *The Journal of Theological Studies*, XXII, pp. 356–61. But the borrowed pieces there are longer than the several half-verses of Matthew in our passage, and there is little insertion of odd words and phrases from one source into the text borrowed from the other.

there at once gives us, by parallel reasoning, a simple solution of our own problem.

It is well known[1] that the data in the Marcan tradition are: (1) agreements of all three Gospels; (2) agreements of Matthew and Mark against Luke, and of Mark and Luke against Matthew; (3) relative absence of agreements of Matthew and Luke against Mark. It must be agreed that these data leave us with a choice between three hypotheses:[2]

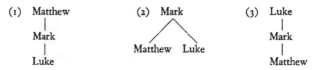

(1) Matthew
    |
    Mark
    |
    Luke

(2) Mark
    /   \
Matthew Luke

(3) Luke
    |
    Mark
    |
    Matthew

Every serious scholar recognizes that to explain Mark as a conflation of Matthew and Luke is a surrender of critical principles. And of course it is agreed that no. (3), involving dependence of Mark on Luke, is not the correct solution.

In the passage now under discussion, however, the data are: (1) agreements of all three Gospels; (2) agreements of Mark and Matthew against Luke, and of Matthew and Luke against Mark; (3) relative absence of agreements between Mark and Luke against Matthew. By applying the same reasoning as is to be accepted with reference to the Marcan tradition we are left with a choice, in explanation of these data, between three hypotheses:

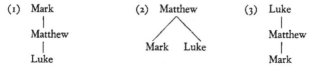

(1) Mark
    |
    Matthew
    |
    Luke

(2) Matthew
    /   \
  Mark   Luke

(3) Luke
    |
    Matthew
    |
    Mark

We reject no. (3), because it would imply that Luke existed before Mark, and it is agreed that in fact St Luke used Mark in the Marcan tradition. And whichever of the other two hypotheses we prefer, we find that, in this Q passage, *Luke derives from Matthew*. To explain Matthew here as a conflation of Mark and Luke (i.e. Q) is a surrender of critical principle exactly similar to the surrender that would be involved in explaining Mark, in the ordinary 'triple tradition', as a conflation of Matthew and Luke.

[1] *Vide* ch. v *infra*.   [2] *Vide* p. 2, n. 1 *supra*.

If we now turn back to the three parallel texts, we note that Matthew's version is a more harmonious one, in semi-poetic (Semitic?) rhythm, than either of the others, a result not likely to be achieved by the conflation of the wording of two prose sources. And examining Luke, we see that the author has changed 'field' into 'garden', possibly because he felt that a single seed of mustard would be lost in a field (he has a curiously literal, numerative, mind); and he has omitted the statements that the seed is the smallest of seeds and the plant the greatest of herbs, perhaps to save space, perhaps because he disliked the hyperbole, which is, however, obviously authentic. Thus his divergences from Matthew do not suggest fidelity to an independent source but the play of his own editorial temperament.[1] His dependence on Matthew may be the explanation of his use here (alone in Luke and Acts except Acts xxi. 26 and probably, with the future, Luke xiii. 35) of ἕως with the indicative; Matthew has this usage in our passage, and also at i. 25, ii. 9, v. 25 where the meaning is 'while', xxiv. 39.

There can thus be no doubt that the application of sound critical principles to these parallel passages, so far from making necessary or recommending the Q hypothesis, tells strongly against that hypothesis. The passages which follow in this chapter will reinforce this inference, and the whole set, taken together, make it practically impossible to deny Luke's immediate dependence on Matthew.

(2) *On giving Scandal*

The Lucan passage is again in non-Marcan context, and its agreements with Mark against Matthew (εἰ, περίκειται and ἔρριπται εἰς, cf. βέβληται εἰς) may therefore be regarded as due to reminiscence rather than copying. As in the previous case, we have agreements of all three Gospels, agreements of Matthew and Mark against Luke,

---

[1] It is one of the paradoxes to which Streeter has been driven by his theories, that he supposes the Lucan versions of Q passages to be, on the whole, more faithful to their original than the Matthaean. 'It is probable that, allowance being made for a slight polishing of the Greek, the form in which the Q sayings appear in Luke is...on the whole more original' (*op. cit.* p. 291). He is thus brought into contradiction with the conclusions of Harnack's careful and thorough study of the Q passages in *The Sayings of Jesus*. Cf. also Burney, *The Poetry of our Lord*, p. 88 (quoted below, p. 31).

6

THE Q HYPOTHESIS TESTED

and agreements of Matthew and Luke against Mark. The natural explanation is therefore, as before, that Matthew is the intermediary between Mark and Luke; that is, that Matthew copied Mark or *vice versa*, while Luke copied Matthew.[1]

Mark ix. 42	Matt. xviii. 6, 7	Luke xvii. 1 b, 2
καὶ ὃς ἂν σκανδαλίσῃ ἕνα τῶν μικρῶν τούτων τῶν πιστευόντων, καλόν ἐστιν αὐτῷ μᾶλλον εἰ περίκειται μύλος ὀνικὸς περὶ τὸν τράχηλον αὐτοῦ καὶ βέβληται εἰς τὴν θάλασσαν.	ὃς δ' ἂν σκανδαλίσῃ ἕνα τῶν μικρῶν τούτων τῶν πιστευόντων εἰς ἐμέ, συμφέρει αὐτῷ ἵνα κρεμασθῇ μύλος ὀνικὸς περὶ τὸν τράχηλον αὐτοῦ καὶ καταποντισθῇ ἐν τῷ πελάγει τῆς θαλάσσης. 7. οὐαὶ τῷ κόσμῳ ἀπὸ τῶν σκανδάλων· ἀνάγκη γάρ ἐστιν ἐλθεῖν τὰ σκάνδαλα, πλὴν οὐαὶ τῷ ἀνθρώπῳ δι' οὗ τὸ σκάνδαλον ἔρχεται.	ἀνένδεκτόν ἐστιν τοῦ τὰ σκάνδαλα μὴ ἐλθεῖν, οὐαὶ δὲ δι' οὗ ἔρχεται· 2. λυσιτελεῖ αὐτῷ εἰ λίθος μυλικὸς περίκειται περὶ τὸν τράχηλον αὐτοῦ καὶ ἔρριπται εἰς τὴν θάλασσαν, ἢ ἵνα σκανδαλίσῃ τῶν μικρῶν τούτων ἕνα. (Underlined are Luke's agreements with Mark against Matthew.)

If, however, we seek to explain Matthew's agreements with Luke against Mark by the dependence of both of them on Q, we have to face the problem of *all* Luke's agreements with Mark (explained by the natural hypothesis as agreements directly with Matthew and so indirectly with Mark, together with Lucan reminiscence of Mark). Thus either (*a*) Luke *v.* 2 is copied from Mark, with which it agrees nearly verbatim, though the order is inverted. This will imply the odd coincidence that *both Matthew and Luke have independently* decided to combine Mark and Q in this passage. It will also offend against the canon that Luke does not copy Mark in non-Marcan contexts. As Streeter observes (*op. cit.* p. 204): 'While there is no reason to suppose that Luke would have religiously avoided introducing an odd saying or a word or two from Mark in his central section, yet as a matter of fact he has done so, if at all, to an extent that is practically negligible.' We shall discover cases, however, where Luke's 'reminiscence' almost amounts to copying.[2] Or (*b*) Luke *v.* 2, despite its virtual identity with Mark, is nevertheless derived from Q. But this (i) fails to explain Luke's τῶν μικρῶν τούτων ἕνα, which is explained in the other two Gospels by the

---

[1] For the same reason as before, we cannot make Luke the source of Matthew.

[2] λυσιτελεῖ is a Lucan stylistic alteration (perhaps more probably of Matthew's συμφέρει than of Mark's καλόν ἐστιν). λίθος μυλικός (more vague than μύλος ὀνικός, *mola asinaria*) is also probably secondary. Of course Luke xvii. 1 b is less original in form than Matt. xviii. 7; cf. Harnack, *Sayings of Jesus*, p. 28.

7

previous context, showing that our Lord had an actual child there as the illustration of his words; (ii) produces such a close similarity between Q and Mark here as would strongly suggest the dependence of one on the other, with the consequence that the relations in this short passage would be as follows:

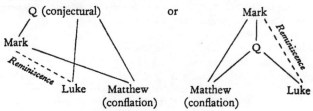

i.e. no less than five relationships, a conjectural source, and a conflation!

It must be emphatically stated that, whichever horn of the dilemma, whether Luke's conflation of Mark and Q, or Mark's dependence on Q (or vice versa), is adopted, the Q solution is repugnant to critical good sense.

The natural and adequate solution is of course:

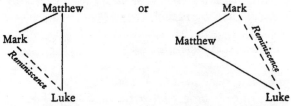

i.e. three relationships, no conjectural source and no conflation. Readers may be reminded that the superiority of the Copernican heliocentric over the Ptolemaic geocentric theory was precisely that it 'saved the appearances' with a greater economy and simplicity of assumed motions.

(3) *The Beelzebub Controversy*

As in the two instances already discussed, Luke's version of this controversy is in non-Marcan context; so is his separate verse, xii. 10. Verse 18*b* may be a reminiscence of Mark iii. 30, and the phrase τῷ εἰς τὸ ἅγιον πνεῦμα βλασφημήσαντι in xii. 10 may be a reminiscence of Mark iii. 29. Luke xi. 17 ἐφ' ἑαυτήν may be from

THE Q HYPOTHESIS TESTED

Mark iii. 23–30	Matt. xii. 25–32	Luke xi. 17–23; xii. 10
καὶ προσκαλεσάμενος αὐτοὺς ἐν παραβολαῖς ἔλεγεν αὐτοῖς· πῶς δύναται σατανᾶς σατανᾶν ἐκβάλλειν; 24. καὶ ἐὰν βασιλεία ἐφ᾽ ἑαυτὴν μερισθῇ, οὐ δύναται σταθῆναι ἡ βασιλεία ἐκείνη. 25. καὶ ἐὰν οἰκία ἐφ᾽ ἑαυτὴν μερισθῇ, οὐ δυνήσεται ἡ οἰκία ἐκείνη σταθῆναι. 26. καὶ εἰ ὁ σατανᾶς ἀνέστη ἐφ᾽ ἑαυτόν, ἐμερίσθη καὶ οὐ δύναται στῆναι ἀλλὰ τέλος ἔχει.	εἰδὼς δὲ τὰς ἐνθυμήσεις αὐτῶν εἶπεν αὐτοῖς· πᾶσα βασιλεία μερισθεῖσα καθ᾽ ἑαυτῆς ἐρημοῦται, καὶ πᾶσα πόλις ἢ οἰκία μερισθεῖσα καθ᾽ ἑαυτῆς οὐ σταθήσεται. 26. καὶ εἰ ὁ σατανᾶς τὸν σατανᾶν ἐκβάλλει, ἐφ᾽ ἑαυτὸν ἐμερίσθη· πῶς οὖν σταθήσεται ἡ βασιλεία αὐτοῦ; 27. καὶ εἰ ἐγὼ ἐν Βεελζεβοὺλ ἐκβάλλω τὰ δαιμόνια, οἱ υἱοὶ ὑμῶν ἐν τίνι ἐκβάλλουσιν; διὰ τοῦτο κριταὶ ἔσονται ὑμῶν. 28. εἰ δὲ ἐν πνεύματι θεοῦ ἐγὼ ἐκβάλλω τὰ δαιμόνια, ἄρα ἔφθασεν ἐφ᾽ ὑμᾶς ἡ βασιλεία τοῦ θεοῦ.	αὐτὸς δὲ εἰδὼς αὐτῶν τὰ διανοήματα εἶπεν αὐτοῖς· πᾶσα βασιλεία διαμερισθεῖσα ἐφ᾽ ἑαυτὴν ἐρημοῦται, καὶ οἶκος ἐπὶ οἶκον πίπτει. 18. εἰ δὲ καὶ ὁ σατανᾶς ἐφ᾽ ἑαυτὸν διεμερίσθη, πῶς σταθήσεται ἡ βασιλεία αὐτοῦ; ὅτι λέγετε ἐν Βεελζεβοὺλ ἐκβάλλειν με τὰ δαιμόνια. 19. εἰ δὲ ἐγὼ ἐν Βεελζεβοὺλ ἐκβάλλω τὰ δαιμόνια, οἱ υἱοὶ ὑμῶν ἐν τίνι ἐκβάλλουσιν; διὰ τοῦτο αὐτοὶ κριταὶ ἔσονται ὑμῶν. 20. εἰ δὲ ἐν δακτύλῳ θεοῦ ἐκβάλλω τὰ δαιμόνια, ἄρα ἔφθασεν ἐφ᾽ ὑμᾶς ἡ βασιλεία τοῦ θεοῦ.
27. ἀλλ᾽ οὐ δύναται οὐδεὶς εἰς τὴν οἰκίαν τοῦ ἰσχυροῦ εἰσελθὼν τὰ σκεύη αὐτοῦ διαρπάσαι, ἐὰν μὴ πρῶτον τὸν ἰσχυρὸν δήσῃ, καὶ τότε τὴν οἰκίαν αὐτοῦ διαρπάσει.	29. ἢ πῶς δύναταί τις εἰσελθεῖν εἰς τὴν οἰκίαν τοῦ ἰσχυροῦ καὶ τὰ σκεύη αὐτοῦ ἁρπάσαι, ἐὰν μὴ πρῶτον δήσῃ τὸν ἰσχυρόν, καὶ τότε τὴν οἰκίαν αὐτοῦ διαρπάσῃ;	21. ὅταν ὁ ἰσχυρὸς καθωπλισμένος φυλάσσῃ τὴν ἑαυτοῦ αὐλήν, ἐν εἰρήνῃ ἐστὶν τὰ ὑπάρχοντα αὐτοῦ· 22. ἐπὰν δὲ ἰσχυρότερος αὐτοῦ ἐπελθὼν νικήσῃ αὐτόν, τὴν πανοπλίαν αὐτοῦ αἴρει, ἐφ᾽ ᾗ ἐπεποίθει, καὶ τὰ σκῦλα αὐτοῦ διαδίδωσιν. 23. ὁ μὴ ὢν μετ᾽ ἐμοῦ κατ᾽ ἐμοῦ ἐστιν, καὶ ὁ μὴ συνάγων μετ᾽ ἐμοῦ σκορπίζει.
28. ἀμὴν λέγω ὑμῖν ὅτι πάντα ἀφεθήσεται τοῖς υἱοῖς τῶν ἀνθρώπων τὰ ἁμαρτήματα καὶ αἱ βλασφημίαι, ὅσα ἂν βλασφημήσωσιν·	30. ὁ μὴ ὢν μετ᾽ ἐμοῦ κατ᾽ ἐμοῦ ἐστιν, καὶ ὁ μὴ συνάγων μετ᾽ ἐμοῦ σκορπίζει. 31. διὰ τοῦτο λέγω ὑμῖν, πᾶσα ἁμαρτία καὶ βλασφημία ἀφεθήσεται τοῖς ἀνθρώποις, ἡ δὲ τοῦ πνεύματος βλασφημία οὐκ ἀφεθήσεται. 32. καὶ ὃς ἐὰν εἴπῃ λόγον κατὰ τοῦ υἱοῦ τοῦ ἀνθρώπου, ἀφεθήσεται αὐτῷ·	xii. 10. καὶ πᾶς ὃς ἐρεῖ λόγον εἰς τὸν υἱὸν τοῦ ἀνθρώπου, ἀφεθήσεται αὐτῷ· τῷ δὲ εἰς τὸ ἅγιον πνεῦμα βλασφημήσαντι οὐκ ἀφεθήσεται.
29. ὃς δ᾽ ἂν βλασφημήσῃ εἰς τὸ πνεῦμα τὸ ἅγιον, οὐκ ἔχει ἄφεσιν εἰς τὸν αἰῶνα, ἀλλὰ ἔνοχος ἔσται αἰωνίου ἁμαρτήματος. 30. ὅτι ἔλεγον· πνεῦμα ἀκάθαρτον ἔχει.	ὃς δ᾽ ἂν εἴπῃ κατὰ τοῦ πνεύματος τοῦ ἁγίου, οὐκ ἀφεθήσεται αὐτῷ οὔτε ἐν τούτῳ τῷ αἰῶνι οὔτε ἐν τῷ μέλλοντι.	

Mark, or from Matt. xii. 26 ἐφ᾽ ἑαυτόν. Otherwise there are no agreements of Luke with Mark against Matthew, and as before we must choose between Q and Luke's direct dependence on Matthew. It should be noted that, in the introduction to the passage quoted, Luke xi. 14 finds its real parallel not in Matt. xii. 22, 23, but in the twin of this passage at Matt. ix. 32, 33. And Luke v. 16, which at first sight looks like a parallel to Matt. xii. 38, the verse immediately succeeding the Beelzebub discourse in Matthew, is in fact parallel to Mark viii. 11, Matt. xvi. 1. These complications are discussed in the next chapter (pp. 25, 27).

Streeter's views on the Beelzebub controversy changed between about 1911 and 1924. In the *Oxford Studies in the Synoptic Problem*, pp. 169–71, he argues the case for Mark's dependence on Q in this passage. He points out that Matt. xii. 27, 28 and Luke xi. 19, 20 are original in this context, since they are pointless except as a reply to the challenge 'By Beelzebub he casts out devils'. Q, then, he infers, must also have contained Matt. xii. 24, Luke xi. 15.[1] He notes also that Matt. vv. 25, 26 agree with Luke against Mark not only in twelve words but in the general form and construction of the sentences; they therefore were also in Q, which—he further argues—contained also Matt. xii. 32, Luke xii. 10, 'though probably as in Luke in a different context'. It will be observed that by now we have attributed to Q the contents of the whole passage, Matt. xii. 22–32, except vv. 23, 29 and 31; and *there is no reason why these also should not have belonged to it*.[2] This is an unconscious admission that Luke xi. 14–23 and xii. 10 may be explained perfectly well by direct dependence on Matthew, with some slight reminiscence of Mark. It is hardly necessary to add that the application of normal critical principles shows that Matthew, here again, is the middle term between Mark and Luke, and that therefore—whether Matthew depends on Mark or vice versa—the proper conclusion is that Luke depends on Matthew.

In *The Four Gospels*, however, Streeter abandons his previous

---

[1] Thus Q was not only discourse. The difficulty is to prevent Q's growth. It tends continually to become a Gospel, in fact to become Matthew.

[2] Verse 23a or its equivalent is guaranteed as Q by Luke xi. 14b; v. 29 or its equivalent by Luke xi. 21. And it is not reasonable to suppose that, having deserted Mark for Q in the whole of the rest of this section, Matthew inserted v. 31 from Mark.

view that Mark is here dependent on Q, and maintains that Matthew has 'carefully conflated'[1] Mark and Q; attributing to him, as a glance at the underlinings in the passages as set out above will show, a virtuosity as superhuman as it would be futile. Luke, supposed to be relatively pure Q, simply gives Lucan style and vocabulary except where it agrees with Matthew. Note the following:

Luke xi. 17. αὐτός.
διανοήματα (cf. Luke's fondness for κατανοέω).
διαμερισθεῖσα (Matthew 1; Mark 1; Luke 6. Luke prefers compounds with διά).
οἶκος ἐπὶ οἶκον πίπτει (?) (reminiscence of Mark xiii. 2 or Matt. xxiv. 2?).
xi. 18. δὲ καί.
διεμερίσθη.
xi. 19. αὐτοί.
xi. 20. ἐν δακτύλῳ θεοῦ (cf. Exod. viii. 19; xxxi. 18; Deut. ix. 10, Ps. viii. 4 = R.V. viii. 3. Luke has many LXX reminiscences).
xi. 21. φυλάσσῃ.
εἰρήνη.
τὰ ὑπάρχοντα.
xi. 22. ἐπελθών.
ἐπεποίθει.
διαδίδωσιν.
xii. 10. πᾶς ὅς.
τῷ... βλασφημήσαντι (participle).

And on the other hand, note v. 19 διὰ τοῦτο (elsewhere in Luke only xi. 49 = Matt. xxiii. 34; xii. 22 = Matt. vi. 25; xiv. 20 preceded by καί; Acts once, in quotation); cf. Matthew here, in the two passages referred to, and also xii. 31; xiii. 13; xiii. 52; xiv. 2; xviii. 23; xxi. 43; xxiv. 44. συνάγειν (xi. 23) is a favourite word with Matthew, rare in Luke; common in Acts of meetings. Luke xi. 21, 22 is a pleasant Greek prose version, but Matt. xii. 29, with its Semitic *inclusio*, is doubtless far closer to what our Lord actually said. Thus, whatever his source, Luke has rewritten it, and its vocabulary cannot be distinguished from that of Matthew.

If we now turn back to Matthew itself, we find a passage of harmonious literary and logical architecture, superior in both respects to Mark's and Luke's versions: a general principle receives two illustrations and an application (vv. 25, 26), a dilemma is followed

[1] P. 211.

by its justification (*vv.* 27-9),[1] and this by a summary of the argument (*v.* 30, which may be regarded as a general principle stated personally); and the implied conclusion is made the basis of a solemn warning to the Pharisees, who have ascribed a work of the Holy Spirit to diabolic power. The ensuing passage, *vv.* 33-7, carries on the same harmonious line of thought, in similar flowing rhythm; it is without a parallel in Mark, and the Lucan parallel is in a different context.

Can we believe that, for the creation of the first of these harmonious paragraphs (*vv.* 25, 26), Matthew found in Mark precisely what he needed to insert into the middle of the Q passage? And that, for the last of them, he found his first ἀφεθήσεται in Mark, and the last two in Q? In that case, we can only say that his two sources complemented each other, with a preordained harmony, like the two pieces of a wishbone. The alternative is to say that these harmonies existed ready-made in Q; in other words that Q in this passage is indistinguishable from Matthew. In fact, Q *is* Matthew.

There are two further observations to be made in this connexion: (1) Luke xii. 10 is a typical Lucan mitigation of a severe saying; in its Lucan context it almost seems to contradict the verse which it follows. (2) Luke's δακτύλῳ θεοῦ may seem to some more original than Matthew's πνεύματι θεοῦ. But the latter prepares the way for the warning about blasphemy against the Holy Spirit and our explanation of Luke's variation as a Septuagintalism is therefore probably correct.

APPENDIX TO SECTION 3

The Marcan version of the Beelzebub controversy is in a section of Mark (iii. 20-35) omitted by Luke, who here inserts his Little Interpolation. To the last five verses of this omission (Mark iii. 31-5, immediately following the Beelzebub controversy) there is a parallel

---

[1] Note how the triumph over the Kingdom of Satan, evidenced by the success of our Lord's exorcisms, proves that the opposite Kingdom, that of God, has arrived: Satan could not be despoiled if our Lord had not 'bound' him already, thus inaugurating God's Reign. This point is obscured in Mark through the absence of anything to correspond to Matthew's *v.* 28. It was probably to point this contrast that Matthew here writes βασιλεία τοῦ θεοῦ. Elsewhere, except xxi. 31, 43, he always prefers βασιλεία τῶν οὐρανῶν, or τοῦ πατρὸς σοῦ (μοῦ κτλ.), or βασιλεία without a genitive.

at Luke viii. 19–21; the Matthaean parallel is in the 'Marcan tradition' context, at Matt. xii. 46–50:

Mark iii. 31–5	Matt. xii. 46–50	Luke viii. 19–21
καὶ ἔρχεται ἡ μήτηρ αὐτοῦ καὶ οἱ ἀδελφοὶ αὐτοῦ, καὶ ἔξω στήκοντες ἀπέστειλαν πρὸς αὐτὸν καλοῦντες αὐτόν. 32. καὶ ἐκάθητο περὶ αὐτὸν ὄχλος, καὶ λέγουσιν αὐτῷ· ἰδοὺ ἡ μήτηρ σου καὶ οἱ ἀδελφοί σου καὶ αἱ ἀδελφαί σου ἔξω ζητοῦσίν σε. 33. καὶ ἀποκριθεὶς αὐτοῖς λέγει· τίς ἐστιν ἡ μήτηρ μου καὶ οἱ ἀδελφοί μου; 34. καὶ περιβλεψάμενος τοὺς περὶ αὐτὸν κύκλῳ καθημένους λέγει· ἴδε ἡ μήτηρ μου καὶ οἱ ἀδελφοί μου. 35. ὃς ἂν ποιήσῃ τὸ θέλημα τοῦ θεοῦ, οὗτος ἀδελφός μου καὶ ἀδελφὴ καὶ μήτηρ ἐστίν.	ἔτι αὐτοῦ λαλοῦντος τοῖς ὄχλοις, ἰδοὺ ἡ μήτηρ καὶ οἱ ἀδελφοὶ αὐτοῦ εἱστήκεισαν ἔξω ζητοῦντες αὐτῷ λαλῆσαι. [47. εἶπεν δέ τις αὐτῷ· ἰδοὺ ἡ μήτηρ σου καὶ οἱ ἀδελφοί σου ἔξω ἑστήκασιν ζητοῦντές σοι λαλῆσαι.] 48. ὁ δὲ ἀποκριθεὶς εἶπεν τῷ λέγοντι αὐτῷ· τίς ἐστιν ἡ μήτηρ μου, καὶ τίνες εἰσὶν οἱ ἀδελφοί μου; 49. καὶ ἐκτείνας τὴν χεῖρα ἐπὶ τοὺς μαθητὰς αὐτοῦ εἶπεν· ἰδοὺ ἡ μήτηρ μου καὶ οἱ ἀδελφοί μου· 50. ὅστις γὰρ ἂν ποιήσῃ τὸ θέλημα τοῦ πατρός μου τοῦ ἐν οὐρανοῖς, αὐτός μου ἀδελφὸς καὶ ἀδελφὴ καὶ μήτηρ ἐστίν.	παρεγένετο δὲ πρὸς αὐτὸν ἡ μήτηρ αὐτοῦ καὶ οἱ ἀδελφοὶ αὐτοῦ, καὶ οὐκ ἠδύναντο συντυχεῖν αὐτῷ διὰ τὸν ὄχλον. 20. ἀπηγγέλη δὲ αὐτῷ ὅτι ἡ μήτηρ σου καὶ οἱ ἀδελφοί σου ἑστήκασιν ἔξω ἰδεῖν σε θέλοντες. 21. ὁ δὲ ἀποκριθεὶς εἶπεν πρὸς αὐτούς· μήτηρ μου καὶ ἀδελφοί μου οὗτοί εἰσιν οἱ τὸν λόγον τοῦ θεοῦ ἀκούοντες καὶ ποιοῦντες. (Underlined are possible reminiscences of Mark; but they may all be accidental similarities.)

On general principles we should suppose that Luke, being in non-Marcan context, is not derived from Mark. If Matt. xii. 47 is authentic,[1] Luke's passage is if anything more akin to Matthew's than to Mark's, and as usual in such cases is covered by the formula: dependence on Matthew, (possible) reminiscence of Mark, Lucan modification of Matthew's wording.[2] To suppose that Matthew has here conflated Mark with Q (especially as Q gave him nothing that he could not find in Mark) would be unnatural and an offence against sound criticism.

(4) *The Mission Charge*

The long section of Matt. ix. 35–x. 16, the former half of a great architectural whole of discourse, has partial parallels at no less than

---

[1] Omitted by ℵ*B, etc., it is square-bracketed by Huck and is usually regarded as an interpolation or at best as doubtfully authentic. But the omission was probably due to homœoteleuton, and I regard Mark iii. 32 and Luke viii. 20, taken together, as early evidence for the verse's genuineness.

[2] For Luke viii. 21 οἱ τὸν λόγον τοῦ θεοῦ ἀκούοντες καὶ ποιοῦντες, cf. vi. 47 πᾶς ὁ... ἀκούων μου τῶν λόγων καὶ ποιῶν αὐτούς. Cf. Matt. vii. 24.

13

Mark vi. 8–11	Matt. x. 9–15	Luke x. 4–12
καὶ παρήγγειλεν αὐτοῖς ἵνα μηδὲν αἴρωσιν εἰς ὁδὸν εἰ μὴ ῥάβδον μόνον, μὴ ἄρτον, μὴ πήραν, μὴ εἰς τὴν ζώνην χαλκόν, 9. ἀλλὰ ὑποδεδεμένους σανδάλια, καὶ μὴ ἐνδύσησθε δύο χιτῶνας. 10. καὶ ἔλεγεν αὐτοῖς· ὅπου ἐὰν εἰσέλθητε εἰς οἰκίαν, ἐκεῖ μένετε ἕως ἂν ἐξέλθητε ἐκεῖθεν.	μὴ κτήσησθε χρυσὸν μηδὲ ἄργυρον μηδὲ χαλκὸν εἰς τὰς ζώνας ὑμῶν, 10. μὴ πήραν εἰς ὁδὸν μηδὲ δύο χιτῶνας μηδὲ ὑποδήματα μηδὲ ῥάβδον· ἄξιος γὰρ ὁ ἐργάτης τῆς τροφῆς αὐτοῦ. 11. εἰς ἣν δ' ἂν πόλιν ἢ κώμην εἰσέλθητε, ἐξετάσατε τίς ἐν αὐτῇ ἄξιός ἐστιν· κἀκεῖ μείνατε ἕως ἂν ἐξέλθητε. 12. εἰσερχόμενοι δὲ εἰς τὴν οἰκίαν ἀσπάσασθε αὐτήν. 13. καὶ ἐὰν μὲν ᾖ ἡ οἰκία ἀξία, ἐλθάτω ἡ εἰρήνη ὑμῶν ἐπ' αὐτήν· ἐὰν δὲ μὴ ᾖ ἀξία, ἡ εἰρήνη ὑμῶν πρὸς ὑμᾶς ἐπιστραφήτω.	μὴ βαστάζετε βαλλάντιον, μὴ πήραν, μὴ ὑποδήματα· μηδένα κατὰ τὴν ὁδὸν ἀσπάσησθε. 5. εἰς ἣν δ' ἂν εἰσέλθητε οἰκίαν, πρῶτον λέγετε· εἰρήνη τῷ οἴκῳ τούτῳ. 6. καὶ ἐὰν ᾖ ἐκεῖ υἱὸς εἰρήνης, ἐπαναπαήσεται ἐπ' αὐτὸν ἡ εἰρήνη ὑμῶν. εἰ δὲ μήγε, ἐφ' ὑμᾶς ἀνακάμψει. 7. ἐν αὐτῇ δὲ τῇ οἰκίᾳ μένετε ἔσθοντες καὶ πίνοντες τὰ παρ' αὐτῶν· ἄξιος γὰρ ὁ ἐργάτης τοῦ μισθοῦ αὐτοῦ. μὴ μεταβαίνετε ἐξ οἰκίας εἰς οἰκίαν. 8. καὶ εἰς ἣν ἂν πόλιν εἰσέρχησθε καὶ δέχωνται ὑμᾶς, ἐσθίετε τὰ παρατιθέμενα ὑμῖν. 9. καὶ θεραπεύετε τοὺς ἐν αὐτῇ ἀσθενεῖς καὶ λέγετε αὐτοῖς· ἤγγικεν ἐφ' ὑμᾶς ἡ βασιλεία τοῦ θεοῦ.
11. καὶ ὃς ἂν τόπος μὴ δέξηται ὑμᾶς μηδὲ ἀκούσωσιν ὑμῶν, ἐκπορευόμενοι ἐκεῖθεν ἐκτινάξατε τὸν χοῦν τὸν ὑποκάτω τῶν ποδῶν ὑμῶν εἰς μαρτύριον αὐτοῖς.	14. καὶ ὃς ἂν μὴ δέξηται ὑμᾶς μηδὲ ἀκούσῃ τοὺς λόγους ὑμῶν, ἐξερχόμενοι ἔξω τῆς οἰκίας ἢ τῆς πόλεως ἐκείνης ἐκτινάξατε τὸν κονίορτον ἐκ τῶν ποδῶν ὑμῶν. 15. ἀμὴν λέγω ὑμῖν, ἀνεκτότερον ἔσται γῇ Σοδόμων καὶ Γομόρρων ἐν ἡμέρᾳ κρίσεως ἢ τῇ πόλει ἐκείνῃ.	10. εἰς ἣν δ' ἂν πόλιν εἰσέλθητε καὶ μὴ δέχωνται ὑμᾶς, ἐξελθόντες εἰς τὰς πλατείας αὐτῆς εἴπατε· 11. καὶ τὸν κονιορτὸν τὸν κολληθέντα ἡμῖν ἐκ τῆς πόλεως ὑμῶν εἰς τοὺς πόδας ἀπομασσόμεθα ὑμῖν· πλὴν τοῦτο γινώσκετε, ὅτι ἤγγικεν ἡ βασιλεία τοῦ θεοῦ. 12. λέγω δὲ ὑμῖν ὅτι Σοδόμοις ἐν τῇ ἡμέρᾳ ἐκείνῃ ἀνεκτότερον ἔσται ἢ τῇ πόλει ἐκείνῃ.

three places in Mark and four in Luke, not to mention the list of the apostles in Acts. It is, moreover, immediately followed by a section, x. 17–22, which has a parallel in Mark xiii, and which Burney suggested was a loan from Q. Our present concern is with x. 9–15, its parallel in Mark vi. 8–11, and Luke x. 4–12, a Lucan parallel in non-Marcan context. Luke ix. 3–5 is a parallel, in Marcan context, to Mark vi. 8–11, and may be disregarded here.

Luke x. 4–12 is from the Mission of the Seventy, an incident not related in the other Gospels. St Luke seems to have filled out the incident with material which, in the other two Gospels, is connected with the Mission of the Twelve, and we must allow for the fact that the influence of his peculiar source may be present in his version of this Q passage. It has no Marcan reminiscences, but there may be one a few verses earlier (x. 1 ἀνὰ δύο; cf. Mark vi. 7 δύο δύο). As in the instances we have previously examined, the solution dictated by normal critical considerations is that Matthew (agreeing as it does with Mark against Luke and with Luke against Mark, besides the agreements of all three) is the intermediary between the other two; so that Mark and Matthew are directly connected, and Luke is derived from Matthew; for as usual we reject the hypothesis of Lucan priority.

Once again Streeter has to explain the data by Q overlapping Mark, and Matthew conflating Mark and Q; the contents of Q being sought in Luke. He says (*The Four Gospels*, p. 190): 'Matt. x. 5–16 is clearly a conflation of the Q discourse, given by Luke as the Charge to the Seventy, with Mark's discourse on the Mission of the Twelve. Matthew has additional matter both at the beginning and the end', though, as we have seen, Burney has thought fit to assign x. 17–22 to Q; and Luke x. 9 suggests that at least some part of Matt. x. 7, 8 is from Q—as usual it is very difficult to keep Q from engrossing all its Matthaean context. 'But', says Streeter, 'in the central part of his version of the discourse (Matt. x. 9–16a) there is hardly a word which is not to be found either in Mark vi. 7–11 or in Luke x. 1–12.' Again (p. 248) he refers to this passage as an example of 'the almost meticulous care with which Matthew conflates Mark and Q...the only real additions he has to make are the words "gold" (*v.* 9) and "Gomorrha" (*v.* 15).... There is another point to notice. The necessity[1] of conflating the Marcan and the Q versions has led Matthew entirely to rearrange the order of the

---

[1] Why 'necessity'?—the word conceals the real weakness of Streeter's case; there was *no* necessity, and the procedure attributed to Matthew is gratuitous and futile.

sections in Q, which we may presume to be preserved in Luke x. 4 ff.'

I venture to suggest that these two passages from *The Four Gospels* constitute an implicit condemnation of the Q hypothesis which dictated them. To explain the agreements of Matthew and Luke against Mark in the paragraph under consideration by appeal to a conjectural source is to introduce into the problem an entirely unnecessary, disturbing and complicating element. Without it, as indicated above, a natural solution is provided by the normal application of the principles of comparative documentary criticism. The reader is invited to consider the full and dotted underlinings in the passage as set out above, the former indicating the loans from Q, and the latter those from Mark, which Matthew may be supposed to have made if we accept Streeter's view. Such motiveless, and extremely difficult, patchwork composition and 'invisible mending' are so improbable psychologically and artistically as to constitute a very grave objection to the Q hypothesis.

If we examine Luke we find that many of his differences from Matthew can be explained, as usual, as Lucan stylistic variants:

Luke x. 4. βαστάζω (Matthew 3, including a quotation; Mark 1; Luke 5; Acts 4).
βαλλάντιον (Luke 4; rest of N.T. o).
κατά c. acc.

x. 5. οἶκος (Matthew 9; Mark 12; Luke 32).

x. 6. εἰ δὲ μήγε.

x. 7. ἐσθίειν καὶ πίνειν (Matthew 4; Mark 1; Luke 14).

x. 8. παρατίθημι (Matthew 2; Mark 3; Luke 5; Acts 4).

x. 10. πλατείας (Matthew 2, including a quotation; Mark 1; Luke 3; Acts 1).

x. 11. κολλάομαι (Matthew 1, quotation; Luke 2; Acts 5).
ἀπομάσσομαι (rest of N.T. o; but cf. ἐκμάσσω Luke 2, John 3 only).

There are, however, a few details in Luke that are hardly derivable from Matthew ('salute no one', cf. II Kings iv. 29; 'son of peace'— but Luke is fond of this Semitic use of 'son of', and the substitution of the householder for the house may have been suggested by Matthew, v. 11, 'seek out who is worthy'; 'eating and drinking what they provide'—but this may be a development of Matthew's 'the labourer is worthy of his hire'; but not 'heal their sick and tell them the Kingdom of God is at hand for you', for this could be obtained from Matt. x. 7, 8). Here we may perhaps see the influence of the source from which Luke obtained the incident of the Seventy.

A certain fusion of Q material with other material can be detected elsewhere in Luke; for example, in the episode of the Centurion's servant, in the parable of the Great Supper, and in the episode of the meal at the Pharisee's house. This, it may be argued, is a different procedure from the interlacing conflation of the whole of two overlapping sources to which Matthew is supposed, on the Q hypothesis, to have had recourse.

A few words may be added on the wider context from which our quotation of Matthew is an extract.

(a) Matt. ix. 35 is probably paraphrased, in Lucan style, at Luke viii. 1. On this, see p. 51 *infra*.

(b) Matt. ix. 37, 38 is almost identical with Luke x. 2, and Luke x. 3 is an anticipation of Matt. x. 16a. Thus Luke fills the gap caused by his omission of Matt. x. 1–8, from which section, however, Luke x. 9 is constructed, to explain—as St Luke's omission of Matt. x. 1–8 made necessary—what the missioners were to do during their stay in a place; after which follows our passage.

(c) It is worth while to read over the whole section, Matt. ix. 35–x. 16, allowing it to make on the mind its native impression of superb, internally coherent,[1] unity. The mission of the Twelve is represented as a derivation from, and an extension of, our Lord's own ministry, its motive being His compassion for the multitudes, too numerous for His own immediate activities to touch. The Twelve are therefore summoned and empowered—the enumeration of them being a natural parenthesis—and they are told what regions to make for, what to preach and what good works to perform. They are given personal directions about equipment (or dispensing with equipment), and about their behaviour in the places they visit; and the punishment of those who reject them is foretold—a fate analogous to that of the places that turned a deaf ear to our Lord Himself and refused the evidence of His miracles (cf. xi. 20–4). Details, some of them easily overlooked, link part with part of this section (cf. ix. 35 πόλεις...καὶ...κώμας (special source? or Q?) with x. 11 πόλιν ἢ κώμην (Q?); κηρύσσων τὸ εὐαγγέλιον τῆς βασιλείας (special source? or Q?) with x. 7 κηρύσσετε...ἤγγικεν ἡ βασιλεία τῶν

---

[1] In general it may be said that Matthew's Q passages belong to their contexts by intrinsic right, Luke's by editorial collocation, the link in the latter case being often not a developing idea, but a verbal association.

οὐρανῶν (special source? or will Q be suggested, since Luke ix. 2, in the parallel to Mark vi. 6–13, seems to be connected?); θεραπεύων πᾶσαν νόσον καὶ πᾶσαν μαλακίαν (editorial?) with x. 1b θεραπεύειν πᾶσαν μαλακίαν[1] (editorial? or perhaps Q, since Luke ix. 1b has νόσους θεραπεύειν as an agreement with Matthew against Mark?); ix. 36 πρόβατα μὴ ἔχοντα ποιμένα (from Mark vi. 34?) with x. 6 τὰ πρόβατα τὰ ἀπολωλότα (special source?); ix. 38 ἐργάτας (Q?) with x. 10 ὁ ἐργάτης (Q?); x. 1 ἔδωκεν ἐξουσίαν (Mark?) with x. 8b δωρεὰν ἐλάβετε, δωρεὰν δότε (special source? It immediately succeeds the command to exercise the powers bestowed in x. 1); x. 5 ἀπέστειλεν (from Mark vi. 8?) with x. 16 ἀποστέλλω (Q? though it produces an *inclusio*); x. 5b ὁδόν... πόλιν (special source?) with x. 10a πήραν εἰς ὁδόν (Mark?) and x. 11a εἰς ἣν δ' ἂν πόλιν (Q?)). It will be noticed that these pairs of connected phrases show a marked indifference to the alleged diversity of sources. Yet Harnack's verdict, after a searching examination, was that Matthew had been very conservative in his editing of Q.

If such signs of unitary composition and homogeneous texture are too little emphasized in many studies of the Synoptic problem, it is perhaps due, sometimes, to the fact that critics approach Matthew with a prejudice. Dependence on Mark, Q and a special Jerusalem source is something which they do not discover by direct scrutiny of this Gospel, but something which they are compelled to assume because, for other reasons, the Two-Document hypothesis has been accepted. In reality it is preposterous to explain this unity as produced by combining—as in the case in question is supposed—three Marcan passages, conflating a Q passage with one of them in the way suggested by Streeter, and perhaps adding a few verses from some third source.

Contrast with the unity, harmony and logic of Matthew here the results achieved by St Luke, that practised editor and compiler, in Luke x. 1–12; where the disciples are first brought to a house, then reference is made to their arrival at a city, and they are then to 'eat' in a 'city'. This seems to be the kind of rather clumsy effect that might be supposed to result from the editing of sources. We may compare with it the dislocation produced by Luke's substitution of the preaching at Nazareth for the Marcan call of Simon and his

[1] Cf. iv. 23 (editorial?).

partners; with the result that our Lord's miracles at Capernaum are mentioned in the synagogue at Nazareth before they have been narrated in St Luke's own Gospel.

(5) The Dual Precept of Charity

Mark xii. 28–34	Matt. xxii. 35–40	Luke x. 25–8
καὶ προσελθὼν εἷς τῶν γραμμάτεων, ἀκούσας αὐτῶν συνζητούντων, ἰδὼν ὅτι καλῶς ἀπεκρίθη αὐτοῖς, ἐπηρώτησεν αὐτόν· ποία ἐστίν ἐντολή πρώτη πάντων; 29. ἀπεκρίθη ὁ Ἰησοῦς ὅτι πρώτη ἐστίν· ἄκουε, Ἰσραήλ, κύριος ὁ θεὸς ἡμῶν κύριος εἷς ἐστιν, 30. καὶ ἀγαπήσεις κύριον τὸν θεόν σου ἐξ ὅλης τῆς καρδίας σου καὶ ἐξ ὅλης τῆς ψυχῆς σου καὶ ἐξ ὅλης τῆς διανοίας σου καὶ ἐξ ὅλης τῆς ἰσχύος σου.	(34. οἱ δὲ Φαρισαῖοι ἀκούσαντες....) 35. καὶ ἐπηρώτησεν αὐτὸν εἷς ἐξ αὐτῶν νομικὸς πειράζων αὐτόν. 36. διδάσκαλε, ποία ἐντολή μεγάλη ἐν τῷ νόμῳ; 37. ὁ δὲ ἔφη αὐτῷ· ἀγαπήσεις κύριον τὸν θεόν σου ἐν ὅλη τῇ καρδίᾳ σου καὶ ἐν ὅλη τῇ ψυχῇ σου καὶ ἐν ὅλη τῇ διανοίᾳ σου.	καὶ ἰδοὺ νομικός τις ἀνέστη ἐκπειράζων αὐτὸν λέγων· διδάσκαλε, τί ποιήσας ζωὴν αἰώνιον κληρονομήσω; 26. ὁ δὲ εἶπεν πρὸς αὐτόν· ἐν τῷ νόμῳ τί γέγραπται; πῶς ἀναγινώσκεις; 27. ὁ δὲ ἀποκριθεὶς εἶπεν· ἀγαπήσεις κύριον τὸν θεόν σου ἐξ ὅλης τῆς καρδίας σου καὶ ἐν ὅλη τῇ ψυχῇ σου καὶ ἐν ὅλη τῇ ἰσχύι σου καὶ ἐν ὅλη τῇ διανοίᾳ σου,
31. δευτέρα αὕτη· ἀγαπήσεις τὸν πλησίον σου ὡς σεαυτόν. μείζων τούτων ἐντολὴ οὐκ ἔστιν.	38. αὕτη ἐστιν ἡ μεγάλη καὶ πρώτη ἐντολή. 39. δευτέρα ὁμοία αὐτῇ· ἀγαπήσεις τὸν πλησίον σου ὡς σεαυτόν. 40. ἐν ταύταις ταῖς δυσὶν ἐντολαῖς ὅλος ὁ νόμος κρέμαται καὶ οἱ προφῆται.	καὶ τὸν πλησίον σου ὡς σεαυτόν.
32. καὶ εἶπεν αὐτῷ ὁ γραμματεύς· καλῶς, διδάσκαλε, ἐπ᾽ ἀληθείας εἶπες ὅτι εἷς ἐστιν καὶ οὐκ ἔστιν ἄλλος πλὴν αὐτοῦ. 33. καὶ τὸ ἀγαπᾶν αὐτὸν ἐξ ὅλης τῆς καρδίας καὶ ἐξ ὅλης τῆς συνέσεως καὶ ἐξ ὅλης τῆς ἰσχύος, καὶ τὸ ἀγαπᾶν τὸν πλησίον ὡς ἑαυτὸν περισσότερόν ἐστιν πάντων τῶν ὁλοκαυτωμάτων καὶ τῶν θυσιῶν. 34. καὶ ὁ Ἰησοῦς ἰδὼν αὐτὸν ὅτι νουνεχῶς ἀπεκρίθη, εἶπεν αὐτῷ· οὐ μακρὰν εἶ ἀπὸ τῆς βασιλείας τοῦ θεοῦ....		28. εἶπεν δὲ αὐτῷ· ὀρθῶς ἀπεκρίθης· τοῦτο ποίει, καὶ ζήσῃ.

Luke x. 25–8, concerning the precept of charity, is one of the few passages in Luke that have a non-Marcan context and yet show some considerable influence of Mark (Mark xii. 28–34). It has also, if we follow the ordinary texts, some links with Matthew's parallel to that passage. Despite first appearances, the influence of the Marcan version in Luke's is strong. It is remarkable that St Luke puts into the lawyer's mouth the combination of the two precepts of charity (Deut. vi. 5, Lev. xix. 18), whereas in Matthew and Mark this conjunction is attributed to our Lord. It is not certainly found in any Jewish tradition that could have been a source for the Christian combination; the apparent exceptions in the apocryphal Testaments of the Twelve Patriarchs (Issachar v. 2; vii. 6, Benjamin iii. 3–5, Dan. v. 3) are regarded by Lagrange[1] as being some of the Christian interpolations in the extant texts of the Testaments. It is indeed reasonable to hold that the epoch-making combination was first effected by our Lord Himself. How then does St Luke come to attribute it to the lawyer? Probably under the influence of Mark xii. 28–34, where the scribe, *echoing our Lord's words*, says that to love God and one's neighbour as oneself is better than all holocausts and sacrifices. In other words, the combination does occur on the lips of the scribe in Mark (though originally made by our Lord) and Luke has felt justified in making use of this fact. It is an interesting illustration of St Luke's editing.

This explanation of Luke's version seems to be borne out by the resemblance between Mark xii. 34 καὶ ὁ Ἰησοῦς ἰδὼν αὐτὸν ὅτι νουνεχῶς ἀπεκρίθη, εἶπεν αὐτῷ· οὐ μακρὰν εἶ ἀπὸ τῆς βασιλείας τοῦ θεοῦ and Luke x. 28 εἶπεν δὲ αὐτῷ· ὀρθῶς ἀπεκρίθης· τοῦτο ποίει, καὶ ζήσῃ, where our Lord's words have been adjusted to the lawyer's initial question.

It will further be observed that Luke agrees with Mark (xii. 30) in giving four members in the love of God precept, and in using ἐξ with the first of them; while Matthew, Mark xii. 33 and the Old Testament have only three members, and Matthew and the Old Testament have the preposition ἐν. Further, Luke appends the second precept of charity immediately to the first, as in Mark xii. 33, against Mark xii. 31 and Matthew.

Turning to Matthew's version, we note Streeter's remark (*op. cit.* p. 320) that Matthew is mainly following Mark, but Luke 'seems to derive the incident from another source. Hawkins suggests that the incident might have stood in Q.' Luke's placing of the incident in non-Marcan context would certainly suggest that he had another

---

[1] *Judaisme avant Jésus-Christ*, p. 124, n. 4.

source for it (though he had a good reason for placing it here, as an introduction to the story of the Good Samaritan). But this time Streeter does not suggest that Matthew has conflated Mark and Q. On the contrary, he seeks to remove agreements of Luke with Matthew against Mark by manipulating the evidence of the textual tradition: (1) νομικός (apart from this passage) is found in no Gospel except Luke; 'this fact practically compels us to accept as original its omission in Matthew by 1 &c., e, Syr.S., Arm., Orig. Mt.' We would be inclined to agree—if that were all. (2) 'διδάσκαλε in Luke is omitted by D and by Marcion as quoted by Tertullian.' This seems weak authority for its rejection; but since, as we have shown, Luke probably had the Marcan version very much in his mind, διδάσκαλε might, if necessary, be derived from Mark xii. 32.

Nevertheless, there are other agreements of Matthew and Luke against Mark: (1) (ἐκ)πειράζων. (2) ὁ δὲ (εἶπεν πρός). (3) ἐν τῷ νόμῳ. (4) ἐν (three times for Mark's ἐξ in the quotation). (5) The omission of the quotation from Deut. vi. 4 (Mark xii. 29 b). On the whole, it seems better to take this as a further instance, like those previously discussed, where the choice lies between 'Matthew conflating Mark and Q' and 'Luke depending on Matthew. As usual, it is natural to accept the latter solution.[1]

The five sets of passages discussed in this chapter are obviously crucial for the determination of the relations between Matthew and Luke in all the (genuine) Q passages. It will be observed that in each case, provided we admit that Luke was written subsequently to Mark, and that he is often 'reminiscent' of passages that he is not

---

[1] (1) It should be mentioned that there is a variant ἐν for ἐξ in the first member of Luke's quotation. (2) The objection may be made that the above analysis presents Luke here as a conflation of Matthew and Mark, whereas we have refused to admit, in the previous cases discussed and in this case, that Matthew is a conflation of Mark and Q. It should, however, be noticed that (a) Luke omits much from both his sources, while Matthew is regularly supposed to preserve the full contents of both his 'sources'; (b) Luke's version here, though short and simple, is inferior in content to those of his sources, whereas Matthew is regularly superior to Mark and Q; (c) the conflation of sources is specially apparent in Luke's variation from ἐξ (if the reading is genuine) to ἐν in v. 27—precisely the opposite phenomenon to Matthew's repeated ἀφεθήσεται in xii. 31, 32, which is taken over by Mark from v. 31, and by Luke from v. 32.

directly copying,[1] the natural interpretation of the evidence is that, while Matthew and Mark are directly connected, *Luke is dependent on Matthew*; and in each case the appeal to Q is unnecessary and embarrassing. The five cases are not all equally impressive, the fifth giving perhaps less certain results than any of the others. But while each of the first four is strong by itself, the cumulative force of all five, taken together, is practically irresistible. Only the most powerful considerations, extraneous to these passages themselves, would justify us in refusing to admit the dependence of Luke on Matthew and to reject the Q hypothesis forthwith and finally.

[1] Both of these assumptions will be granted by the Two-Documentarians.

CHAPTER II

ARGUMENTS FOR Q

The advocates of the Two-Document hypothesis show no sign, as a rule, of having noticed that the passages where they are forced to suggest that Matthew conflated Mark and Q can be quite easily explained by the direct dependence of Luke on Matthew. Yet there is no other easy explanation. This is an interesting example of the way in which prepossession by a theory can blind critical intuition— for there is an element of intuition in comparative documentary criticism; the power to 'see' natural lines of relationship and directions of dependence, like the power to 'see' the Hidden Princess in the picture-puzzles of our childhood.

Streeter, however, gives (*op. cit.* p. 183) two reasons for refusing to admit that St Luke used Matthew:

(1) After the Temptation story, Luke's Q passages are never inserted in the place in the Marcan outline which they occupy in Matthew. Streeter infers that, if St Luke used Matthew, he 'must have proceeded with the utmost care to tear every little piece of non-Marcan material he desired to use from the context of Mark in which it appeared in Matthew—in spite of the fact that contexts in Matthew are always exceedingly appropriate [a welcome admission]—in order to re-insert it into a different context of Mark having no special appropriateness'.

The argument might seem more plausible if, less than twenty pages earlier, Streeter had not himself made the felicitous observation that, half-a-dozen or so odd verses apart, Marcan and non-Marcan material alternate in Luke in great blocks. In other words, as Mr H. G. Jameson succinctly put it, *Luke does not attempt to insert his Q matter into Marcan contexts at all.* St Luke has taken Mark as his source for the Marcan tradition, and just as he hardly ever inserts fragments of Mark into his non-Marcan blocks, so he will not interpolate into his Marcan contexts either verses from Matthew or material from his special sources.

There is evidence, indeed, that he made an attempt (iii. 1–iv. 13) to fuse Matthew, Mark and another source or sources. He presumably (and very naturally) decided that this was a far too complicated editorial procedure, though he was driven to resort to combination again in the Passion narrative (he takes none of Matthew's peculiar Passion material, but he no doubt wanted to preserve his own special additions to the story as it appears in Mark, and he was pressed for room). From iv. 13 till the opening of the Passion story, with the exception of his big blocks of non-Marcan matter, he follows Mark exclusively for the main sequence of his narrative.[1] Having decided on this course, if he wished subsequently to make use of pieces of Matthew that were built up in Matthew's Marcan sections, he would find it necessary to go through Matthew marking off all that was identical with Mark. The remainder was at his disposal, to fit into the great non-Marcan blocks of his Gospel. His procedure is entirely natural, and our ignorance of his precise motives for preferring Mark to Matthew cannot justify us in neglecting the proofs offered above of his use of Matthew in the five crucial instances.

But there is strong evidence from order tending to show that St Luke, in his Q passages, was using as his source the Q passages in Matthew and not a separate Q. The matter is examined at some length in Jameson's *Origin of the Synoptic Gospels*.[2] In particular, he seems to recognize on more than one occasion that the passage facing him in his source is one member of a Matthaean doublet, and to turn thereupon to the other member of the same doublet in another part of Matthew:

(a) We have already seen that Luke's version of the Mission charge to the Seventy ends with x. 12, the warning that 'it will be more tolerable for Sodom in that day than for' the city that rejects the missionaries. The verse seems to be taken almost word for word from the passage of Matthew (or Q) that he has been following in

---

[1] Why not Matthew? Wo do not know. But if he preferred the *Anschaulichkeit* of Mark, he would not be alone in his preference. And he may well have believed that Mark was a transcript of St Peter's preaching and have valued it for that reason. Moreover, there was this disadvantage about the use of Matthew—that Matthew was already a full-blown, and a very Palestinian, Gospel.

[2] Blackwell's (1922). See ch. 8.

the previous verses (Matt. x. 7–15). Plainly, such a verse followed here in Luke's source, whether it was Matthew or Q.

But in Matthew this verse is the first member of a doublet,[1] the second member (xi. 24) being appended to the prophecy of Capernaum's punishment, and echoing the warning to Chorazin and Bethsaida a few verses earlier. It cannot be regarded as a coincidence that *Luke x. 12 is immediately followed by the Woes to Chorazin, Bethsaida and Capernaum*, including the warning to the first two; this is a genuine Q passage. And it cannot be maintained that in Q the order was as in Luke, and that Matthew has broken up one long Q passage (represented by Luke x. 3–16), using the fragments, with a repeat of x. 15 at xi. 24, in two separate contexts. For (a) Matt. xi. 21–4 is an elaborate 'poem' in which the two 'stanzas' both work up to the refrain 'It shall be more tolerable for. . .in the day of judgment than for you'; it is quite obvious that the omission, in Luke, of the refrain after the second stanza wrecks the aesthetic whole. The refrain is therefore in its right place in Matt. xi. 24 and in its *wrong place* at Luke x. 12 which is parallel to Matt. x. 15; and this parallelism cannot be regarded as a coincidence. (b) The passage about Chorazin, Bethsaida and Capernaum has no business in a Mission charge to disciples. It does not give a warning of punishment for possible future rejection of our Lord's envoys; it foretells the punishment of these cities, where our Lord Himself had taught and worked miracles, for their past and present refusal to obey his own personal summons to them to repent. In Luke's placing of the passage it has, however, to be accommodated, very awkwardly, to the context of a Mission charge; coming as it does between the injunction to 'shake the dust off your feet' and *v.* 16: 'He that heareth you heareth Me', etc.

We thus have a very strong combination of indications that Luke's source contained both Matt. x. 9–15 and xi. 21–4 (or their equivalents) and that Luke is responsible for combining these two passages. We further note that the source contained the doublet.

(b) We have already mentioned that whereas Luke xi. 14–23 (the Beelzebub controversy) as a whole is parallel to the same controversy in Matt. xii. 22–32, yet the introductory miracle (Luke xi. 14) is taken *not from Matt. xii. 22, 23 but from Matt. ix. 32, 33*, these two

[1] No. (4) in Hawkins's list of Matthew's doublets.

Matthaean passages forming no. (17) in Hawkins's list of Matthaean doublets. The fact is incontrovertible:

Matt. (A) xii. 22, 23	Luke xi. 14	Matt. (B) ix. 32, 33
τότε προσηνέχθη αὐτῷ δαι-	καὶ ἦν ἐκβάλλων δαιμόνιον	προσήνεγκαν αὐτῷ ἄνθρωπον
μονιзόμενος τυφλὸς καὶ κωφός·	καὶ αὐτὸ ἦν κωφόν· ἐγένετο	κωφὸν δαιμονιзόμενον. 33. καὶ
καὶ ἐθεράπευσεν αὐτόν, ὥστε	δὲ τοῦ δαιμονίου ἐξελθόντος	ἐκβληθέντος τοῦ δαιμονίου
τὸν κωφὸν λαλεῖν καὶ βλέπειν.	ἐλάλησεν ὁ κωφός· καὶ ἐθαύ-	ἐλάλησεν ὁ κωφός. καὶ ἐθαύ-
23. καὶ ἐξίσταντο πάντες οἱ	μασαν οἱ ὄχλοι. τινὲς δὲ ἐξ	μασαν οἱ ὄχλοι λέγοντες....
ὄχλοι καὶ ἔλεγον...·	αὐτῶν....	

Luke agrees with Matthew (B) against (A) in omitting the blindness and the word 'all'; he further agrees with (B) against (A) in the verb 'to cast out', the genitive absolute, the phrase 'the dumb man spoke' and the word 'wondered'; in fact the whole of his *v.* 14*b* except the Lucan initial verb is plainly the same as the parallel part of Matthew (B). Yet after *v.* 15 the Lucan passage runs parallel with the continuation of Matthew (A). By analogy with the case just examined ('more tolerable for Sodom') we shall naturally suppose that Luke is copying a source which, like Matthew, contained both members of the doublet, and in which member (A) (the *second* member) introduced the Beelzebub controversy; and that Luke, on meeting member (B), has turned on to member (A) for the continuation of the story.

The adherent of the Q hypothesis may argue that Luke xi. 14–23 gives the original Q sequence, and that Matthew, having begun to utilize the Q passage at ix. 32, 33, broke off and then at xii. 22, 23 repeated the used verses with some alterations and continued as in Q. But the Q hypothesis is still not at the end of its troubles. For between *vv.* 15 and 17ff. (our Lord's reply to the Pharisaic challenge) St Luke has inserted *v.* 16:

Luke xi. 16	Cf. Matt. (A) xii. 38
ἕτεροι δὲ πειράзοντες σημεῖον ἐξ οὐρανοῦ ἐзήτουν παρ' αὐτοῦ.	τότε ἀπεκρίθησαν αὐτῷ τινες τῶν γραμματέων καὶ Φαρισαίων λέγοντες· διδάσκαλε, θέλομεν ἀπό σου σημεῖον ἰδεῖν.

The above verse from Matthew follows immediately upon the Beelzebub controversy, and is followed by the discourse on Jonah, the Ninevites, the Queen of the South and the seven other spirits more wicked than himself. In Luke the Beelzebub controversy is immediately followed by the 'seven other spirits' and two verses peculiar to Luke, after which we have the sign of Jonah to the Ninevites. Thus we must suppose a literary connexion between Luke xi. 16 and Matt. xii. 38. But it would seem that the verse is in its correct place in Matthew and has been displaced in Luke; for whereas in Matthew its request is at once answered, the reply to it in Luke, when it does come, has to be prefaced with a fresh introduction: 'While the crowds were thronging to (him) he began to say', etc.[1]

And as if this were not enough, it will be noticed that Matt. xii. 38, 39 a is the first member of a doublet (no. (9) in Hawkins's list) of which the second member (xvi. 1, 2 a) or its Marcan parallel, or more probably both, have exerted their influence on Luke xi. 16:

Matt. (B) xvi. 1	Luke xi. 16	Mark viii. 11
καὶ προσελθόντες οἱ Φαρισαῖοι καὶ Σαδδουκαῖοι πειράζοντες ἐπηρώτων αὐτὸν σημεῖον ἐκ τοῦ οὐρανοῦ ἐπιδεῖξαι αὐτοῖς.	ἕτεροι δὲ πειράζοντες σημεῖον ἐξ οὐρανοῦ ἐζήτουν παρ' αὐτοῦ.	καὶ ἐξῆλθον οἱ Φαρισαῖοι καὶ ἤρξαντο συνζητεῖν αὐτῷ, ζητοῦντες παρ' αὐτοῦ σημεῖον ἀπὸ τοῦ οὐρανοῦ πειράζοντες αὐτόν.

(Luke agrees with Mark against Matthew (B) in ζητεῖν and παρ' αὐτοῦ. He agrees with Matthew (B) against Mark in ἐξ, in the position of πειράζοντες and in the use of the participle without an object. He agrees with Matthew (B) against (A) in the absence of direct speech and in πειράζοντες and ἐξ οὐρανοῦ.)

With the hypothesis that Luke is using Matthew we shall again say that St Luke, arriving at one member of a Matthaean doublet, turns to the second member (xvi. 1); or perhaps it would be enough to say that he shows his knowledge of the second member, and of the Marcan passage to which it is parallel—and the awkward result of his reminiscence is that the request for a sign *from heaven* hangs in the air in his text (as it does in that of Mark viii. 11).[2]

What the believer in Q is going to make of this complication it is impossible to conjecture. Will he resign himself to the view that

---

[1] J. M. Creed, in his commentary on Luke, agrees that Luke xi. 16 has been displaced by the author of the Gospel from its original Q context, and that xi. 29 a is editorial.

[2] As a clue to the Lucan verse's provenance it is comparable with 'one of these little ones' in xvii. 2. The phrase 'from heaven' has its explanation in Matt. xvi. 1-4, if we accept the longer text there; as to which see pp. 141 f. below.

Q contained Matt. ix. 32, 33, xii. 22–45, xvi. 1–4, all in this order?
But in that case 'Q' is obviously a sub-title for 'Matthew'. It is
surely clear that Q can only be salvaged at the cost of all critical
principles.

(c) Matt. (A) xvii. 20	Luke xvii. 5, 6	Matt. (B) xxi. 21
ὁ δὲ λέγει αὐτοῖς· διὰ τὴν ὀλιγοπιστίαν ὑμῶν· ἀμὴν γὰρ λέγω ὑμῖν, ἐὰν ἔχητε πίστιν ὡς κόκκον σινάπεως, ἐρεῖτε τῷ ὄρει τούτῳ· μετάβα ἔνθεν ἐκεῖ, καὶ μεταβήσεται, καὶ οὐδὲν ἀδυνατήσει ὑμῖν.	καὶ εἶπαν οἱ ἀπόστολοι τῷ κυρίῳ· πρόσθες ἡμῖν πίστιν. 6. εἶπεν δὲ ὁ κύριος· εἰ ἔχετε πίστιν ὡς κόκκον σινάπεως, ἐλέγετε ἂν τῇ συκαμίνῳ ταύτῃ· ἐκριζώθητι καὶ φυτεύθητι ἐν τῇ θαλάσσῃ, καὶ ὑπήκουσεν ἂν ὑμῖν.	ἀποκριθεὶς δὲ ὁ Ἰησοῦς εἶπεν αὐτοῖς· ἀμὴν λέγω ὑμῖν, ἐὰν ἔχητε πίστιν καὶ μὴ διακριθῆτε, οὐ μόνον τὸ τῆς συκῆς ποιήσετε, ἀλλὰ κἂν τῷ ὄρει τούτῳ εἴπητε· ἄρθητι καὶ βλήθητι εἰς τὴν θάλασσαν, γενήσεται.

Matthew (B) has a close parallel in Mark xi. 22, 23. The two passages
from Matthew are no. (11) in Hawkins's list of Matthaean doublets.
'Faith as a grain of mustard' is an agreement of Luke with Matthew
(A) against (B) (and Mark). But it would seem that Luke looked
up the other member of the doublet; for ἐκριζώθητι καὶ φυτεύθητι
seems to be a reflexion of ἄρθητι καὶ βλήθητι. And why has Luke
'this sycamine tree' in place of 'this mountain' (both Matthaean
passages and Mark)? The answer is probably to be found in
Matthew's (B): οὐ μόνον τὸ τῆς συκῆς ποιήσετε. Matthew (B)
(and Mark) follow immediately upon the disciples' surprise at the
withering of the fig-tree, and our Lord says: 'If you have faith you
will be able not only to wither a fig-tree but to move this mountain',
doubtless the Mount of Olives. One cannot help suspecting that
Luke either shrank from the idea of moving anything as big as
a mountain, or else was aware that he had not placed the incident
in the vicinity of a mountain; he therefore suggests something
greater, no doubt, than withering a fig-tree but not open to the
objection which he felt to the Matthaean passage. And therefore
(having the withering of the tree in his mind), though he begins
with an 'if' clause in the present indicative, his apodosis is that
regular for a past conditional, and so suggests an actual historical
situation: 'You would have said to this tree (not, as I said, "be
withered", but) be uprooted and cast into the sea, and it would have
obeyed you (as it has obeyed me).'

The data might, it is true, be explained in part by reminiscence
of Mark instead of by reference to Matthew (B). But Matthew's

οὐ μόνον τὸ τῆς συκῆς ποιήσετε gives a neater point of insertion for Luke's συκαμίνῳ and the case has to be considered along with those just discussed.

(*d*) It is suggested in the next chapter (p. 42) that St Luke at vi. 43 turns from Matt. vii. 17 (the good tree and its fruit) to Matt. xii. 33 (these forming no. (3) of Hawkins's list of Matthaean doublets) and conflates the two similar passages for an obvious reason.

Such are some of the reasons that make it seem probable that St Luke knew his source for the Q passages in the order, and with the repetitions, of Matthew.

(2) Streeter's second objection runs as follows: 'Sometimes it is Matthew, sometimes it is Luke, who gives a saying in what is clearly the more original form' (*op. cit.* p. 183). Streeter here gives no examples of the latter phenomenon; and it must be remembered that we cannot be sure, in every case where Matthew and Luke seem to report the same saying, that there is a literary connexion between them. Whether we believe in Q or not, we are bound to admit that St Luke had other sources besides St Matthew (or Q) and St Mark, and one of his peculiar sources may occasionally 'overlap' St Matthew or Q.[1] Thus, the occasional greater originality of the Lucan version of a saying would not necessarily disprove Luke's dependence on Matthew in other passages. And we must remember the subjective element that is only too liable to enter into judgements of greater or less originality. In this field, it is the accumulation of instances that can lead to a relatively certain inference.

For examples of Matthew's alleged modifications of Q we may turn to Harnack's important study, translated into English under the title *The Sayings of Jesus*.[2] It is at first sight disturbing to find that Harnack manages to bring forward no less than eighty-four instances where he thinks such modifications may, with varying degrees of probability, and occasionally with certainty, be detected. But it must be remembered that Harnack's object is not to prove the existence of Q. The truth of the Q hypothesis is presupposed by him, and this means that he frequently and naturally regards tricks

---

[1] A fairly certain case is the incident of the healing of the Centurion's servant, see p. 46. And Streeter was confident that Luke's version of the Lost Sheep derived from a different source from that of the Matthaean version.

[2] Translated by J. R. Wilkinson (Williams and Norgate, 1908).

of Matthaean style, occurring in Matthew's Q passages and absent from their parallels in Luke, as modifications of Q. Thus, to take two striking cases, wherever πατὴρ ὁ οὐράνιος (or ὁ ἐν (τοῖς) οὐρανοῖς) or βασιλεία τῶν οὐρανῶν occurs in such a passage, it is automatically stigmatized by Harnack as an editorial modification since these phrases are notoriously typical of Matthew as a whole.

Now, in view of the fact that Harnack discovers about *six hundred* Lucan modifications of Q, or about seven times as many as the alleged Matthaean modifications, it is not in itself surprising that Matthaean characteristics should be found in Matthew's Q passages and be missing from their Lucan parallels, since Luke obviously edited the style of his source drastically. In particular, the phrases instanced above never occur in either Q or non-Q passages of Luke, who no doubt disliked in them the barbarous plural of οὐρανός and was probably aware that it was a Jewish circumlocution for God, unintelligible to ordinary Gentile readers; and who may have feared, for the same class of readers or hearers, the materialistic ring of πατὴρ οὐράνιος, etc., the sky-God among the Greeks being Zeus. But he does use πατὴρ ὁ ἐξ οὐρανοῦ once (xi. 13); and it is in a Q passage where Matthew has πατὴρ ὁ ἐν τοῖς οὐρανοῖς. Harnack in this case is compelled to say that the original Q text was as in Luke, and that Matthew has substituted his own favourite phrase. To some it will appear more probable that Matthew's phrase is original and that Luke has, in this one instance, allowed himself to depict God as in heaven—for a very good reason: the Q passage in question is an *a fortiori* argument from the kindness of human fathers to that of the heavenly Father, and the latter concept could not therefore be removed by Luke if he wished to use the passage at all.

It may therefore be claimed that much of the evidence adduced by Harnack for Matthaean modification of Q depends for its validity on the previous establishment of the truth of the Q hypothesis and cannot be used in recommendation of that hypothesis without begging the question.[1] Harnack's total of eighty-four is very considerably reduced once this point is grasped.[2]

[1] Indeed, in view of the fact that emerges from Harnack's study, that Matthew made very few, if any, changes in his Q material, the presence of the Matthaeanisms becomes an additional argument against the Q hypothesis and in favour of our identification of Q with Matthew.

[2] Matthew's Q passages sometimes have the name Ἰησοῦς where it is missing

On a review of Harnack's alleged instances of Matthaean modification of Q perhaps only the following deserve separate discussion:
(1) Matt. iv. 5 'Holy City' (Luke *ad loc.* and Gospel of the
Hebrews: 'Jerusalem'). 'The bias of a Christian of Jerusalem',
says Harnack, has led to Matthew's use of a Jewish mode of referring
to Jerusalem. Q, if it existed, was of course notably free from
Palestinian bias. Yes, because—on our view—Luke has selected
from Matthew such material as would suit his own universalistic
outlook, and where necessary has changed the wording of his
borrowings to make them thus suitable. Hence this example cannot,
without begging the question, be used as an argument to prove the
truth of the Q hypothesis.

(2) Matt. iv. 10 ὕπαγε, Σατανᾶ (om. Luke). Harnack asks what
reason St Luke could have had for omitting these words, if they
were in his source (*op. cit.* p. 44). The answer is very simple. It is
after the third and last temptation, according to Matthew's order,
that Satan is thus commanded to depart, and in the next verse he
duly leaves our Lord. In Luke, however, this is the second of the
three temptations, so the command to depart must be omitted, since
Satan cannot be allowed to flout our Lord's order and yet he is still
present in the third Lucan (cf. the second Matthaean) temptation.

(3) Matt. v. 3 μακάριοι οἱ πτωχοὶ τῷ πνεύματι. (Luke vi. 20 om.
τῷ πνεύματι. For the simple πτωχοί see also Matt. xi. 5 πτωχοὶ
εὐαγγελίζονται.) But Luke would have three reasons for the
omission: (*a*) He is interested in the problems of literal wealth and
poverty; cf. his parable of Dives and Lazarus, the parable of the

---

from the Lucan parallel. The Holy Name is considerably more frequent in Matthew
as a whole than in Luke as a whole, so that this is a stylistic difference between the
two authors and tends against the Q hypothesis. Again, the vocatives Κύριε and
διδάσκαλε in Matthaean Q passages are sometimes absent from the Lucan parallels.
The absence of these vivid touches in Luke is a sign that he is further away from
eyewitness actuality than Matthew.

Harnack alleges, in discussing Matt. xi. 16, that Matthew often destroys the
Semitic parallelism of Q. But it is scarcely possible to discover a clear instance of
this. It is of course patent, on the other hand, that Luke very frequently destroys
a parallelism preserved in Matthew (Burney, *The Poetry of Our Lord*, pp. 87–8).
Burney sums up as follows: 'If we admit that parallelism is a sign of originality
we must assign to Matthew the palm for having (at least in such cases as can be
tested by this criterion) preserved the sayings of Q in a more original form than
Luke.'

man who built new granaries, and the episode of the man who wished our Lord to settle a dispute about an inheritance. (*b*) He is also especially interested in the Holy Spirit and would recoil from the sound of a phrase which might seem to praise a deficiency in spiritual endowment. (*c*) The beatitude of 'the poor' is, in Luke but not in Matthew, contrasted with the 'Woe' to 'the rich'; 'rich in spirit' might seem a still odder 'Woe' than 'poor in spirit' as a Beatitude, so Luke omits 'in spirit' and preserves the parallelism.

(4) Matt. v. 32 παρεκτὸς λόγου πορνείας (om. Luke). Harnack admits that St Luke (xvi. 18) has been influenced by Mark and 'has completely changed' what he supposes to have been the original meaning of the Q source of Matt. v. 32. If, as seems not improbable, the 'exception' in Matthew would not have been understood in Palestinian circles (and in the Aramaic of which Matthew here may be supposed to be a translation) as permission to divorce a wife for adultery, then Luke's omission of it is entirely understandable (for the phrase was only too liable to be misunderstood by Gentiles), and Matthew's text is not a mitigation of primitive austerity.[1]

(5) Matt. vi. 9 ff., the Lord's Prayer, cf. Luke xi. 2–4. Harnack prefers, to the ordinary text of Luke, that given by Marcion, and holds that the first three petitions and the last petition in Matthew are accretions, urging that Luke would certainly not have passed over the seventh petition if it had existed in his source. Creed, however, does not accept Marcion's text. Luke's omission of 'Thy will be done', etc., may be due to his dislike for οὐρανός (except in the physical sense) and to the fact that for him θέλημα means not will in general, but a particular decree. Not much can be built upon the absence from Luke of Matthew's last clause.

(6) Matt. vi. 20 οὐρανῷ. Harnack prefers Luke's οὐρανοῖς (xii. 33), because the plural is much rarer in Luke than in Matthew, so that the plural may be supposed to have stood in the source. But, curiously enough, the plural is also the accepted reading at Luke xviii. 22, representing the Marcan singular.

(7) Harnack thinks that Matt. vii. 16–18 and xii. 33 derive from two sources (Hawkins suggested that both passages were from a single source), and that St Matthew has 'intermingled the forms'. He finds the original Q, by reference to Luke vi. 44, 43, partly in

[1] On the Matthaean exception, see Bonsirven, *Enseignements de Jésus*, p. 196 n. 3.

each of the Matthaean passages. The truth is probably that in xii. 33 St Matthew is adapting his own previous passage, and that the 'intermingling' of two forms is the work of Luke in vi. 43, 44.[1]

(8) Matt. x. 32, 33 twice has the phrase 'before My Father in heaven'; the Lucan parallel (xii. 8, 9) has 'before (once ἔμπροσθεν, which is the word in the Matthaean parallels, and once ἐνώπιον) the angels of God'. Though Luke has altered other words in his source here, Harnack is sure that 'the angels of God' is original, and thinks that Matthew has substituted 'My Father in heaven', and that this substitution is 'connected with the evangelist's Christological position'. Cf. also Luke xv. 10 'joy before the angels of God' (no parallel in Matthew). Harnack may be influenced by his general conviction that 'Father in heaven', as a Matthaean peculiarity, cannot have occurred in Q; but we have pointed out that this conviction presupposes the truth of the Q hypothesis. Assuming, for the sake of argument, that Luke depends on Matthew, we cannot forget that St Luke avoids the title 'Father in heaven' wherever he can. He usually substitutes 'God'; but he could not conveniently do so here;[2] for it is a question of those who confess or deny God (the Son) on earth being acknowledged or denied before God the Father in heaven. To write 'acknowledged (or denied) before God' will obviously not suit this context. St Luke therefore substitutes for the contrast between our Lord and His heavenly Father a contrast between 'before men' and 'before the angels of God'. In that case the same phrase in Luke xv. 10 will be a reminiscence, stimulated by Matt. xviii. 14 (parallel to Luke xv. 7) 'before your Father in heaven'.

(9) Matt. x. 34 uses statement where the Lucan parallel (xii. 51) has a question, and Harnack thinks that the latter form is original, as St Luke has 'often obliterated' the interrogative form elsewhere. But St Luke has a certain weakness for questions, at least when addressed to our Lord: x. 29 (no parallel); xiii. 23 (om. Matthew); xvii. 37 (om. Matthew).

---

[1] For the former suggestion, see ch. IX below; for the latter, see pp. 43 f.

[2] I assume that St Luke, like St Paul, believed in the divinity of Christ. As Creed says, with reference to the pre-existence of our Lord, 'there is no reason to suppose that Luke was conscious of differing from Paul' (*The Gospel according to St Luke*, p. lxxiv).

(10) Matt. x. 39, 'He that loses his life *for my sake* [om. Luke] shall find it'. The words in italics are, says Harnack, interpolated by Matthew from Mark viii. 35, owing to 'the influence of Christological dogma' (*op. cit.* p. 111). But St Luke has probably omitted the words owing to the context chosen by him for this saying. In Matthew the theme is the cost of following Christ, and Harnack thinks that x. 37 is probably 'Q unaltered'; he also assigns x. 38 to Q (*op. cit.* p. 143): a man who loves his family more than our Lord is not worthy of him, nor one who does not 'take up his cross' —but he who loses his life for him will find it. The Q passage itself— if we accept the Q hypothesis—loses its logical and rhetorical climax if 'for My sake' is omitted. But in Luke the verse has been incorporated in a context dealing with the fate of believers in the period of trial at the fall of Judaism or the end of the world, when safety will be found only in desperate measures and the normal promptings of the self-preserving instinct will be fatal; the idea of 'losing one's life for Christ's sake' would be irrelevant here, the motive in view being rather one's own safety.

(11) Matt. xi. 27, ἐπιγινώσκει. Harnack thinks that this present tense is perhaps a dogmatic alteration of an original ἔγνω. Further, Luke has the simple verb γινώσκειν and Harnack thinks that Matthew's compound can therefore scarcely be original. Appealing to Marcion and patristic quotations, he suggests that the original was preserved by Luke in the past tense ἔγνω (though this is read by no Greek MS. of the Gospel). Lagrange (*ad loc.*) replies that the present tense would not suit Marcion's dogmatic system, and that the past tense would also be convenient for non-Marcionite Christians in controversy with the Jews. He sums up: 'Instead of concluding that ἔγνω is original in Luke and his source, we find that it is an ancient variant, found only in the Fathers, and hardly ever preferred to the exclusion of γινώσκει; it suggested itself automatically when it was desired to prove that the Jews had not had the true knowledge of God.' He stigmatizes Harnack's hypothetical reconstruction of an original Q text here as fantasy.[1] At least it must be agreed that Harnack's case is too weak to be used as an argument against the originality of Matthew.

[1] It is perhaps fair to say that, within limits set by a good critical conscience, Harnack wanted to exclude from Q anything that suggested an orthodox Christology.

(12) Matt. xii. 40, 'As Jonah was in the belly of the whale for three days and three nights', etc. (om. Luke). Harnack regards this as a Matthaean addition to Q, since 'it would never have been omitted by St Luke if he had read it in his source' (*op. cit.* p. 23). But St Luke probably omitted it because our Lord was 'in the heart of the earth' for only two nights, not three. St Luke has an arithmetical bent—cf. xii. 52, where he has counted up the members of the household referred to in Matt. x. 35.

(13) Matt. xii. 22 describes a man as blind and dumb, and Luke xi. 14 appears at first to describe the same man only as dumb. But Luke is here following not Matt. xii. 22 but Matt. ix. 32 (see p. 25 above), where deafness only, and not blindness, is mentioned.

(14) Matt. xxiii. 23 καὶ τὴν πίστιν (om. Luke xi. 42) is regarded by Harnack as only very doubtfully original to Q. Perhaps what is meant is not 'faith' but 'faithfulness', in which case Luke's omission is hardly decisive.

(15) Matt. xxiii. 27; cf. Luke xi. 40. Harnack thinks that Luke's 'unseen tombs' must be original. But it is possible that St Luke knew that 'whited sepulchres' would be unfamiliar to his Gentile readers and preferred therefore to give a text that could be interpreted by reference to Num. xix. 16. He was intimately acquainted with the LXX.

(16) Matt. xxiii. 34; cf. Luke xi. 49. For Matthew's ἰδοὺ ἐγώ Luke has ἡ σοφία τοῦ θεοῦ εἶπεν. In the Lucan phrase Harnack (*op. cit.* p. 103) sees a reference to an apocryphal scripture, which Matthew would have found in Q and omitted. But neither Lagrange nor Creed is prepared to concede that Luke's phrase implies such a reference. The meaning is obscure: a reference to the (Pauline) doctrine of Christ as the Wisdom of God has been suggested; or—if 'God in his wisdom' is meant—we may refer to such passages as II Chron. xxiv. 19 ff. In the same verse St Luke has, as Harnack admits, substituted ἀποστόλους for Matthew's σοφοὺς καὶ γραμματεῖς, and it is possible that Matthew's σοφούς suggested to him his own ἡ σοφία τοῦ θεοῦ.

(17) In the verse just discussed, and in xxiii. 35, Harnack thinks that σταυρώσετε καὶ ἐξ αὐτῶν μαστιγώσετε ἐν ταῖς συναγωγαῖς ὑμῶν (cf. xx. 19 μαστιγῶσαι καὶ σταυρῶσαι), ἀπὸ πόλεως εἰς πόλιν (cf. x. 23) and the two occurrences of δίκαιος (all omitted

3-2

by Luke xi. 49, 50) are secondary. But (*a*) St Luke's need to abbreviate when possible, in order not to exceed the length of an ancient book, must not be forgotten; (*b*) he has restricted the purview of the passage to prophets and apostles, perhaps under the influence of I Thess. ii. 15, where the Jews are accused of having killed their own prophets and driven 'us' out; (*c*) hence he changes 'righteous blood' to 'blood of all the prophets'; (*d*) it would indeed be devotion to his own ideology for Matthew to add the epithet 'just' to Abel's name! On the other hand, its omission by Luke is not at all surprising, though by his editing of his source St Luke has managed to convey the impression that Abel was a prophet.

The collection of instances just considered includes what is probably a fair sample of those that can be most plausibly argued to show Matthew's modification of Q. It must be admitted that it is not an impressive list and that it is quite insufficient to prove Matthew's secondariness. And in fact the total number of such instances is itself an argument against Q, since it is scarcely credible that St Matthew could have welded a source into his other material with such slight and rare alterations of its text and with such a harmonious integration of text and context.

To sum up: Streeter's two arguments in favour of Q prove on examination to be too insecure to support the hypothesis of a conjectural document, with the complexities thus introduced, even were there no positive arguments against the hypothesis. But the positive arguments adduced in chapter I retain their full force, and the conclusion is inevitable that the Q hypothesis must be discarded unless a closer examination of the remaining Q passages forces it upon us. To such an examination we must now address ourselves.

CHAPTER III

THE GREAT SERMON

The Great Sermon in Luke comprises thirty verses (vi. 20–49), while Matthew's Sermon on the Mount extends to a hundred and seven (v. 3–vii. 27). But they are the same sermon. Each begins with Beatitudes and ends with the simile of the two houses; and there is hardly anything in Luke's sermon, apart from the Woes and about three long verses, that does not find a parallel in Matthew's.

Matthew's sermon forms an integral feature of the Gospel considered as an architectural whole. The first group of disciples has been called, and a general description has been given of the popular movement of which Jesus was the centre. 'Many crowds followed him from Galilee and Decapolis and Jerusalem and Judaea and beyond the Jordan.[1] And seeing the crowds he went up into the mountain; and when he had sat down his disciples came to him. And opening his mouth he taught them saying. . . .' Thus the sermon seems to be addressed not to 'crowds' but to the disciples, and it proves to be a manifesto of the new religion with special reference to Judaism.

Luke's sermon introduces the Little Interpolation. It is preceded by some editorial manipulation, Luke having, most unusually, inverted the order of two sections of Mark (Mark iii. 13–19, 7–12). This inversion enables him to identify the Mountain of Matt. v. 1 with that of Mark iii. 13, while by describing here the choosing of the Twelve he provides a suitable inner circle as an audience for the sermon. He puts the sermon on a Level Place, perhaps because a 'mountain' seemed uncongenial for purposes of preaching (for St Matthew 'mountain' may have meant 'the hill country'); and St Luke wants the sermon to be addressed to a wider audience than the disciples, though it begins with a passage specially directed to them. How 'editorial' all this is may be seen by comparing Luke vi. 17 with its Marcan original iii. 7: Luke presents (a) a crowd

[1] An enumeration from a Galilaean standpoint. Luke's at vi. 17 is from a world-wide viewpoint.

of disciples, and (*b*) much multitude of the people; this division corresponds with vi. 20 'lifting up His eyes upon His disciples' and vi. 27 'But to you which hear I say' (cf. vi. 17 'who came *to hear* Him'); Mark has no such distinction in this passage.

A priori, it would not be unreasonable to suppose that the two evangelists had separate sources for a sermon which—at least as reported in Matthew—was, we may presume, of high significance in the spiritual formation of the new religious movement. And indeed it is, to say the least, not improbable that some of the peculiar matter in Luke's sermon does represent a special sermon-source. But it cannot be maintained that the two versions only differ as independent records of the same sermon. For the Lucan version is practically destitute of the special Palestinian-Jewish colouring and relevance that are so pervasive in Matthew's. St Luke has given us neither simply a variant record, nor simply an untendencious abridgment, of the sermon more fully preserved in Matthew. Unless we can bring ourselves to believe the preposterous notion that Matthew has taken a sermon of universalistic tenour and deliberately 'Judaized' it by setting it back into a Jewish thought-world and making it echo Palestinian controversies and reflect a Palestinian environment, we are bound to conclude that either St Luke or his source has edited the sermon so as to bleach out these contingent elements; and in view of the general cast of his mind and the drift of his Gospel as a whole, we need not attribute this editorial activity to any other hand than his own. The following considerations tend to suggest that St Luke, whose use of Matthew in passages where we have Mark as a criterion has been demonstrated in chapter I, at least turned to Matthew for help in editing any special source of the Great Sermon which he may have had.

(1) vi. 23 ἰδοὺ γὰρ ὁ μισθὸς ὑμῶν πολὺς ἐν τῷ οὐρανῷ; cf. Matt. v. 12. Μισθός occurs ten times in Matthew, once in Mark, once in John and once in Acts.[1] In Luke, besides this instance, it occurs at vi. 35—where its presence can again be explained by the context of the Matthaean parallel v. 46—and at x. 7 where,

---

[1] Acts i. 18, where the thirty pieces of silver are described as Judas's 'reward of unrighteousness', perhaps with a reminiscence of Zach. xi. 12 (LXX). If so, there would seem to be no case of the employment of μισθός by St Luke, except under the influence of a source.

curiously enough, it represents Matthew's τροφή; but τροφή ('sustenance') is more fitted to the context than μισθός ('hire'). What has happened is that Luke has there substituted μισθός from Matt. xx. 8 (the parable of the Labourers in the Vineyard) where the *labourers* are to be given their *hire*—this is a normal instance of Lucan reminiscence, valuable as showing St Luke's knowledge of a part of Matthew which is outside their common contexts. (In our passage, St Luke has changed 'heavens' to the singular; but then he has the plural only four times in all in his Gospel.)

(2) vi. 24 ἀπέχετε τὴν παράκλησιν ὑμῶν. The Woes, in which this phrase occurs, have no parallel in Matthew. St Luke's word for 'receive' would normally have been ἀπολαμβάνειν (in this sense Matthew 0, Mark 0, Luke 5, John 0); cf. xvi. 25, where the rich man (cf. here 'Woe to you rich') is told: 'You have received (ἀπέλαβες) your good things in your life, and Lazarus likewise (his) evil things; but now he is comforted (παρακαλεῖται), and you are tormented.' But Matthew has ἀπέχουσιν τὸν μισθὸν αὐτῶν three times in the sermon (vi. 2, 5, 16) and the verb has this sense nowhere else in Gospels or Acts. It therefore seems probable that it is the influence of Matthew's sermon that has here deflected St Luke from the (to him) more obvious ἀπολαμβάνειν or ἔχειν. It is worth noting that Matthew's three uses of the verb come in the passages on Almsgiving, Prayer, and Fasting, a highly Judaic section of the sermon.

(3) vi. 27 ἀλλ' ὑμῖν λέγω τοῖς ἀκούουσιν. Here our Lord seems to address no longer only the disciples but the 'much multitude of the people who came to hear him'. One cannot but feel the 'editorial character' of this transition. It is therefore of considerable interest to note the Matthaean parallel v. 43 f.: ἠκούσατε ὅτι ἐρρέθη· ἀγαπήσεις τὸν πλησίον σου καὶ μισήσεις τὸν ἐχθρόν σου. ἐγὼ δὲ λέγω ὑμῖν, ἀγαπᾶτε τοὺς ἐχθροὺς ὑμῶν κτλ. St Luke has dropped the reference to the Law in accordance with his usual practice of bleaching out points of special Jewish interest, but his ἀκούουσιν (cf. ἠκούσατε) betrays his indebtedness, coming as it does at the very point where he resumes his use of Matthew.

(4) St Luke, in the passage just discussed, inserts two clauses between his parallels to Matthew's 'love your enemies' and 'pray

39

for them that persecute you'. The second of these inserted clauses runs: εὐλογεῖτε τοὺς καταρωμένους ὑμῖν. It is possible that there is a connexion here with Rom. xii. 14 εὐλογεῖτε τοὺς διώκοντας ὑμᾶς εὐλογεῖτε καὶ μὴ καταρᾶσθε. The other clause inserted by St Luke—καλῶς ποιεῖτε τοῖς μισοῦσιν ὑμᾶς—may be connected with Matt. v. 43 μισήσεις τὸν ἐχθρόν σου, which he had omitted a moment before.

(5) vi. 31; cf. Matt. vii. 12 καθὼς θέλετε ἵνα ποιῶσιν. This use of ἵνα with the subjunctive after θέλειν occurs only here in Matthew and Luke–Acts. This suggests direct literary connexion.

(6) vi. 35f. ἔσται ὁ μισθὸς ὑμῶν πολύς, καὶ ἔσεσθε υἱοὶ τοῦ ὑψίστου. ὅτι αὐτὸς χρηστός ἐστιν ἐπὶ τοὺς ἀχαρίστους καὶ πονηρούς. γίνεσθε οἰκτίρμονες καθὼς ὁ πατὴρ ὑμῶν οἰκτίρμων ἐστίν. Luke's combination of indebtedness and idiosyncrasy comes out interestingly here. A few verses earlier, where Matthew has τίνα μισθὸν ἔχετε;, St Luke wrote ποία ὑμῖν χάρις ἐστίν;, substituting χάρις (Matthew 0, Mark 0, Luke 8) for μισθός. But now, when he is getting back to Matthew after a digression, he uses the μισθός phrase from Matt. v. 12; cf. Luke vi. 23. He then takes Matthew's ἔσεσθε (v. 48), and so back to υἱοί, etc. He changes Matthew's τοῦ πατρὸς ὑμῶν τοῦ ἐν οὐρανοῖς to ὑψίστου, thus missing the point of 'sons of your Father' (but he implies it by retaining 'Father' in v. 36). χρηστός is weak for ἥλιον ἀνατέλλει and βρέχει. Ἀχαρίστους is due partly to his own ποία χάρις, partly to his phrase about lending without hope of return (it should decide us in favour of the reading μηδέν in v. 35). Then γίνεσθε is substituted for Matthew's ἔσεσθε from Matthew's own ὅπως γίνησθε. Οἰκτίρμονες is perhaps due to a sense that Matthew's τέλειοι ὡς τέλειος required explanation or softening.

Two further points: Luke vi. 33 τὸ αὐτὸ ποιοῦσιν is a 'weariness phenomenon'; Matthew has the phrase here and also just before. St Luke had expanded in the former instance; here he copies. Had he not had Matthew before him he would perhaps have said: κατὰ τὰ αὐτὰ ποιοῦσιν. On the other hand, 'publicans', and especially 'Gentiles' (Matthew) he prefers to bleach out into 'sinners'.

St Luke's Sermon has, over and above what is paralleled in Matthew, the Woes and vi. 34, 35a, 37b, 38a. It would perhaps be going too far to suppose that he composed these verses out of the suggestions found in Matthew (the Woes, in particular, by contrast with the Beatitudes). But if he had a separate source for these verses, there is some probability that it was in Aramaic; for the influence of Matthew's Greek extends into these verses, and such of the Greek in them as is not Matthaean is generally rather strikingly Lucan, and is in fact often linked with the vocabulary not of the Third Gospel only, but of Acts. In any case, there is little in the evidence so far considered to encourage belief that St Matthew and St Luke had a common Greek source for the Sermon. There are passages in Matthew's Sermon that may have been spoken at other times and been 'edited' into the Sermon by St Matthew (e.g. v. 25 f., vi. 7–15, the *Pater Noster*, vii. 6, vii. 7–11) and most of these have parallels in Luke outside the Sermon. But Matt. v. 25 f. is more original than Luke xii. 57–9, which betrays Lucan editing; as also does the Lucan *Pater Noster* (xi. 2–4).

It may be noted that Luke xi. 9–13 adds to Matt. vii. 7–11 the question, 'Or again if he ask an egg will he give him a scorpion?' It might be suggested that Luke here gives the full Q text, but it should be observed that snakes and scorpions occur together also at Luke x. 19 (reminiscent of Ps. xc (xci)), and the mention of a snake in Matt. vii. 10, Luke xi. 11 may have reminded St Luke of that verse. In other respects Luke's divergences from Matthew in this passage show some striking Lucanisms.

More important, as a possible argument for Q, is the comparison of Luke vi. 43 f. with Matt. vii. 15–20 and xii. 33, for here Luke can be represented as intermediary between the two passages of Matthew, since each of them has its own links with the Lucan version. Since it cannot be supposed that Matthew used Luke, it might be argued that all three passages derive from an original in Q. The alternative is that Luke here has 'conflated' the two Matthaean passages.[1] And it is possible to suggest a reason for such conflation: St Luke determined to omit from his Sermon the instructions on prayer, as well as the treatment of the Mosaic Law. In fact, after the Woes he has

---

[1] On Matthew's Doublets see ch. IX below. Generally speaking, they show the author repeating himself, not copying different sources. It is probable that Matt. xii. 33 is a shortened reproduction of vii. 16–20; note that in ch. vii the tree is 'good' or 'corrupt', the fruit is 'fair' or 'bad'; this nuance is missing in ch. xii, which also lacks the Semitic *inclusio* of the earlier passage.

narrowed the Sermon down practically to the theme of love of neighbour. Hence after the Mote and Beam passage (vi. 41f.; cf. Matt. vii. 3–5) he omits a longish passage of Matt. (vii. 6–14). The next section is ours, *By their fruits*, etc., which suggests to his mind the idea (congenial to his purpose in the Sermon) that if you want to do good you must *be* good. However, *as it stands in Matthew's Sermon*, the section is given quite a different bearing by its opening verse: 'Beware of false prophets, who come to you in sheep's clothing, but within they are ravening wolves; *from their fruits you shall know them.*' Here the point is not 'if you want to do good, *be* good' but 'if you want to judge whether another man is good, examine whether he does good'. Obviously, then, St Luke must drop Matt. vii. 15; but then the next verse loses its connexion. Not unnaturally, he turns to the other member of the doublet (Matt. xii. 33) for inspiration, which he gets, along with the useful conclusion ὁ ἀγαθὸς ἄνθρωπος κτλ. The result of this procedure is that his own version fuses the two in Matthew.

We now turn to examine Lucan passages outside the Sermon that have their parallels in Matthew's Sermon:

(1) Matt. v. 13

ὑμεῖς ἐστε τὸ ἅλα τῆς γῆς· ἐὰν δὲ τὸ ἅλα μωρανθῇ, ἐν τίνι ἁλισθήσεται; εἰς οὐδὲν ἰσχύει ἔτι εἰ μὴ βληθὲν ἔξω καταπατεῖσθαι ὑπὸ τῶν ἀνθρώπων.

Luke xiv. 34–5

καλὸν οὖν τὸ ἅλα· ἐὰν δὲ καὶ τὸ ἅλα μωρανθῇ ἐν τίνι ἀρτυθήσεται; 35. οὔτε εἰς γῆν οὔτε εἰς κοπρίαν εὔθετόν ἐστιν· ἔξω βάλλουσιν αὐτό. ὁ ἔχων ὦτα ἀκούειν ἀκουέτω.

The Lucan passage is not in Marcan context, but it has reminiscences, in the words καλόν and ἀρτύειν, of Mark ix. 50. Its language shows Luke's editorial hand, and Harnack (*op. cit.*) concludes that the original form of the saying is accurately preserved in Matthew.

(2) Matt. v. 15

οὐδὲ καίουσιν λύχνον καὶ τιθέασιν αὐτὸν ὑπὸ τὸν μόδιον, ἀλλ' ἐπὶ τὴν λυχνίαν, καὶ λάμπει πᾶσιν τοῖς ἐν τῇ οἰκίᾳ.

Luke xi. 33

οὐδεὶς λύχνον ἅψας εἰς κρυπτὴν τίθησιν οὐδὲ ὑπὸ τὸν μόδιον, ἀλλ' ἐπὶ τὴν λυχνίαν, ἵνα οἱ εἰσπορευόμενοι τὸ φέγγος βλέπωσιν.

Here again Harnack's verdict is that 'in Q it ran as St Matthew gives it'. Lucan are οὐδείς, ἅψας, εἰσπορευόμενοι. In the combination εἰς κρυπτήν...ὑπὸ τὸν μόδιον there may be a reminiscence of Mark iv. 21. Luke's verse is in poor contextual sequence, both backwards and forwards.

(3)　　Matt. v. 18

ἀμὴν γὰρ λέγω ὑμῖν, ἕως ἂν παρέλθῃ ὁ οὐρανὸς καὶ ἡ γῆ, ἰῶτα ἓν ἢ μία κεραία οὐ μὴ παρέλθῃ ἀπὸ τοῦ νόμου, ἕως ἂν πάντα γένηται.

Luke xvi. 17

εὐκοπώτερον δέ ἐστιν τὸν οὐρανὸν καὶ τὴν γῆν παρελθεῖν, ἢ τοῦ νόμου μίαν κεραίαν πεσεῖν.

Harnack (p. 56) regards ἀμὴν γὰρ λέγω ὑμῖν and ἕως ἂν πάντα γένηται as perhaps secondary, but the rest of Matthew's text as identical with Q. Luke's version is poorly linked with its context. Reviewing Matt. v. 3–20, it will be noticed that νν. 14 and 16 cohere closely with the Q νν. 13 and 15 (Luke's ἵνα... τὸ φέγγος βλέπωσιν is probably from Matt. v. 16 ὅπως ἴδωσιν ὑμῶν τὰ καλὰ ἔργα), and that Q thus tends, as often, to grow out like a cancer into the Matthaean context of the actual verses guaranteed to it by Luke's use of them. And it will be further noticed that this section of Matthew's Sermon is preceded by the Beatitudes, of which Luke has a version, and is followed by a 'Jewish' section which Luke would naturally omit. There is nothing to prevent Q from having contained all the first twenty verses of Matthew's Sermon in the order and sequence in which Matthew gives them. Q in fact always threatens to identify itself not only with the text of Matthew's so-called Q passages, but with Matthew as a whole. In other words the Q hypothesis is one that tends to destroy itself.

(4) Matt. v. 31, 32; cf. Luke xvi. 18, on Divorce. We have already discussed this passage (p. 32 *supra*). Harnack accepts the whole of Matthew's *v.* 32 as Q, except ἐγὼ δὲ λέγω ὑμῖν ὅτι and παρεκτὸς λόγου πορνείας. It will be noted that there is no reason why ἐγὼ δὲ λέγω ὑμῖν ὅτι should not be original, except that it would carry with it *v.* 31 and, presumably, the whole context.

(5)　　Matt. vi. 19–21

μὴ θησαυρίζετε ὑμῖν θησαυροὺς ἐπὶ τῆς γῆς, ὅπου σὴς καὶ βρῶσις ἀφανίζει, καὶ ὅπου κλέπται διορύσσουσιν καὶ κλέπτουσιν· 20. θησαυρίζετε δὲ ὑμῖν θησαυροὺς ἐν οὐρανῷ, ὅπου οὔτε σὴς οὔτε βρῶσις ἀφανίζει, καὶ ὅπου κλέπται οὐ διορύσσουσιν οὐδὲ κλέπτουσιν. 21. ὅπου γάρ ἐστιν ὁ θησαυρός σου, ἐκεῖ ἔσται καὶ ἡ καρδία σου.

Luke xii. 33, 34

πωλήσατε τὰ ὑπάρχοντα ὑμῶν καὶ δότε ἐλεημοσύνην· ποιήσατε ἑαυτοῖς βαλλάντια μὴ παλαιούμενα, θησαυρὸν ἀνέκλειπτον ἐν τοῖς οὐρανοῖς, ὅπου κλέπτης οὐκ ἐγγίζει οὐδὲ σὴς διαφθείρει. 34. ὅπου γάρ ἐστιν ὁ θησαυρὸς ὑμῶν ἐκεῖ καὶ ἡ καρδία ὑμῶν ἔσται.

Harnack appears to regard all three verses of Matthew as original Q, except that he would substitute Luke's plural 'heavens' for Matthew's singular (see p. 32 *supra*), and does not decide between σου and ὑμῶν in the last verse. A special interest is attached to Luke xii. 33 *a*, apparently a variation on the theme of Matt. vi. 19. Matthew says, 'Do not accumulate earthly wealth'; Luke (*remembering the Rich Man* who was to have 'treasure in heaven' if he gave up his earthly wealth to follow Christ, Matt. xix. 21; Mark x. 21; Luke xviii. 22) says, '(On the contrary) sell what you have and give alms':

Matt. xix. 21	Luke xii. 33
πώλησόν σου τὰ ὑπάρχοντα καὶ δὸς πτωχοῖς, καὶ ἕξεις θησαυρὸν ἐν οὐρανῷ.	πωλήσατε τὰ ὑπάρχοντα ὑμῶν καὶ δότε ἐλεημοσύνην...θησαυρὸν ἀνέκλειπτον ἐν τοῖς οὐρανοῖς.

Thus Luke appears to show knowledge of a Marcan section of Matt. (xix. 21, the parallels in Mark and Luke lacking ὑπάρχοντα). Lucan are δότε ἐλεημοσύνην, βαλλάντια (ἀνέκλειπτον is a N.T. *hapax legomenon*, but cf. Luke xvii. 1 ἀνένδεκτον N.T. *hapax*; ἐκλείπω Luke 3, Hebrews 1, elsewhere in N.T. 0; note especially xvi. 9 ἵνα ὅταν ἐκλίπῃ κτλ.), ἐγγίζει.

(6) Matt. vi. 22–34; cf. Luke xi. 34–6, xvi. 13, xii. 22–31. Harnack comments: 'The variants in St Luke, in so far as they are of a stylistic character, appear throughout as secondary readings.' Luke xi. 34–6 and xvi. 13 are less happily placed in their contexts than the Matthaean parallels. Luke xii. 22 perhaps opens with some editorial words, to weld together two passages not joined in a source. Luke xii. 26 looks like an editorial gloss; and the phrase τί περὶ τῶν λοιπῶν μεριμνᾶτε; is probably a reminiscence of Mark iv. 19. Matthew's rhythms seem original.

(7) Matt. vii. 13, 14	Luke xiii. 23, 24
εἰσέλθατε διὰ τῆς στενῆς πύλης· ὅτι πλατεῖα [ἡ πύλη] καὶ εὐρύχωρος ἡ ὁδὸς ἡ ἀπάγουσα εἰς τὴν ἀπώλειαν, καὶ πολλοί εἰσιν οἱ εἰσερχόμενοι δι' αὐτῆς· 14. ὅτι στενὴ [ἡ πύλη] καὶ τεθλιμμένη ἡ ὁδὸς ἡ ἀπάγουσα εἰς τὴν ζωήν, καὶ ὀλίγοι εἰσὶν οἱ εὑρίσκοντες αὐτήν.	εἶπεν δέ τις αὐτῷ· κύριε, εἰ ὀλίγοι οἱ σωζόμενοι; ὁ δὲ εἶπεν πρὸς αὐτούς· 24. ἀγωνίζεσθε εἰσελθεῖν διὰ τῆς στενῆς θύρας, ὅτι πολλοί, λέγω ὑμῖν, ζητήσουσιν εἰσελθεῖν καὶ οὐκ ἰσχύσουσιν.

Matthew's passage is quite well placed, though without explicit links. Luke's version is without context backwards, hence probably the (editorial?) question that introduces it (cf. Luke xxii. 49; Acts i. 6), which is perhaps derived from Matthew's 'There are few that find it'. Forwards, Luke's version links up with a passage recalling first the Matthaean parable of the Foolish Virgins and then Matt. vii. 22 f.

Matthew's version is an injunction to set out on the difficult road which leads through this life to life eternal. Luke's refers to a situation at the *end* of this life's struggles, when the good will be admitted to the heavenly home, while the bad are driven away; hence Luke's 'door' for Matthew's 'gate'; hence also the future tenses in Luke, where Matthew has the present. Matthew's version seems more original, for it will surely be too late to 'struggle' to enter in when the Last Day comes, and the fact that Luke has this awkwardness is presumably due to his attempt to weld together material of disparate provenance. Even so, *v.* 25 is appended somewhat abruptly, and Creed points out that in *v.* 24 the emphasis falls on the narrowness of the door, in *v.* 25 on the fact that it is closed. The Matthaean passage has the simplicity and rhythm of originality. One may, in fact, suspect that Luke xiii. 23–30 is an editorial and reminiscent patchwork. With it and its language compare Luke xi. 5–10, Matt. xxv. 10–12, vii. 22 f., viii. 11 f., xx. 16 (note, in Luke xiii. 30, the characteristic softening of the language, 'there are last who shall be first, and there are first who shall be last').

The Sermon ended, Matthew continues: 'And it came to pass, when Jesus had finished these words, the crowds were astonished at His teaching', etc. There follow the descent from the mountain and the cleansing of a leper, and then, after the entry into Capernaum, the centurion's request leads to the healing of his servant.

Luke had copied from Mark the sentence about the effect of the teaching (iv. 32), and had also taken from Mark the healing of the leper (v. 12–16). But apart from these omissions, his continuation follows Matthew exactly, with some Lucan change of vocabulary: 'When he had completed all His words in the ears of the people, he went into Capernaum', and there the centurion's servant is healed. (For πληροῦν 'complete', not of time, cf. Acts xiv. 26, xix. 21; ῥῆμα Matt. 5, Mark 2, Luke 19, John 12, Acts 14; for εἰς τὰς ἀκοὰς τοῦ λαοῦ cf. Acts xvii. 20 and note Luke vi. 17, the introduction to the Sermon, editing Mark.) Harnack emphasizes the importance of this parallelism between the two Gospels, 'for from this it follows with certainty that even in Q large portions of the Sermon on the Mount occurred together, and that the Sermon was followed by the Cure of the Centurion's Servant in Capernaum'. These are significant admissions; we note how Q, from being a collection of sayings and discourses, threatens to become a Gospel, discourse and incidents being linked together by narrative. It is further of great importance to observe that Matthew's ὅτε ἐτέλεσεν κτλ. is a Matthaean formula, recurring at xi. 1, xiii. 53, xix. 1, xxvi. 1. Luke borrows the formula on this occasion alone.

The episode of the Centurion's servant is one in which Luke's fusion of Matthew and a special source is most evident. The special source is represented by the description of the sick person as δοῦλος, while Matthew, and Luke when copying Matthew, call him παῖς.[1] Luke's μὴ σκύλλου, interpolated into Matthew's κύριε, οὐκ εἰμὶ ἱκανός κτλ., looks like a reminiscence of the Jairus incident (Luke viii. 49; cf. Mark v. 35).

We may now summarize and review our discussion of the Great Sermon. Luke's Sermon is introduced by some considerable editorial manipulation of Marcan material, and his choice of context for it indicates that in his source for the Sermon itself it was indeed a Sermon on 'the Mount'. It is the same Sermon as the one recorded by St Matthew, as exordium and peroration prove, together with the fact that there are, besides the Woes, at most only a few verses in it that could not be derived from Matthew's—than which, however, it is far shorter. But while not simply a variant record, it is not a mere précis or abridgment of Matthew's Sermon, for it is constructed—after the Woes—in the main so as to be a discourse on the duty of charity towards one's fellow-men.

Either then our Lord preached a sermon on this theme, which Matthew has expanded, 'Judaized' (i.e. set back into a Jewish thought-world and made relevant to Palestinian controversies), and so transformed into a quasi-original Christian manifesto; or St Luke

---

[1] Matt. viii. 9, 'my slave (δοῦλος)' does not refer to the sick servant, but to any one of the slaves of the centurion.

has transformed a sermon of the latter type into a shorter one on a more generalized theme.

Not only does the former solution offend against what we may call the historical law of entropy (it involves putting back the clock of history and an inversion of the principles of historical development),[1] but its falsity is indicated by the following considerations: (*a*) Luke vi. 27 ἀλλὰ ὑμῖν λέγω τοῖς ἀκούουσιν appears to be an adaptation of Matt. v. 43 f. And since the 'inner and outer circles' arrangement was edited into his materials by Luke at vi. 17 (μαθητῶν …λαοῦ), we may be excused for suspecting that, wishing to convey our Lord's message in a form prepared for a Gentile reading-public, he has deliberately selected teaching of the most universal kind—charity towards one's fellow-men being a thing of universal appeal and yet implicitly covering the whole Christian ethical system[2]—out of a sermon of a more particular colour. (*b*) It is interesting to note that, apart from Matt. vii. 6, 15, there is nothing in Matthew's Sermon that St Luke does not copy somewhere in his Gospel, except passages that have a particular reference to the Jewish Law or to Jewish religious practice. It would be somewhat surprising, if St Matthew has expanded a Sermon of the Lucan type, that he should find nothing not also at St Luke's disposal except this Judaic material. (*c*) Our conclusion is reinforced by some traces of Matthew's vocabulary in Luke's Sermon: μισθός, ἀπέχετε, ὁ πατὴρ ὑμῶν, τὸ αὐτὸ ποιοῦσιν. (*d*) Luke's ὑψίστου spoils the sense in its effort to avoid the phrase 'your Father in heaven'. In view of this, the weakness of χρηστός and οἰκτίρμονες becomes significant. (*e*) The divergences from Matthew's vocabulary in Luke's Sermon are, as regularly in Luke's Q passages, specifically 'Lucan'; in other words, the formula 'Matthew's style *plus* Luke's style' covers the Greek of Luke's Sermon adequately without appeal to a non-Matthaean Greek source. (*f*) Luke xi. 33, xvi. 18, xii. 33 f., xii. 22–31 seem secondary when compared with the corresponding passages of Matthew's Sermon, and Luke xii. 33 f. also shows the influence of Matt. xix. 21. (*g*) The immediate sequel of the Sermon in Luke is equivalent to the sequel to Matthew's Sermon on the

---

[1] It would be a case, not merely of selecting material of special Palestinian interest, but of impregnating a whole un-Jewish sermon with the atmosphere of Palestine.

[2] Cf. Rom. xiii. 10, 'Love is the fulfilment of the law'.

Mount, except that Luke lacks here what he had copied elsewhere from Mark.

Such arguments against our solution as may be derived from a comparison of Luke xi. 9–13 with Matt. vii. 7–11 and of Luke vi. 43 f. with Matt. vii. 15–20 and xii. 33 cannot carry weight against the multiple converging indications of Luke's direct dependence on the Matthaean Sermon. And it must always be remembered that the simple and economical solution is that of direct dependence, not that of coincident use of a conjectural source.

CHAPTER IV

FURTHER EVIDENCE

The conclusion drawn from our five crucial instances (chapter i) has stood the test of application to the problems raised by a comparison of Matthew's Sermon on the Mount with Luke's Great Sermon and other passages of Luke. We now extend our test to other passages where there is, or may be, literary connexion between the first and third Gospels.

(1) A passage from Matthew's version of the healing of the Centurion's servant, lacking in the parallel version of Luke, but found at Luke xiii. 28-30, of which we have already discussed *v*. 30.

<table>
<tr><td>Matt. viii. 11 f.</td><td>Luke xiii. 28 f.</td></tr>
<tr><td>λέγω δὲ ὑμῖν ὅτι πολλοὶ ἀπὸ ἀνατολῶν καὶ δυσμῶν ἥξουσιν καὶ ἀνακλιθήσονται μετὰ Ἀβραὰμ καὶ Ἰσαὰκ καὶ Ἰακὼβ ἐν τῇ βασιλείᾳ τῶν οὐρανῶν. 12. οἱ δὲ υἱοὶ τῆς βασιλείας ἐξελεύσονται εἰς τὸ σκότος τὸ ἐξώτερον. ἐκεῖ ἔσται ὁ κλαυθμὸς καὶ ὁ βρυγμὸς τῶν ὀδόντων.</td><td>ἐκεῖ ἔσται ὁ κλαυθμὸς καὶ ὁ βρυγμὸς τῶν ὀδόντων, ὅταν ὄψεσθε Ἀβραὰμ καὶ Ἰσαὰκ καὶ Ἰακὼβ καὶ πάντας τοὺς προφήτας ἐν τῇ βασιλείᾳ τοῦ θεοῦ, ὑμᾶς δὲ ἐκβαλλομένους ἔξω. 29. καὶ ἥξουσιν ἀπὸ ἀνατολῶν καὶ δυσμῶν καὶ βορρᾶ καὶ νότου καὶ ἀνακλιθήσονται ἐν τῇ βασιλείᾳ τοῦ θεοῦ....</td></tr>
</table>

(a) The phrase 'There shall be weeping and gnashing of teeth' is a Matthaean formula, occurring six times in that Gospel. This is the only occasion of its use by Luke. We may compare Luke's use, at the end of the Sermon, of a Lucan modification of the formula for the ends of Matthew's discourses (καὶ ἐγένετο ὅτε ἐτέλεσεν κτλ.). Are we to assume that Matthew picked up both these phrases from a single use of each in Q, and turned them into recurrent refrains?

(b) It will be noticed that Luke's order apparently involves treating ἐκεῖ as a temporal adverb, a meaning it has perhaps nowhere else in the New Testament (Liddell and Scott give one reference to Sophocles and one to Demosthenes for this meaning of ἐκεῖ). Creed says: 'The ἐκεῖ shows that the wording has been disarranged' in Luke.

(c) Luke's 'all the prophets' and 'and north and south' are typical Lucan completions ('all' is a favourite word with Luke); Matthew has a starker, more original, ring. Indeed, the whole Lucan context ~~is misty and vague, while~~ its Matthaean parallels are in general vivid and clear-cut. Harnack says that 'ye shall see' reminds one of the parable of Dives and Lazarus. 'From the time when the master of the house is roused' (xiii. 25) is a reminiscence of Matt. xxiv. 43, from which verse of Matthew Luke passes on to the parable of the Ten Virgins, a little lower down, for his scene before the shut door (*vv.* 25–7). The master of the house and his 'rising up' are unexplained in Luke, and barely congruous with the following Messianic banquet. In short, Lucan psychology and literary criticism combine to show that Matt. viii. 11 f. is more original than Luke xiii. 28–30, and that the whole paragraph in Luke can be explained by the use of various Matthaean passages, but hardly vice versa.

(2) The Baptist and Christ, Matt. xi. 2–19; cf. Luke vii. 18–35. This is a typical Q passage, our Lord's words being recorded in almost identical Greek by both evangelists. Luke has, beyond Matthew, *vv.* 20, 21 and 29f. Of *v.* 21 Creed says: 'This verse is very awkwardly interpolated by Luke', and of *vv.* 29f.: 'It is not at all clear whether these verses are intended to be read as a historical statement introduced by' the evangelist; 'this seems to be the most satisfactory interpretation...although the return to direct speech in *v.* 31 without further introduction is awkward.... The passage was perhaps introduced here to provide an interpretation by anticipation of *v.* 35 *infra.*' These phenomena strongly suggest that Luke has been 'editing' a text indistinguishable from Matthew's, and his variations from Matthew betray Lucan style and psychology: vii. 18, περί, πάντων; 19, τίνας; 20, οἱ ἄνδρες; 21, ἐχαρίσατο; 22, asyndeton in place of Matthew's rhythmical three pairs; 24, πρός; 25, ἱματισμῷ, ἐνδόξῳ, ὑπάρχοντες; 28, προφήτης, inserted to make the statement less apparently sweeping; 31, double question; 32, ἐκλαύσατε; 33, insertion of ἄρτον and οἶνον (since John did eat *something*, and did not drink wine, Luke i. 15); 35, πάντων. Thus Q, if it be supposed to have existed, must have been, so far as we can see, indistinguishable from Matthew, and it is reasonable to regard Luke's *v.* 19b as an insertion to prepare the way for what follows. Matthew has, beyond Luke, *vv.* 12–15, which Luke may have omitted because of their obscurity and narrower Jewish interest. Part of the omitted passage has a parallel at Luke xvi. 16, upon which Creed comments:

'From the literary point of view the version given' in Luke 'may be confidently pronounced secondary' as compared with Matthew's; *vv*. 17 and 18 in the same chapter are from the Sermon on the Mount.

The section on the Baptist is splendidly placed in Matthew: the Christian movement has taken a great step forward in the sending forth of the apostles, and it is set in contrast first (here) with John the Baptist, then with the Jews in general, then in particular with the places in which Christ had worked many miracles; after which, by a kind of *inclusio*, we revert to the core of the Christian revelation itself, hidden from wise and prudent and revealed to little ones. Compared with this, the Lucan setting is tame.

(3) Luke viii. 1 seems to be a paraphrase of Matt. ix. 35, despite difference of wording and context:

Matt. ix. 35 ff.; x. 1	Luke viii. 1 f.
καὶ περιῆγεν ὁ Ἰησοῦς τὰς πόλεις πάσας καὶ τὰς κώμας, διδάσκων ἐν ταῖς συναγωγαῖς αὐτῶν καὶ κηρύσσων τὸ εὐαγγέλιον τῆς βασιλείας καὶ θεραπεύων πᾶσαν νόσον καὶ πᾶσαν μαλακίαν.... 37. τότε λέγει τοῖς μαθηταῖς αὐτοῦ.... x. 1. τοὺς δώδεκα μαθητὰς αὐτοῦ.	καὶ ἐγένετο ἐν τῷ καθεξῆς καὶ αὐτὸς διώδευεν κατὰ πόλιν καὶ κώμην κηρύσσων, καὶ εὐαγγελιζόμενος τὴν βασιλείαν τοῦ θεοῦ, καὶ οἱ δώδεκα σὺν αὐτῷ, 2. καὶ γυναῖκές τινες, αἳ ἦσαν τεθεραπευμέναι ἀπὸ πνευμάτων πονηρῶν καὶ ἀσθενειῶν....

Luke's wording is in the main a series of Lucan equivalents for that of Matthew (as shown by underlining, above). Luke uses the passage as an introduction to the parables of the kingdom; Matthew had used it as an introduction to the Mission Charge, and has a doublet-twin to introduce the Sermon on the Mount (iv. 23). In view of the other evidence of St Luke's use and treatment of Matthew, one may be forgiven for suspecting that there is indebtedness here also. Otherwise we have to admit a very striking coincidence.

(4) The Mission of the Seventy, etc., Luke ix. 57–x. 24. Luke ix. 57–62 has a partial parallel at Matt. viii. 19–22. The words of our Lord, so far as they occur in both, are practically identical, but *v*. 60*b* is absent from Matthew. Διαγγέλλειν is a Lucan word, and the discrepancy between ἀκολούθει μοι and ἀπελθὼν διάγγελλε may indicate that Luke is expanding—Creed says the clause was 'probably added by Luke'. Verses 61 and 62 are also peculiar to

Luke, and Creed says 'Luke may have added it to provide a setting for a great saying'.

The Mission of the Seventy has been dealt with in chapter 1 above. The story of this Mission is peculiar to Luke, and the material for it has been eked out with matter from the Matthaean Mission of the Twelve, St Luke having used the Marcan Mission of the Twelve in its own context. Besides the points noticed in chapter 1, it may be observed that the instructions to the Seventy end with a verse (16) similar to one of the concluding verses (x. 40) of the Matthaean Mission of the Twelve. Luke's use of Matt. xi. 21–3 at Luke x. 13–15 has been noted in chapter 11. Luke x. 21 f. is a curtailed reproduction of Matt. xi. 25–30. Luke has omitted the wonderful concluding verses of Matthew's version: 'Come unto Me', etc.; yet their relevance to the preceding Matthaean context is at once clear, when we note that the 'wise and prudent' from whom the revelation is withheld are typically the scribes and Pharisees who (Matt. xxiii. 4; cf. Luke xi. 46) *bind heavy burdens and lay them on men's shoulders*; whereas the burden of those who *learn* from the only Revealer of the Heavenly Father is a *light* one. Στραφεὶς πρὸς τοὺς μαθητὰς εἶπεν (Luke x. 23) is one of St Luke's frequent explanatory additions (στραφείς: Matthew 2, Luke 7 or 8); like 'He rejoiced in the Holy Spirit' in *v.* 21. Thus once again what is non-Matthaean in a Lucan Q passage turns out to be characteristically Lucan, and hence is no indication of another source; Q, as usual, is indistinguishable from Matthew.[1] Finally, Luke x. 23 f. is parallel to Matt. xiii. 16 f., but Luke omits 'your ears because they hear' despite the rhythmical balance with the next verse 'to see...and hear'. Luke's 'kings' may be due to reminiscence, for example, of the Psalm *Deus, Deus meus*, considered as the prayer of King David. The 'in private' of *v.* 23 shows St Luke's awareness that the occasion in Matthew when our Lord spoke these words to His disciples was when He was about to explain (to them and not to the crowds) the parable of the Sower; as he remembered from Mark, these explanations were given 'in private' (Mark iv. 34).

[1] Creed, who appears inclined to accept Norden's verdict that 'the integral text' of this great *rhesis* is preserved in Matthew, suggests that St Luke 'modified the source with a view to the setting in which he has placed it, i.e. the occasion of the return of the seventy disciples'.

The cumulative force of the evidence afforded by the comparison of Luke ix. 57–x. 24 with the parallels in Matthew is strong. It can hardly be believed that the data could be so adequately met by the hypothesis of direct dependence on Matthew if in fact both Gospels were dependent on an unknown source.

(5) Luke xi. 24–6; cf. Matt. xii. 43–5; the 'Seven other spirits'. The wording is almost identical, but the contexts differ. In Matthew the passage occurs in a reply to a request for a sign, and it means that the Jews, having been purged of their spirit of unbelief under the Old Covenant, are in danger of reverting to infidelity and thus of succumbing to other faults, if they do not now go on to make a positive act of faith in the new revelation, for which their past purification was intended to prepare them. In Luke the passage comes in the Beelzebub controversy, and the result is that it reads like a comment on diabolic possession in the literal sense—the more so if, with Huck, we omit the word σχολάζοντα in Luke, which gives the point to the passage in Matthew. It is easier to believe that Luke has emptied of its deeper meaning a Matthaean passage, by altering its context, than that Matthew, by clever placing (and the interpolation of σχολάζοντα?), has put a new and significant colour on a piece of Q.

Luke xi. 29–32 proceeds (somewhat awkwardly, after an interjection from a woman in the crowd, and a piece of Lucan editing) to answer the request for a sign (xi. 16); cf. Matt. xii. 38–42 (see p. 26 *supra*). Luke substitutes prose for Matthew's poetry. And note the 'fatigue phenomenon'; in the second half of the passage his variations from Matthew are much less numerous than in the first—only τῶν ἀνδρῶν inserted before the former τῆς γενεᾶς ταύτης, but not before the latter (the effort to modify ceasing here entirely). For Luke xi. 33 cf. Matt. v. 15 and p. 42 *supra*.

(6) Luke xi. 37–xii. 1; cf. Matt. xxiii. 25 f., 23, 6 f., 27, 4, 29–31, 34–6, 13, and for Luke xii. 1 see Matt. xvi. 6, 12; cf. Mark viii. 15.

As Creed observes, these denunciations of the Pharisees and the lawyers are all of them closely paralleled in Matt. xxiii, but the Matthaean denunciations are much longer than the Lucan, and the method of arrangement is entirely different. 'Much of the material in Matthew not found in Luke has a pronounced Jewish colouring, and would be of less interest to Luke's readers.' In Matthew...we have a series of seven "woes". In Luke there are six "woes", of which three are pronounced upon Pharisees and three upon "lawyers" (i.e. the scribes). But there is something artificial about this arrangement. The dividing verse (45) is a somewhat clumsy division. Moreover the second "woe" of the second series (v. 47f.) does not appear to be especially appropriate to lawyers....Luke's conclusion is abrupt and much less impressive' than Matthew's. 'The scene is laid at a Pharisee's dinner-table...but there can be little doubt that *vv.* 37, 38 is a setting provided by Luke.' Perhaps we may suggest that St Luke had an authority, independent of Matthew, for some words spoken by our Lord at a Pharisee's table, and has fitted in his borrowings from Matt. xxiii to this context, as he fitted in part of the Matthaean Mission charge to his Mission of the Seventy. Wellhausen's suggestion that Luke xi. 41 'give alms' is due to a misunderstanding of the Aramaic *dakki* as if it were *ʒakki* is famous; but it is not free from difficulties[1] and it will be noticed that, if accepted, this suggestion proves not only that, for this verse, Luke was not dependent on Matthew, but that neither of them was dependent for it on Q; since Q (if it existed) was used, as the evidence overwhelmingly proves, in an identical Greek translation by both evangelists. Thus, on Wellhausen's hypothesis, the verse is no argument against Luke's dependence on Matthew in genuine Q passages; while, if we reject the theory that the two evangelists are here dependent on different sources (i.e. that this is not a Q saying), we have Harnack's verdict that 'St Matthew has the more original text'.

(7) Luke xii. 2–12; cf. Matt. x. 26–33, xii. 32, x. 19f. A more normal Q passage, as is shown by the coincidence in order with Matthew over a sequence of eight verses. Luke's modifications are often in his own style: συγκεκαλυμμένον, ἀνθ᾽ ὧν, πρὸς τὸ οὖς, the cheapening of the sparrows (Lucan inasmuch as Luke likes to suit his readers' circumstances and to play with figures), ἐνώπιον, 'officers and authorities' (vague and more comprehensive than 'governors and emperors', and likely to happen more often), ἐν αὐτῇ τῇ ὥρᾳ, perhaps εἰσφέρωσιν for παραδῶσιν. In *v.* 8 καὶ ὁ υἱὸς τοῦ

---

[1] It seems doubtful whether the verb *ʒakki* in Aramaic can mean 'give alms', either absolutely or with a direct object of the thing given. And such a construction would be required to explain our verse of Luke.

ἀνθρώπου is a reminiscence of Luke ix. 26, Mark viii. 38, from which context St Luke also got his 'angels'. In *v.* 10 βλασφημήσαντι is a reminiscence of Mark iii. 29. Matthew is more balanced and has better Semitic rhythm, and here and there we see St Luke changing one member of Matthew's pairs of parallels (*v.* 3 ὅσα...ὅ, *vv.* 8f. ὁμολογήσει active...ἀπαρνηθήσεται passive). We conclude that Q and Matthew are indistinguishable, that is, that Q is an unnecessary hypothesis.

(8) Luke xii. 35–8, with its injunction to have one's 'light burning', has been compared to the parable of the Ten Virgins (Matt. xxv), but the situation is very different: in Matthew the master is inside the house, while in Luke it is the servants who are inside, the master being outside and knocking. And apart from the marriage-motif and the words it entails, the wording is very different. The Lucan passage is closely connected with Luke xvii. 7–10, where note εὐθέως, παρελθών, ἀνάπεσε (cf. ἀνακλινεῖ here), περιζωσάμενος, διακόνει.

The more striking direct influence would seem to be Mark xiii. 33–7. There, as here, the servants are to be vigilant in the house, as the Master may be expected at any watch of the night—'lest coming suddenly he find you sleeping'; cf. in our passage 'blessed are those servants, whom the lord when he comes will find watching...and if he comes in the second and if in the third watch, and finds them thus...'.[1] Note that for St Luke (who looks back at our Lord's words from a later date) the first watch is already past. Thus we may suppose a substratum of independent tradition worked up into shape by St Luke with the help of memories of Mark xiii and a vague influence of the knowledge of Matt. xxv.

Luke xii. 39–46; cf. Matt. xxiv. 43–51. Here the slave waiting for his master gives place to the householder watching for the thief, but Mark is not forgotten, and in *v.* 41 Mark's ὃ δὲ ὑμῖν λέγω πᾶσιν λέγω (xiii. 37) has been metamorphosed into a question put into St Peter's mouth: κύριε, πρὸς ἡμᾶς τὴν παραβολὴν ταύτην λέγεις, ἢ πρὸς πάντας;, and this again introduces the Matthaean simile of the steward, *vv.* 42 ff. It may be noted that ἄρα in Matthew draws a lesson from the general teaching on the uncertainty about the

[1] Roughly speaking, the thought of this is from Mark, the language is largely from Matt. xxiv. 46.

55

Last Day which has been the theme of the preceding paragraphs; in Luke the same particle appears to answer St Peter's question by saying, 'Of course this teaching is meant specially for you, the steward whom I intend to leave in charge of my Church' (or for the apostles as a body, since each shares in the stewardship). Of these rival contexts for ἄρα Matthew's has the stronger claim to originality; for the introductory question or request is a Lucan idiosyncrasy; cf. x. 29, xi. 1 (answered by the *Pater Noster*), xii. 13, xiii. 23 (in a passage which we have argued to be secondary to Matthew), xvii. 5, 37 (cf. also, though these are not questions or petitions: xiii. 1, xiv. 15, xi. 45 and xv. 1f.; in the last case the introduction seems to be drawn from the Marcan tradition). Here again we see how intimacy with St Luke's psychology and editorial practice enables us to perceive that Q is indistinguishable from Matthew.

(9) Luke xii. 49–56; cf. Matt. x. 34–6, xvi. 2f. Luke xii. 49 has verbal links with Matt. x. 34; the following three verses are parallel to Matthew, with changes: in *v.* 51*a* the wording is altered for variety, Matthew's wording having been utilized already in *v.* 49; in *v.* 51*b* διαμερισμόν is less violent and obscure than Matthew's obviously more original μάχαιραν; *v.* 52 illustrates Luke's numerative, glossing trend—he has counted up the three pairs in Matthew and correctly made them five (the daughter-in-law's mother-in-law being the same person as the mother of the man and his sister); in *v.* 53 the use of the passive voice escapes attributing the feuds to Christ's agency. (Incidentally the quotation from Micah is in consequence blurred.)

Verses 54–6 are either a variant tradition, or a Lucan adaptation for non-Palestinian readers, of the saying recorded at Matt. xvi. 2f., the authenticity of which they strongly support, since the difference of vocabulary precludes the suggestion that Matthew has been 'harmonized' with Luke.

(10) Luke xiii. 34f.; cf. Matt. xxiii. 37–9, the lament over Jerusalem. In Matthew this passage comes as a magnificent (but perhaps editorial) climax to the Woes on the Pharisees. As regards its position in Luke we may quote Creed: 'If the lament is spoken, as Luke represents it, while Jesus is on the way to Jerusalem; how can Jesus say, "ye shall not see me until ye shall say Blessed is he..."' —unless, indeed, Luke thought that the salutation referred to the

triumphal entry, xix. 38?/But that gives a very bald sense, and leaves the last words and the preceding lament without any intelligible connexion.' To this we may add Harnack's comment on the variant wording: 'Even here the text of St Matthew shows itself to be the more ancient.'

(11) Luke xiv. 15–24, the Great Supper; cf. Matt. xxii. 1–10, the Wedding Feast. Each evangelist has features or whole episodes, in these somewhat similar passages, that are lacking or abridged in the other, and there is no identity of language beyond what the identical subject-matter might explain. Luke has one notable Syriacism ἀπὸ μιᾶς, and his parable might almost be a direct translation from an Aramaic source. In other words, this is not an ordinary Q passage.

(12) Luke xiv. 25–7; cf. Matt. x. 37–9. The Lucan passage may be a re-writing of the Matthaean, with reminiscence of Mark viii. 34 and parallels (whence the crowd, and εἴ τις ἔρχεται). The verbal links are not many, but Lucan style (prose for poetry, etc.) will in large measure account for the divergence.

(13) Luke xv. 1–10, the Lost Sheep and the Lost Drachma; cf. Matt. xviii. 12–14, the Lost Sheep. Streeter (*The Four Gospels*, p. 244) came to the conclusion that Luke and Matthew had different sources for the parable of the Lost Sheep; in other words that this is not a Q passage. Luke's parables of Sheep and Drachma certainly form a pair, with parallel pattern and numerous parallels of language. It is, however, not impossible that St Luke has utilized the language of Matthew's version for the rendering into Greek of the parable of the Lost Sheep; and *v.* 7 seems to show a reminiscence of Luke v. 31f. The data would be adequately met by the supposition that Luke obtained his pair of parables in an Aramaic version. Note that in Luke the sheep is 'lost' not 'wandering'; cf. Matt. xv. 24 'lost sheep of the House of Israel'. '[Joy] before the angels of God' may be a Lucan variant for Matthew's [θέλημα] ἔμπροσθεν τοῦ πατρὸς ὑμῶν τοῦ ἐν οὐρανοῖς. Cf. the same variant in Luke xii. 8f.; cf. Matt. x. 32f. Harnack, on our passage, says: 'Here the text of Luke is shown to be everywhere secondary.'

(14) Luke xvii. 3–6, Forgiveness and Faith; cf. Matt. xviii. 15, 21f., xvii. 20. In the two verses before this passage St Luke had been reproducing Matt. xviii. 6f. on scandal (see chapter I *supra*). Now in *vv.* 3f. he seems to be skimming over the surface of the Matthaean

section immediately following xviii. 6f.: προσέχετε ἑαυτοῖς is Lucan (note the dative after προσέχειν) for Matt. xviii. 10 ὁρᾶτε; the remainder of this verse is a stunted torso of the elaborate passage Matt. xviii. 15–17, the last two words anticipating Matt. xviii. 21f., which is again incompletely represented by Luke xvii. 4. All this is important, as it shows that Luke had a long piece of Matthew (most inadequately represented in Luke) before him, and that this piece was in Matthew's order.

Here an odd thing happens: Mark xi. 20–5 appends the idea of forgiveness to that of faith. In our passage reminiscence of that section of Mark leads St Luke to append the idea of faith (from Matt. xvii. 20, but affected by reminiscence of Mark xi. 22f.; cf. Matt. xxi. 21) to that of forgiveness (see p. 28 *supra*).

Thus these four verses admirably illustrate St Luke's indebtedness to his predecessors, and also the curious mixture of copying, reminiscence and modification that (together, of course, with independent material on occasion) underlies so much of his Gospel. They also serve to illustrate the vast superiority of Matthew's claim to originality.

(15) Luke xvii. 22–37, the Revelation of the Son of Man; cf. Matt. xxiv. 26–40 and Luke ix. 24 with its parallels. *Vv.* 22–5 are not very close to their Matthaean parallel; but *v.* 27, after its fourth word, becomes verbally identical (with omissions) with Matthew except that Luke has ἀπώλεσεν for ἦρεν. *Vv.* 28f. are without parallel in Matthew; for *v.* 31 cf. Matt. xxiv. 17f.; *v.* 32 is peculiar; *v.* 33 probably carries a reminiscence of Luke's own ix. 24; for *vv.* 34f. cf. Matt. xxiv. 28.

It must be admitted that the coupling, in Luke only, of the days of Lot with the days of Noah would seem to tell strongly in favour of the Q hypothesis, since the pair of closely parallel historical allusions, with a similar pattern of language, reminds one of the pairs of parables for which both Matthew and Luke provide evidence; although Creed remarks that if the Lot passage was in Q its omission by Matthew is remarkable. It is possible that Luke is drawing on an independent source, and it will be noted that in *v.* 31 the author is plainly copying Mark xiii. 15f. or its Matthaean parallel, while *vv.* 33 and 37 again show his editorial hand. Details follow:

Luke's borrowings from Matt. xxiv cease at Matt. xxiv. 28 and recommence at Matt. xxiv. 37 (it is indeed possible that Luke xvii. 31

is from Matthew and not from Mark; ἐν τῷ ἀγρῷ suggests Matthew, but εἰς τὰ ὀπίσω Mark. Luke's ordinary practice is not to use Mark outside Marcan contexts; but this is not an invariable rule.[1] Incidentally it may be suspected that Luke's τὰ σκεύη in this verse is a reminiscence of Matt. xii. 29 or its Marcan parallel, where there is a question of entering the house to plunder τὰ σκεύη). The intervening verses of Matthew (xxiv. 29–36) are parallel to Mark xiii. 24–32, which Luke follows at xxi. 25 ff. It is perhaps easier to explain this as due to St Luke's having excerpted from Matthew, omitting what was already to be found in Mark, than to suppose that both Matthew and Luke have succeeded in utilizing practically the whole of a rather long Q section, the one as framework for a Marcan passage, the other independently.

On our view, Luke's v. 34 is a delayed utilization of Matt. xxiv. 40 (see Luke xv. 10 for a similar phenomenon); ταύτῃ τῇ νυκτί may be a reminiscence of Lot's flight; but it may also be due to Matt. xxiv. 43, where the thief comes in the watches of the night. V. 37a is a Lucan editorial question, and the placing of the Vultures seems more original in Matthew—Creed suggests that the saying has been transposed by Luke to make a conclusion to the paragraph. Ἐπισυναχθήσονται in this verse (for Matthew's συναχθήσονται) may be a memory of the same verb in Matt. xxiv. 31 or its Marcan parallel.

On the whole, Luke's section is so suspiciously patchwork that it can afford only precarious support for the Q hypothesis, though the Lot reference must be conceded to be impressive.

(16) Luke xix. 11–27; cf. Matt. xxv. 14–30. The parable of the Pounds and the parable of the Talents. This is a mixed example, like that of the Wedding-Feast and the Great Supper. The parallelism of language is imperfect, and the hypothesis of literary connexion in Greek hardly becomes imperative till Luke xix. 21 ff. The two parables differ considerably in detail, and it may well be that they are not variants of the same parable, but were spoken at different times by our Lord. Matthew's story shows no sign of mutilation, and is more simply 'parabolic' than Luke's, though the line between parable and allegory should not be drawn too sharply.

---

[1] Luke's uneasy paraphrase of Mark xiii. 14–16 at Luke xxi. 21 f. suggests that he had already written xvii. 31 with its utilization of Mark xiii. 15 f. or its Matthaean parallel.

It is reasonable to hold that Luke's parable is from an Aramaic source, translated and embellished with the help of Matthew.

After the investigation of the Q passages conducted in this and the preceding chapters we may now review the case against the Q hypothesis. A hypothesis which introduces a conjectural document and multiplies, instead of reducing, literary relationships is suspect *a priori*. It imposes a burden of proof upon its supporters, and we have argued, in chapter II, that the reasons, alleged by Streeter against the natural supposition that Luke's Q passages are directly derived from Matthew, are unconvincing. Moreover Q never succeeds in becoming more than a vague, Protean entity, whose contents and character elude definition; an entity which tends to multiply into an Antiochene, an Ephesian and a Roman Q. All that one can say about it is, that it must have been in Greek, and that it was free from Palestinian and Jewish colouring to a degree that seems extremely remarkable in such an early Christian document, and indeed reminds one of Luke itself.

But we have shown, in chapter I, grave positive objections to the hypothesis. In the only passages where such a test can be applied we found that Matthew proves to be a 'middle-term' between Mark and Luke in passages where, on the opposing theory, Mark and Q overlapped. This result was obtained by objective use of the critical methods that are used to establish Mark's intermediate character in the 'Triple Tradition'. The implication is that the Lucan Q passages are derived from Matthew. In chapters III and IV we have tested this conclusion, first in the Lucan parallels to sections of Matthew's Sermon on the Mount, then elsewhere. We have found abundant support for the theory of direct dependence and little evidence tending against that theory.

Perhaps the most impressive arguments for the Q hypothesis, apart from a probably mistaken interpretation of a fragment of Papias, are (*a*) its general acceptance by a large number of distinguished scholars and their followers. But this appeal to authority is worth little or nothing if the reasons given for such acceptance are inadequate, and if the positive reasons for supposing Luke's direct dependence on Matthew have hardly been realized and never refuted. (*b*) If Matthew is dependent on Mark in the Marcan sections of the first Gospel, a source is required for the non-Marcan material incorporated in those sections. Since this non-Marcan material is often represented in non-Marcan sections of Luke, it is not unnatural, though still unnecessary, to suppose that it is derived by St Luke from the source whence St Matthew took it. The reply to this argument is found by implication in the following chapters, in which the fundamental hypothesis of Matthaean dependence on Mark is examined.

CHAPTER V

THE LACHMANN FALLACY

'A century of discussion', says Streeter,[1] 'has resulted in a consensus of scholars... that the authors of the First and Third Gospels made use either of our Mark, or of a document all but identical with Mark. The former and the simpler of these hypotheses, viz. that they used our Mark, is the one which I hope... to establish beyond reasonable doubt.' In the following pages I assume that it is agreed that 'a document all but identical with Mark'[2] need not be introduced to complicate the argument; we need only consider the three extant Gospels.

Streeter proceeds to set out, under five heads, 'the main facts and considerations which show the dependence of Matthew and Luke upon Mark'. The first three 'heads' comprise the familiar facts that about nine-tenths of Mark's subject-matter is found in Matthew, and rather more than half in Luke, in language 'very largely identical with that of Mark', the majority of Mark's actual words, in any average section of the common matter, being found in one or both of the other Gospels; that Mark's order of sections and incidents is generally found also in Matthew and Luke, and when one of these has an order different from that of Mark, the other usually follows Mark's order; and that Matthew and Luke, in genuinely 'Marcan' passages, never agree together *against Mark* in point of order and very rarely in words, collocation of words, or structure of sentences.

On the basis of this accurate statement of highly important data, Streeter, following in the wake of a distinguished line of critics, and himself not the last in the ranks, rests an inference which is obviously false. As the matter is so vital it may be well to quote his actual words: 'We note, then, that in regard to (a) items of subject-matter, (b) actual words used, (c) relative order of incidents, Mark is in general supported by *both* Matthew and Luke, and in

---

[1] *The Four Gospels*, p. 157.
[2] Whether Ur-Markus or a 'second edition' of Mark.

most cases where they do not both support him they do so alternately [i.e. one or other of them supports him], and they practically never agree together against Mark. This is only explicable [here is the vicious inference] if they followed an authority which in content, in wording, and in arrangement was all but identical with Mark.'

The mistake, though not actually made by Lachmann (1835),[1] is apparently fathered upon him, and it has been repeated over and over again in modern times—for instance by V. H. Stanton (apparently) in 1899,[2] by E. A. Abbott (1901),[3] by Wellhausen (1905),[4] by Burkitt (1906),[5] perhaps by Sir J. Hawkins (1911),[6] by Streeter, as we have just seen (1924), by Bishop Rawlinson (1925),[7] by Bishop Narborough (1928),[8] and by Canon Redlich (1936).[9] Since the argument conceals a schoolboyish[10] error of elementary reasoning at the very base of the Two-Document hypothesis as commonly proposed for our acceptance, we may be for-

---

[1] *De Ordine Narrationum in Evangeliis Synopticis*, in *Studien und Kritiken* (1835), pp. 570 ff. I quote from the Preface to the Second Volume of Lachmann's Edition of the New Testament (Berlin, 1850). Lachmann took it for granted that neither St Matthew nor Luke is dependent on Mark and held that all three Synoptic Gospels depend on a common written or oral source. On this assumption his argument (that the Marcan order of events is a faithful reproduction of the source's order) holds good. It is Lachmann's followers who have inadvertently committed themselves to a fallacy. Lachmann prefaces his inference with the vital proviso (discarded by his modern followers): *Si eos* [sc. St Matthew and St Luke] *exemplar Marci propositum quod imitarentur non habuisse manifestum est.*

[2] 'Gospels', *Hastings Dictionary of the Bible*, p. 239.

[3] 'Gospels', *Encyclopaedia Biblica*, col. 1765, referring only to contents.

[4] *Einleitung in die drei ersten Evangelien*, pp. 43 f.

[5] *The Gospel History and its Transmission*, pp. 36 f.

[6] *Oxford Studies in the Synoptic Problem*, ed. Sanday, p. 29.

[7] *The Gospel according to St Mark*, p. xxxv: 'It is obvious that these facts are most simply explained by the hypothesis' that Mark was a source of Matthew and Luke.

[8] 'The Synoptic Problem', in *A New Commentary on Holy Scripture*: 'It seems to follow', from the data, that either Mark or a document resembling it 'has largely shaped the other two Synoptic Gospels.'

[9] *Student's Introduction to the Synoptic Gospels*, p. 31: 'Each of the three arguments by itself [i.e. common contents, common diction, common arrangement] would not have proved our thesis, but the three arguments together furnish decisive evidence that Mark is the primary Gospel.' That the error should be so persistently propagated may be pleaded as a justification for exposing it once and for all, as the text attempts to do.

[10] Or schoolmasterish; see *infra*.

given for devoting to its refutation more space than it intrinsically deserves.

Burkitt (*op. cit.* p. 37) wrote as follows:

> Lachmann started from the central fact that the common order of the three Synoptic Gospels is Mark's order. 'There is not so much diversity', he says, 'in the order of the Gospel tales as most people imagine. It is indeed very great if you compare the Synoptic Gospels indiscriminately together, or compare Luke with Matthew; but if you compare Mark with both the others separately the diversity is inconsiderable.' And he goes on to draw the conclusion that the order of the narrative, as we have it in Mark, is presupposed by and underlies the narratives in Luke and Matthew.[1]

Since Lachmann's time the investigation has been extended, as we have seen, to cover the very wording of Mark. The theory of a common oral tradition has been (rightly) excluded, though Lachmann did not apparently himself finally close the door upon it. And the gap between 'a tradition embodied in Mark', or Ur-Markus, and Mark itself as we now possess it has been successfully narrowed and in fact almost closed. Thus was reached the firm position held

---

[1] Lachmann's statement runs as follows: *Narrationum evangelicarum ordinis non tanta est quam plerisque videtur diversitas; maxima sane si aut hos scriptores eadem complexione omnes aut Lucam cum Matthaeo composueris, exigua si Marcum cum utroque seorsim* (*Novum Testamentum Graece et Latine*, II, p. xiv). For his inference, see *ibid.* p. xx, where, having premissed that the authors of Matthew and Luke did not have Mark before them, he proceeds: *Quid superest nisi ut illum quem omnes velut sibi praescriptum sequuntur ordinem, prius quam ipsi scriberent, auctoritate ac traditione quadam evangelica constitutum et confirmatum fuisse dicamus?* The clause *prius quam ipsi scriberent* shows that Lachmann was not recommending the theory of his modern followers, that Mark was itself the source of the other two. So also C. H. Weisse (according to Stanton in the article referred to above) took the view that Mark 'more simply and fully embodied a document used by the other two', i.e. Ur-Markus (*Die Evangelische Geschichte*, 1838). He also held that 'Matthew's "Logia"' was also used both in our first and our third Gospel. Here for the first time was' the 'two-document hypothesis' (Stanton, p. 236). It is not without interest that the two-document hypothesis started off with Ur-Markus, which has since been discarded, and apparently with an appeal to Papias (the Logia) which is no longer regarded as essential. Is it necessary to point out that Streeter in 1911 and Burney held Mark to be dependent on Q? Substitute Ur-Markus for Mark, in order to restore to Lachmann's argument its original cogency, and admit that Ur-Markus may have been not merely dependent on Q but *comprised in the same document with it*, and Ur-Markus then becomes indistinguishable from Matthew, on which Mark (our present Mark) will then depend; and Luke must depend on our present Mark (for the Marcan sections) and on Matthew (for the Q passages). The two-document hypothesis can thus be resolved into the hypothesis which is worked out in the course of our present study.

by Streeter, that our present Mark was a written source for Matthew and Luke.

The argument in its modern form was stated by Burkitt in the following way:

> In the parts common to Mark, Matthew, and Luke there is a good deal in which all three verbally agree; there is also much common to Mark and Matthew, and much common to Mark and Luke, but hardly anything common to Matthew and Luke which Mark does not share also. There is very little of Mark which is not more or less adequately represented either in Matthew or in Luke. Moreover, the common order is Mark's order; Matthew and Luke never agree against Mark in transposing a narrative. Luke sometimes deserts the order of Mark, and Matthew often does so; but in these cases Mark is always supported by the remaining Gospel. Now what is the deduction to be drawn from these facts? There is only one answer. We are bound to conclude that Mark contains the whole of a document which Matthew and Luke have independently used, and, further, that Mark contains very little else besides.

And after further examination Burkitt decides that there is no necessity to suppose that the document thus used by Matthew and Luke was in fact any other than Mark itself—Ur-Markus resigns its place to Mark (*ibid.* p. 58).

But once Ur-Markus is rejected, *the terms of the problem are altered.* 'The deduction to be drawn from these facts' is no longer that 'Mark contains the whole of a document which Matthew and Luke have independently used', but that (*a*) there is a relation of dependence, *one way or the other*, between Matthew and Mark, and again between Mark and Luke; (*b*) the similarities between Matthew and Luke in the 'triple tradition' are not, as a rule,[1] due to immediate dependence of Matthew on Luke or *vice versa*, but to the fact that either Matthew or Luke depends on Mark, while the other either depends on Mark *or is Mark's source*. In other words, *Mark is necessarily the connecting-link between Matthew and Luke in these passages, but not necessarily the source of more than one of them.*

The data adduced by Streeter in the 'heads of evidence' referred to at the beginning of this chapter and by Burkitt in the above quotation are quite incapable of giving any indication leading towards a more precise determination of the relations obtaining between the

---

[1] The qualifying clause is intended to allow for possible occasional agreements between Matthew and Luke against Mark, in case these cannot be explained away.

three documents than that stated in the last sentence of the paragraph just written. We are left with three possible 'solutions' of the problem of the 'triple tradition', and none of them is more probable than the other, on the evidence so far presented:

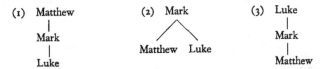

(1) Matthew   (2) Mark   (3) Luke
    | |
   Mark   Matthew Luke   Mark
    | |
   Luke   Matthew

In mathematical terms, the solution which Lachmann's followers consider to be dictated by the facts turns out to have one chance in three of being correct; there is a probability of two to one against it.[1]

We can at once concede that the third solution, supposing as it does that Luke was the original Gospel, is absurd—though for reasons not included in Streeter's first 'three heads' of evidence. Rejecting it, we are left with a choice between solutions (1) and (2), and their claims on our acceptance, up to date, are exactly equal. There is one chance in two that Matthew copied Mark; and there is one chance in two that Mark copied Matthew. To decide between these precisely equal alternatives we must turn to an entirely different set of considerations, and the arguments so far adduced will not give any 'accumulative' force to such further arguments as we may discover.

---

[1] There is unconscious humour in the following passage from E. A. Abbott (*The Fourfold Gospel*, sect. 1, pp. 11 f.): 'Matthew and Luke are in the position of two schoolboys, Primus and Tertius, seated on the same form, between whom sits another, Secundus (Mark). All three are writing (we will suppose) a narrative of the same event....Primus and Tertius copy largely from Secundus. [It may be noted that Abbott begs his question only a little more blatantly than some other Marcan priorists.] Occasionally the two copy the same words; then we have... agreement of three writers. At other times Primus (Matthew) copies what Tertius (Luke) does not....At others, Tertius (Luke) copies what Primus (Matthew) does not....But Primus and Tertius cannot look over one another's shoulders', and hence agreement of them 'against' Secundus is only possible by accident. As the same results (exactly) will follow if Secundus copied from Primus (or Tertius) and was himself copied by Tertius (or Primus), we must hope that Abbott, who was headmaster of a famous school, is not illustrating from real life. Otherwise, it would be interesting to hear what Primus (or Tertius) thought of the acumen and justice of his headmaster.

Is it too much to hope that the 'Lachmann fallacy' will no longer be displayed—with every appearance of superior logic—before the imagination of an unsuspecting public, prone to submit to the claim to reason, and slow to examine its validity? The catena of authors listed above as propagating this fallacy[1] should at least suggest a doubt whether the present dominance of the theory of Marcan priority is really due, as is commonly supposed, to a triumph of honest criticism over traditionalism and fantasy. The truth is probably that Lachmann drew a correct inference on the assumption that the Synoptic Gospels are only indirectly connected by dependence of them all on a lost document or oral tradition; namely that, in that case, the phenomena of order show that the lost document is most faithfully preserved in Mark. This conclusion was the basis of the theory of Ur-Markus as a sort of first 'edition' of Mark and as source for Matthew and Luke. In course of time it was seen that Ur-Markus must have been so similar to Mark as to have been practically identical with it, and the proper step was taken of abandoning this conjectural document. But it was not noticed that by identifying Ur-Markus with Mark the terms of Lachmann's problem were essentially altered and his inference no longer held good. In the theory of Marcan priority Ur-Markus's ghost presides over his own sepulchre.

The data summarized above, though inadequate for the purpose to which Streeter sought to apply them, have nevertheless carried us a long way on the road towards a solution of the Synoptic Problem. They have reduced the nine possible solutions (apart from appeals to oral tradition and conjectural documents) to three, and they enable us, for practical purposes, to exclude the oral theory in its pure form, since the oral tradition (an unwritten Ur-Markus) appealed to would have to be indistinguishable from Mark in order to satisfy the data. Burkitt's critique of Ur-Markus (*op. cit.* pp. 40f.) is sound, and tells equally against the oral hypothesis.

It will be remembered that of Streeter's five 'heads of evidence' we have so far considered only the first three. The fifth turns out to contain no evidence in proof of Streeter's theory, but a series of deductions from it, with a rather closer examination than that

[1] We can add Armitage Robinson to the list; see *The Study of the Gospels* (1902), p. 15 ('The most natural explanation').

5-2

hitherto attempted in *The Four Gospels* of the placing of the 'Marcan tradition' in Matthew and Luke. Thus only the fourth head of evidence contains any argument tending to support the theory of Marcan priority to the exclusion of all other solutions. Not five converging sets of evidence, but one only.

This set is summarized by Streeter as follows: 'The primitive character of Mark is...shown by (*a*) the use of phrases likely to cause offence, which are omitted or toned down in the other Gospels; (*b*) roughness of style and grammar, and the preservation of Aramaic words', and he points out in particular that 'the difference between the style of Mark and of the other two' is the difference which always exists between the spoken and the written word (p. 163); Mark in fact reads like the transcript of the words of 'an impromptu speaker', while 'Matthew and Luke use the more succinct and carefully chosen language of one who writes and then revises an article for publication' (*ibid.*).

Here at last we have an argument deserving serious attention, and it is discussed in later pages of this book.[1] For the moment, it may be enough to say:

(1) The stylistic evidence to which Streeter here appeals is susceptible of a different explanation from that which, in his view, it dictates. It is often taken to indicate, as indeed Streeter's words suggest, that Mark is, practically speaking, not a work of literature but a deposit of oral teaching from the lips of one teacher, and the assumption is often made, not without powerful arguments in its favour, that this oral teaching sprang direct from the recollections of the eyewitness who gave it. Evidence is adduced to suggest that this oral teacher was St Peter, and it is easy to understand the fascination that this idea exerts on many minds and the prejudice it engenders against any theory of a written source behind Mark.

However, as will be pointed out below, Burney (like Streeter in 1911, though on different grounds from his) held that Mark was dependent on Q, and his argument is cogent for those who believe in that 'lost document'; for others it tends directly to suggest Mark's dependence on Matthew. Bishop Rawlinson,[2] again, holds that St Mark's materials came to him from tradition, the arrangement of them being largely his own—this as against those who hold that

---

[1] See pp. 162, 164 ff. [2] Quoted *infra*, p. 108.

Mark is a direct report of St Peter's oral teaching. In this view he was probably influenced by Wellhausen, who in some respects prepared the way for the Form Critics of the last thirty years. Professor Lightfoot [1] summarizes the Form Critics' attitude to Mark as follows: 'We are now bidden to see' in that Gospel 'a compilation of materials of different date, origin, character and purpose, many of which may have had a considerable history—whether oral or literary or both—before they were finally inserted in this Gospel.' Thus a powerful current of thought in modern critical circles tends to see in St Mark *an editor of pre-existing materials*. It is probable that the Form Critics do less than justice to the intrinsic and external arguments for Mark's close connexion with St Peter's oral teaching, but they have prepared the ground for a theory which would accept that connexion *and at the same time look, for an explanation of the signs of editorial work in Mark, not to a purely conjectural evolution of oral or at least sub-literary 'tradition', but to a document lying under our hand and controlling our hypotheses.* [2] We have shown that Streeter's 'stylistic' argument must carry virtually the whole weight of the hypothesis of Marcan priority (I exclude, for the moment, 'higher critical' theories of evolving doctrine and 'legendary accretions'); [3] and the Form Critics (along with Burney and Bishop Rawlinson) have undermined its validity in so far as there is force in their contention that Mark is in the last resort dependent on a source or sources (written or oral) other than the oral teaching of an eyewitness, or indeed of any one teacher.

(2) I therefore suggest that it is desirable, before further examining the stylistic argument, to undertake an investigation (never, so far as I am aware, attempted in modern publications of the Two-Document school) of the actual point-to-point relations revealed

---

[1] *History and Interpretation in the Gospels*, p. 25.

[2] Mark might, for instance, derive from an oral paraphrase or 'Targum' of Matthew.

[3] A quotation from Burkitt (*op. cit.* pp. 38 f.) may be not out of place: 'Far be it from me to disparage the high studies of history and philosophy in favour of literary [or as we should say, documentary] criticism; but as the wise man said, "To everything there is a season", and in the particular study before us the season of literary criticism comes logically first. As long as those who studied the Synoptic Problem attacked it by considering mainly the actual contents of the Gospels, they seemed to be unable to shake off a certain confusion between the earliest Synoptic Gospel and the primitive preaching of Christianity.'

by a comparative study of the texts of either Matthew and Mark, or Mark and Luke, or of both these pairs. I propose that we study the Matthew-Mark pair; I agree, in fact, with the adherents of Marcan priority that Luke is dependent on Mark, and if it emerges from our study of the Matthew-Mark pair that Mark is dependent on Matthew, Luke's dependence on Mark follows automatically.[1]

As I have said, such a study seems never to be offered to the public by the modern Marcan priorists. The reason is, no doubt, that through a combination of false inference (from the first three heads of evidence) with the conclusion to which they have jumped from the fourth 'head', they have supposed that their case is proved, so that this minute documentary comparison is unnecessary. Nevertheless such comparison is of the essence of the kind of criticism involved in a problem such as ours. It can give results practically immune, in their cumulative force, from variable subjective judgements; and if the Marcan priorists believe in their own theory they should welcome the test to which it will be put by such an investigation: if their theory is true, then either our investigation will provide no results, or the results obtained will confirm their theory.

It may not be amiss to draw attention to the fact that our investigation, if it is to have probative value, must be approached with an 'open mind'. Otherwise it will in fact become a study exactly similar to Harnack's study of the Q passages in *The Sayings of Jesus*—a study whose results, as we have seen, can only be used in support of the Q hypothesis after a most searching process of weeding out those among them which depend on a prior acceptance of the hypothesis. This 'open mind', in the matter of the 'triple tradition', is something which the adherents of Marcan priority find it peculiarly difficult to achieve,[2] for the dominant theory is in possession, and it tends to blind the eyes to evidence which, for the unprejudiced, is overwhelmingly cogent. I suggest, then, that we frankly recognize that the first three 'heads of evidence' have not afforded any support to Marcan as against Matthaean priority; and that we put away from our minds, for the time being, the conclusion suggested but not

---

[1] If, however, Matthew depends on Mark, it does not automatically follow that Mark does not depend on Luke.

[2] I write with feeling, having been myself at one time an adherent of the school.

necessitated by the fourth 'head of evidence'. We turn to the first two Gospels and examine them side by side in a purely objective and scientific spirit. Let the argument lead us where it will, and at the end of it we shall be able to decide whether its bearing corroborates, or tends to undermine, the conclusion derived by Marcan priorists from stylistic comparison. Our study will be essentially a study of parallels in their respective contexts.

CHAPTER VI

MATTHEW'S GREAT DISCOURSES

If Mark is divided up into sections (as in Huck's synopsis) it will be found that the following paragraphs are the only ones that have no parallels in Matthew: Jesus in the Synagogue at Capernaum (i. 21–8); Simon goes to Jesus in the Desert Place (i. 35–8); (iv. 21–5 is made up of materials which have parallels in scattered contexts of Matthew); the parable of the Land bearing Seed of itself (iv. 26–9); the Blind Man of Bethsaida (viii. 22–6);[1] the Exorcist who 'followed not the disciples' (ix. 38–41); (ix. 49f. has a partial parallel elsewhere in Matthew); the Widow's Mite (xii. 41–4); (xiii. 33–7 is made up of materials which have parallels scattered about in Matt. xxiv, xxv); the Young Man in Gethsemane (xiv. 51f.); and the last paragraph of the canonical Gospel.

Matthew of course has a great deal that is not in Mark, notably the Infancy narrative, details of the Temptations, some incidents in which St Peter figures prominently, some incidents connected with our Lord's death and resurrection, and especially he has a series of great discourses to which there are only stunted parallels, or stray verses, to correspond in Mark. It is a little, but not much, too strong to describe Mark as equivalent to the purely narrative sections of Matthew's account of our Lord's public ministry and passion, and of the finding of the empty tomb.

The question before us may thus be stated roughly as follows: Did St Mark excerpt from Matthew, or did St Matthew embody the Marcan story in a greater whole? It is proposed in the present chapter to compare Matthew's great discourses or sections of teaching with such parallels as are found in Mark. The following sections will come under review:

Matthew v–vii.   The Sermon on the Mount, of which only odd verses have parallels (out of context in Mark).

---

[1] I disregard for the moment Streeter's suggestion that Mark i. 21–8 and viii. 22–6 have been fused by St Matthew with other incidents.

ix. 37–x. 42.   The Mission Charge; cf. Mark vi. 8–11; xiii. 9–13
                  (both out of context).
xiii. 3–52.   Parables of the Kingdom; cf. Mark iv. 1–34.
xviii. 3–35.   Miscellaneous; cf. Mark ix. 35–50.
xxi. 28–xxii. 14. Parables of Rejection; cf. Mark xii. 1–12.
xxiii.   Denunciations of Scribes and Pharisees; cf. Mark
                  xii. 38–40.
xxiv, xxv.   Fall of Jerusalem and End of the World; cf.
                  Mark xiii. 5–37.

It will be seen that the following discussion takes these sections in
an order which may appear arbitrary. We shall begin with the
Denunciations of the Scribes and Pharisees, the section with a consideration of which we concluded our examination of the Q hypothesis.

I

Matt. xxiii. 1–8

τότε ὁ Ἰησοῦς ἐλάλησεν τοῖς ὄχλοις καὶ
τοῖς μαθηταῖς αὐτοῦ 2. λέγων· ἐπὶ τῆς
Μωϋσέως καθέδρας ἐκάθισαν οἱ γραμματεῖς καὶ οἱ Φαρισαῖοι.... 5. πάντα δὲ
τὰ ἔργα αὐτῶν ποιοῦσιν πρὸς τὸ
θεαθῆναι τοῖς ἀνθρώποις· πλατύνουσιν
γὰρ τὰ φυλακτήρια αὐτῶν καὶ μεγα-
λύνουσιν τὰ κράσπεδα, 6. φιλοῦσιν δὲ
τὴν πρωτοκλισίαν ἐν τοῖς δείπνοις καὶ
τὰς πρωτοκαθεδρίας ἐν ταῖς συναγωγαῖς
7. καὶ τοὺς ἀσπασμοὺς ἐν ταῖς ἀγοραῖς
καὶ καλεῖσθαι ὑπὸ τῶν ἀνθρώπων
ῥαββεί. 8. ὑμεῖς δὲ μὴ κληθῆτε ῥαββεί
κτλ.
[14. οὐαὶ δὲ ὑμῖν, γραμματεῖς καὶ Φαρισαῖοι, ὑποκριταί, ὅτι κατεσθίετε τὰς
οἰκίας τῶν χηρῶν καὶ προφάσει μακρὰ
προσεύχεσθε· διὰ τοῦτο λήμψεσθε περισσότερον κρίμα.]

Mark xii. 37b–40

καὶ ὁ πολὺς ὄχλος ἤκουεν αὐτοῦ ἡδέως.
38. καὶ ἐν τῇ διδαχῇ αὐτοῦ ἔλεγεν·
βλέπετε ἀπὸ τῶν γραμματέων

τῶν θελόντων ἐν στολαῖς περιπατεῖν
καὶ
ἀσπασμοὺς ἐν ταῖς ἀγοραῖς 39. καὶ
πρωτοκαθεδρίας ἐν ταῖς συναγωγαῖς
καὶ πρωτοκλισίας ἐν τοῖς δείπνοις·

40. οἱ κατεσθίοντες τὰς οἰκίας τῶν
χηρῶν καὶ προφάσει μακρὰ προσευχό-
μενοι, οὗτοι λήμψονται περισσότερον
κρίμα.

In both Gospels the immediately preceding paragraph consists
of our Lord's question about the Davidic sonship of Christ. In Mark
the next paragraph is the incident of the Widow's Mite, which is
not found in Matthew; it was perhaps placed here in Mark because
of the reference to 'widows'' houses in the preceding verse. Then
both Gospels agree in giving the prophecy of the destruction of

the Temple. Thus the context in both Gospels is the same, though Mark has added, or Matthew has omitted, the Widow's Mite.

The underlined words and the identity of context compel us to presume that we are here in the presence of a genuine case of dependence—either Matthew has copied Mark or *vice versa*. And the following considerations dictate the inference that Matthew gives the original version, while Mark is secondary:

(1) In Matthew our Lord, after saying that the scribes and Pharisees 'do everything with a view to the impression they hope to create in men', describes their ostentation in three couplets, of which the third states that they 'love to be called Rabbi by men'; this immediately leads on to the injunction 'But be not ye called Rabbi', etc. Thus the Matthaean passage is a unitary whole that cannot be broken up into fragments from different sources.

(2) Matt. xxiii. 5*b*–10 is given by C. F. Burney (*The Poetry of our Lord*, p. 89) as his first example of 'Synthetic Parallelism'. In other words, Mark has an *extract*, which he has turned into prose, from a Matthaean poem.

(3) Still more decisive is the comparison of Matt. *v.* 5*b* with Mark's τῶν θελόντων ἐν στολαῖς περιπατεῖν. Clearly Mark, unwilling to explain what Jewish phylacteries and fringes were, and why specially large ones were signs of religious ostentation, has substituted his own bizarre phrase, which suggests at most mere childish vanity. Matthew cannot possibly be supposed to have invented his version from Mark's jejune phrase, thus giving a vivid Jewish relevance to the picture and (by the same modification) turning the childish vanity into that religious ostentation which exactly fits the Matthaean context. On the contrary, we might almost say that some such text as Matthew's is required as the source of Mark's odd phrase.

(4) We see, too, how Mark's change of φιλοῦσιν to τῶν θελόντων has given him the awkward syntax of a prolate infinitive followed by accusative cases of nouns standing in the same relation to the participle as the infinitive. Matthew's φιλοῦσιν, on the other hand, can quite properly take its accusative nouns *followed by* a prolate infinitive.

(5) Finally, Mark indicates that he is giving us an extract by his introductory formula: καὶ ἐν τῇ διδαχῇ αὐτοῦ ἔλεγεν (cf. Mark iv. 2,

where the same formula conveys the same warning; see pp. 86 f. *infra*).

There can be no question that, if the evidence is approached, as we have asked that it should be, without *parti pris*, the conclusion must be accepted that Mark is here excerpting from Matthew. But, it may be asked, whence—in that case—did Mark derive his *v.* 40? Matthew's *v.* 14 is square-bracketed above, and is usually regarded as not authentic, being omitted by אBDLZΘ1–118–209, 4, 21, etc., sy[s, pal] sa bo arm Or. In some MSS. it is found not after but before *v.* 13. It is, however, probable that these phenomena are due to the early omission of the verse in one line of the MS. tradition by homœoarchomenon, the elaboration of Mark's sentence into a full-blown 'Woe' being rather too much to expect of a cross-harmonizer. (It is, however, inconvenient that the admission of the verse as genuine gives us eight, instead of the (Semitic) seven Woes.)

The treatment of this pair of passages by the Two-Documentarians is not without interest. Streeter (*The Four Gospels*, p. 254) argues that in ch. xxiii Matthew has conflated Q (for the unconflated form of which we are referred to Luke xi. 37–52) with M (a special Matthaean source), and besides placing the resultant discourse in a Marcan context has added in 'a few words from Mark' (and indeed from the chosen context of Mark), 'e.g. πρωτοκλισίας κτλ. Matt. xxiii. 6 = Mark xii. 39'. It will be observed that Streeter appears to be totally unaware of the literary unity of the Denunciations in Matthew (Burney's book came out after the first edition of *The Four Gospels*), and not to perceive the absurdity, from the point of view of ordinary aesthetic sensibility, of making Luke xi. 43 more primitive than its parallel in Matthew. We further observe that again Q and Mark overlap (Luke xi. 43; cf. Mark xii. 38*b*, 39*a*).

Bishop Rawlinson, on the other hand, falls back on Mark's knowledge and use of Q, though for him this symbol here probably represents 'the *Roman* source for the teaching of our Lord, or the version of "Q" which may be assumed to have been current *in Rome*'. He holds that Mark 'appears to presuppose an acquaintance on the part of his readers' with this document (*Commentary on St Mark*, p. xl). This being understood, his comment on our passage of Mark begins as follows: 'These verses contain all that Mark judged it to his purpose to introduce of the long discourse against

Pharisaism which apparently stood in "Q", and which Matthew and Luke (especially the former) reproduce at fuller length. Here certainly it would appear as though Mark were summarizing from memory.' We have given ample reasons for scepticism as to the existence of Q at all, and need not therefore worry too much about the version of it 'current at Rome'. But Bishop Rawlinson is a valuable witness to the strength of the arguments that lead us to suppose that Mark is here extracting from a fuller source that is, so far as the evidence of this passage goes, indistinguishable from Matthew. Is it necessary to point out that, in refusing to admit direct dependence of Mark on Matthew, one is driven to hold that (*a*) Mark used a document here that we cannot differentiate from Matthew, and at the same time (*b*) Matthew recognized that Mark was excerpting, and was fortunate enough to have a copy of the document used by Mark (or of a document indistinguishable from it), which source he proceeded to substitute in full for Mark's extract from it? It can hardly be denied that the conclusions, with reference to this pair of passages, to which the Two-Document hypothesis has driven these two distinguished scholars are themselves a strong confirmation of our contention that the natural explanation of the phenomena is to be sought in dependence of Mark on Matthew.

II

The next two chapters of Matthew comprise the discourse on the Fall of Jerusalem and the End of the World (Matt. xxiv, xxv). The Marcan parallel is xiii. 5–37. Both begin with our Lord's prophecy of the destruction of the Temple; and in both the main discourse is located on the Mount of Olives. In Matthew the discourse, arising out of the double question about the date of the destruction of the Temple and the sign of our Lord's Coming and the End of the Age, begins with a warning about false Christs. A sketch of future history—wars, famines and earthquakes—leads up to the prophecy that Christ's followers will be persecuted and hated. Moreover, there will be defections from within, treachery and mutual hatred. 'False prophets' will cause many to err, sin will increase and charity will grow cold. 'This Gospel of the Kingdom' will be proclaimed throughout the world 'and then will come the end'.

After this tremendous panorama of the future history of the world and the Church, the disciples are warned of a calamity special to Judaea: they will see the Danielic Abomination of Desolation standing in the Holy Place, and must at once flee to escape the horrors of which this will be the prelude. False prophets and false Christs need not be heeded, because the real coming of Christ is to be an absolutely unmistakable event; it will be preceded by a cosmic catastrophe from which flight will be impossible, and then 'the sign of the Son of Man' will appear in the sky, all the nations will mourn, and the Son of Man will be seen coming with the attributes of divine majesty.

A gradual evolution of events within our Lord's own generation will give ample warning of the first disaster (the destruction of the Temple), but no forecast can be made of the date of the second, either by the outside world (xxiv. 37–41) or by the Christians or their leaders (xxiv. 42–xxv. 13). But when Christ does come, He will reward the Christians who have made good use of what has been entrusted to them, and will judge all men by the law of charity (xxv. 14–46).

Apart from one obscurity (the apparent confusion of the lesser and the greater catastrophe in xxiv. 19 f.) the whole passage is a grandiose logical and rhetorical structure, in which passages closely paralleled in Mark cohere inseparably with a great deal of material that is hardly represented at all in Mark, so that no one antecedently could suppose that conflation of sources had occurred.

Let us now examine some of the Marcan parallels to parts of this great discourse:

(i)   Matt. xxiv. 1 ff.

...προσῆλθον οἱ μαθηταὶ αὐτοῦ ἐπιδεῖξαι αὐτῷ τὰς οἰκοδομὰς τοῦ ἱεροῦ. 2. ὁ δὲ ἀποκριθεὶς εἶπεν αὐτοῖς· οὐ βλέπετε ταῦτα πάντα; ἀμὴν λέγω ὑμῖν, οὐ μὴ ἀφεθῇ ὧδε λίθος ἐπὶ λίθον ὃς οὐ καταλυθήσεται. 3. καθημένου δὲ αὐτοῦ ἐπὶ τοῦ ὄρους τῶν ἐλαιῶν
προσῆλθον
αὐτῷ οἱ μαθηταὶ κατ' ἰδίαν λέγοντες
εἰπὲ ἡμῖν,
πότε ταῦτα ἔσται, καὶ τί τὸ σημεῖον τῆς σῆς παρουσίας καὶ συντελείας τοῦ αἰῶνος;

Mark xiii. 1 ff.

...λέγει αὐτῷ εἷς τῶν μαθητῶν αὐτοῦ· διδάσκαλε, ἴδε ποταποὶ λίθοι καὶ ποταπαὶ οἰκοδομαί. 2. καὶ ὁ 'Ιησοῦς εἶπεν αὐτῷ· βλέπεις ταύτας τὰς μεγάλας οἰκοδομάς; οὐ μὴ ἀφεθῇ λίθος ἐπὶ λίθον, ὃς οὐ μὴ καταλυθῇ. 3. καὶ καθημένου αὐτοῦ εἰς τὸ ὄρος τῶν ἐλαιῶν κατέναντι τοῦ ἱεροῦ, ἐπήρωτα αὐτὸν κατ' ἰδίαν ὁ Πέτρος καὶ 'Ιάκωβος καὶ 'Ιωάννης καὶ 'Ανδρέας· 4. εἰπὸν ἡμῖν, πότε ταῦτα ἔσται, καὶ τί τὸ σημεῖον ὅταν μέλλη ταῦτα συντελεῖσθαι πάντα;

We note that there are two questions in Matthew, one relating to the date of the destruction of the Temple, the other to the sign of the second coming and the end of the world. These correspond to the two prophecies in the succeeding discourse, in which the destruction of the Temple is placed within the generation to which our Lord's hearers belonged, while the date of the second coming is left quite uncertain, though its remoteness is implied and the Sign of the Son of Man is predicted. The text of Mark, on the other hand, seems to ask only for the date of the destruction of the Temple and the 'Sign' that the prophecy of that destruction is about to be fulfilled. Yet the answering prophecy in Mark has, as Bishop Rawlinson points out, a much wider scope than that of this question, corresponding rather to the double question in Matthew. In other words, both Gospels imply the double question, but only Matthew gives it.

Assuming that Matthew is here secondary to Mark, we have to suppose that St Matthew noticed the inadequacy of the Marcan question to the Marcan answer and succeeded in elaborating his own double question out of Mark's single question. How lucky for him that Mark already had the word συντελεῖσθαι, to provide the stem for St Matthew's characteristic συντέλεια τοῦ αἰῶνος![1] And we further note that Mark's 'sign when these things'—the prophecy of the destruction of the Temple?—'are about to be accomplished' becomes in Matthew the sign of our Lord's παρουσία, and is taken up again in Matthew (but of course not in Mark) in the reference to the sign of the Son of Man in xxiv. 30. Are we to suppose that St Matthew *invented* the second occurrence, and that the sign of the Coming of the Son of Man is a Matthaean fiction? But if St Matthew went to the length of inventing the idea of this 'sign', why did he not also explain what he meant by it?

There can thus be no doubt that there are good critical grounds for holding that Mark is here dependent on a source indistinguishable from the parallel passage in Matthew. A believer in Q would be well advised to suggest that St Mark has again copied that convenient conjectural document, and that, as so often, St Matthew has noted his dependence and has been able to substitute the original text.

Matt. xxiv. 4–8 is almost identical with Mark xiii. 5–8. The

---

[1] Matthew 5, Hebrews 1, rest of N.T. 0.

disciples are not to be misled by impersonators of Christ; and wars, famines and earthquakes will not prove that 'the end' is imminent; they are only 'the beginning of birth-pangs'. It should be noted that this contrast of end and beginning prepares the way for Matthew's 'and then the end will come' (xxiv. 14, om. Mark *ad loc.*; but the idea is implied in Mark xiii. 10).

(ii) Matt. (A) xxiv. 9–14	Mark xiii. 9–13	Matt. (B) x. 17–22
τότε παραδώσουσιν ὑμᾶς εἰς θλῖψιν	βλέπετε δὲ ὑμεῖς ἑαυτούς· παραδώσουσιν ὑμᾶς εἰς συνέδρια καὶ εἰς συναγωγὰς δαρήσεσθε καὶ ἐπὶ ἡγεμόνων καὶ βασιλέων σταθήσεσθε	προσέχετε δὲ ἀπὸ τῶν ἀνθρώπων· παραδώσουσιν γὰρ ὑμᾶς εἰς συνέδρια, καὶ ἐν ταῖς συναγωγαῖς αὐτῶν μαστιγώσουσιν ὑμᾶς· 18. καὶ ἐπὶ
⟨14. καὶ κηρυχθήσεται τοῦτο τὸ εὐαγγέλιον τῆς βασιλείας ἐν ὅλῃ τῇ οἰκουμένῃ εἰς μαρτύριον πᾶσιν τοῖς ἔθνεσιν, καὶ τότε ἥξει τὸ τέλος.⟩	ἕνεκεν ἐμοῦ, εἰς μαρτύριον αὐτοῖς. 10. καὶ εἰς πάντα τὰ ἔθνη πρῶτον δεῖ κηρυχθῆναι τὸ εὐαγγέλιον. 11. καὶ ὅταν ἄγωσιν ὑμᾶς παραδιδόντες, μὴ προμεριμνᾶτε τί λαλήσητε, ἀλλ' ὃ ἐὰν δοθῇ ὑμῖν ἐν ἐκείνῃ τῇ ὥρᾳ, τοῦτο λαλεῖτε· οὐ γάρ ἐστε ὑμεῖς οἱ λαλοῦντες ἀλλὰ τὸ πνεῦμα τὸ ἅγιον. 12. καὶ παραδώσει ἀδελφὸς ἀδελφὸν εἰς θάνατον καὶ πατὴρ τέκνον, καὶ ἐπαναστήσονται τέκνα ἐπὶ γονεῖς καὶ θανατώσουσιν αὐτούς. 13. καὶ ἔσεσθε μισούμενοι ὑπὸ πάντων διὰ τὸ ὄνομά μου.	ἡγεμόνας δὲ καὶ βασιλεῖς ἀχθήσεσθε ἕνεκεν ἐμοῦ, εἰς μαρτύριον αὐτοῖς καὶ τοῖς ἔθνεσιν. 19. ὅταν δὲ παραδῶσιν ὑμᾶς, μὴ μεριμνήσητε πῶς ἢ τί λαλήσητε· 20. οὐ γὰρ ὑμεῖς ἐστε οἱ λαλοῦντες ἀλλὰ τὸ πνεῦμα τοῦ πατρὸς ὑμῶν τὸ λαλοῦν ἐν ὑμῖν. 21. παραδώσει δὲ ἀδελφὸς ἀδελφὸν εἰς θάνατον καὶ πατὴρ τέκνον, καὶ ἐπαναστήσονται τέκνα ἐπὶ γονεῖς καὶ θανατώσουσιν αὐτούς. 22. καὶ ἔσεσθε μισούμενοι ὑπὸ πάντων διὰ τὸ ὄνομά μου·
καὶ ἀποκτενοῦσιν ὑμᾶς, καὶ ἔσεσθε μισούμενοι ὑπὸ πάντων τῶν ἐθνῶν διὰ τὸ ὄνομά μου. 10. καὶ τότε σκανδαλισθήσονται πολλοὶ καὶ ἀλλήλους παραδώσουσιν καὶ μισήσουσιν ἀλλήλους. 11. καὶ πολλοὶ ψευδοπροφῆται ἐγερθήσονται καὶ πλανήσουσιν πολλούς. 12. καὶ διὰ τὸ πληθυνθῆναι τὴν ἀνομίαν ψυγήσεται ἡ ἀγάπη τῶν πολλῶν. 13. ὁ δὲ ὑπομείνας εἰς τέλος, οὗτος σωθήσεται.		
(verse 14 *vid. supra.*)	ὁ δὲ ὑπομείνας εἰς τέλος, οὗτος σωθήσεται.	ὁ δὲ ὑπομείνας εἰς τέλος, οὗτος σωθήσεται.

Matthew (A) is from the discourse on the destruction of the Temple and the End of the Age, and as far as context goes is therefore parallel to Mark. But the real parallel to Mark is obviously Matthew (B); practically every word of the latter reappears in Mark, which, however, has also *v.* 10 (for which cf. Matt. xxiv. 14), and an extra clause in *v.* 11 (peculiar to Mark).

If Mark is original, St Matthew first borrowed the passage (omitting Mark xiii. 10) for his Mission Charge; and then on arriving at the context in which the passage occurs in Mark he (*a*) abbreviated it ruthlessly; (*b*) inserted his own verses, xxiv. 10–12; (*c*) picked up Mark xiii. 10 which he had omitted in his own chapter x, and thence formed his verse, xxiv. 14*a*.

If Matthew is original, St Mark noticed that Matt. xxiv. 9 is a short doublet-twin of Matt. x. 17–22 (which occurs in the second half of Matthew's Mission Charge, and therefore in a context omitted by St Mark), and has chosen the fuller Matthaean version, into which he has inserted his *v*. 10 from Matt. xxiv. 14*a*; he then omitted Matt. xxiv. 10–13. The following considerations seem decisive in favour of the originality of Matthew:

(1) Matt. x. 17–22 is anything but an intrusion in its Matthaean context. Up to Matt. x. 15 the question of persecution had not been raised; it is hinted at in *v*. 16 and developed in *vv*. 17–22. Then *v*. 23 instructs the disciples how to behave in face of it. As the Mission Charge hitherto has deliberately restricted its horizons to the Jewish-Palestinian world *vv*. 17–22 naturally glance first at persecution by Jewish councils and synagogues, thence proceeding to a hint of a wider mission in the reference to tribunals of governors and emperors. The reference to councils and synagogues is absent from Matt. xxiv. 9, for the horizon there is that required by the more distant future, when Christianity has become not a Palestinian but an ecumenical movement; it is therefore a blemish in Mark xiii. 9 that the Palestinian milieu is implied.

(2) Matt. xxiv. 5–14, in fact, gives a straightforward anticipation of the whole of future history (in reference to the question about the Consummation of the Age), warning the disciples that secular catastrophes must not be taken as signs of the imminent end of history, forecasting, briefly, the world's persecution of the Church, and working up to a poignant climax (om. Mark) which foretells defections from the Church, 'false prophets' and spiritual decay and treason within the Christian body itself; an anticipation devoid of irrelevant instructions about Christian *behaviour* in these circumstances (for the discourse is not exhortatory but informative), and reaching its culmination in the prophecy of the universal proclamation of the 'Gospel of the Kingdom'—'and then will come the end'

(om. Mark), a clause resuming and explaining the earlier 'but not yet is the end' (Matthew and Mark). Is it credible that St Matthew, by editorial work on the material supplied by Mark xiii, could, with the help of the additional verses Matt. xxiv. 10–12—where could they have existed in isolation?—and by drastic abbreviation of Mark and one transposition of genius (moving Mark *v*. 10 to its new position in Matthew), have achieved such superb results?

(3) Mark xiii. 9–13 would in fact be all the better for the omission of *v*. 10, in which πρῶτον is peculiarly odd till we notice that it represents Matthew's 'and then will come the end'. If Matthew is original, we can understand that St Mark should wish to preserve this verse from the Matthaean passage for which he was substituting Matt. x. 17–22, and Matthew's εἰς μαρτύριον αὐτοῖς καὶ τοῖς ἔθνεσιν (x. 18) gave him the hint for its location. We can further understand why Matt. xxiv. 9–14, with its depressing reference to scandals within the Christian body, was rejected by him in favour of the earlier Matthaean passage, which enlarges on a persecution theme which may have been very much to the point for Mark's readers, though it spoils the logical unity of the discourse as found in Matt. xxiv, xxv.

(4) Professor C. F. Burney (*The Poetry of our Lord*, pp. 8f., 118–21) separated Mark xiii. 9–13 out of the context in which it appears in Mark solely on the ground of its rhythmical form, by which it is distinguished from the rest of the chapter, *before* he was aware of the fact that these verses have their true parallel in Matt. x. He also rejected Mark xiii. 10 as a 'gloss', also on rhythmical grounds, before noticing that the verse was absent from Matt. x. 17–22. He further observes that Mark xiii. 9–13, 'though not unsuited to be fitted into an eschatological discourse' such as Mark xiii, is not in itself eschatological—and the setting of the parallel in Matt. x is uneschatological. As Dr Burney accepted the Two-Document hypothesis he suggests, as an explanation of these phenomena, that both Matthew and Mark drew the passage independently from Q, and Bishop Rawlinson (without reference to the stylistic argument) makes the same suggestion. But even if Q could be supposed to have existed, there is no need to introduce it here, as Mark's dependence on Matthew will explain all the phenomena. Moreover, the intrusive character of Mark xiii. 10 and its indubitable literary link with Matt. xxiv. 14 shows that, if Q is to be invoked to save

Mark from dependence on Matthew, Q must have contained not only a passage to serve as a source for Matt. x. 17–22 = Mark xiii. 9–13, but another passage to serve as source for Matt. xxiv. 14, and presumably for the whole paragraph *vv.* 9–14. In other words, when we try to bring in Q to explain literary connexions between Matthew and Mark, exactly the same thing happens as when we use it to explain the connexion in the ordinary Q passages between Matthew and Luke—Q turns out to be indistinguishable from Matthew. The two Gospels run very closely parallel from Matt. xxiv. 15 = Mark xiii. 14 to Matt. xxiv. 36 = Mark xiii. 32, except that Matt. xxiv. 26–8 are without parallel in Mark. These three verses are important in their context, warning the disciples that the Coming of the Son of Man will be unmistakable. Mark also lacks the reference to the Sign of the Son of Man in the sky and that to the Great Trumpet. One effect of these omissions by St Mark is to dispense with obscurities requiring exegesis.

(iii) Matthew	Mark xiii. 33–7
xxv. 13. γρηγορεῖτε οὖν, ὅτι οὐκ οἴδατε τὴν ἡμέραν οὐδὲ τὴν ὥραν.	βλέπετε, ἀγρυπνεῖτε· οὐκ οἴδατε γὰρ πότε ὁ καιρός ἐστιν.
xxv. 14, 15 b. ὥσπερ γὰρ ἄνθρωπος ἀποδημῶν ἐκάλεσεν τοὺς ἰδίους δούλους καὶ παρέδωκεν αὐτοῖς τὰ ὑπάρχοντα αὐτῷ...ἑκάστῳ κατὰ τὴν ἰδίαν δύναμιν, καὶ ἀπεδήμησεν. xxv. 16....ἠργάσατο ἐν αὐτοῖς.	34. ὡς ἄνθρωπος ἀπόδημος ἀφεὶς τὴν οἰκίαν αὐτοῦ καὶ δοὺς τοῖς δούλοις αὐτοῦ τὴν ἐξουσίαν, ἑκάστῳ τὸ ἔργον αὐτοῦ,
xxiv. 45. τίς ἄρα ἐστὶν ὁ πιστὸς δοῦλος καὶ φρόνιμος, ὃν κατέστησεν ὁ κύριος ἐπὶ τῆς οἰκετείας αὐτοῦ...;	καὶ τῷ θυρωρῷ ἐνετείλατο, ἵνα γρηγορῇ.
xxiv. 42 f. γρηγορεῖτε οὖν, ὅτι οὐκ οἴδατε ποίᾳ ἡμέρᾳ ὁ Κύριος ὑμῶν ἔρχεται. ...τὴν οἰκίαν αὐτοῦ.	35. γρηγορεῖτε οὖν· οὐκ οἴδατε γὰρ πότε ὁ κύριος τῆς οἰκίας ἔρχεται,
xxiv. 43. ...εἰ ᾔδει ὁ οἰκοδεσπότης ποίᾳ φυλακῇ ὁ κλέπτης ἔρχεται. xxv. 6. μέσης δὲ νυκτός.	ἢ ὀψὲ ἢ μεσονύκτιον ἢ ἀλεκτοροφωνίας ἢ πρωΐ·
xxiv. 50. ἥξει ὁ κύριος τοῦ δούλου ἐκείνου ἐν ἡμέρᾳ ᾗ οὐ προσδοκᾷ καὶ ἐν ὥρᾳ ᾗ οὐ γινώσκει. Cf. xxv. 6 κραυγὴ γέγονεν· ἰδοὺ ὁ νυμφίος. xxv. 5. ἐνύσταξαν πᾶσαι καὶ ἐκάθευδον. xxv. 32. ...πάντα τὰ ἔθνη.	36. μὴ ἐλθὼν ἐξαίφνης εὕρῃ ὑμᾶς καθεύδοντας.
	37. ὃ δὲ ὑμῖν λέγω, πᾶσιν λέγω, γρηγορεῖτε.

As we have seen, there is very close parallelism between Matt.
xxiv. 15–36 and Mark xiii. 14–32. But at that point Mark proceeds
to the five verses given above, which bring his discourse to an end;
it is quite the longest consecutive discourse in Mark. Matthew,
however, goes on for a further sixty-one verses, comparing the
Second Coming to the Deluge, giving the similes of the Thief in
the Night, of the Servant set over the Household, of the Wise and
Foolish Virgins, and of the Talents: and concluding with the
tableau of the World Judgement (the Sheep and the Goats).

It is quite obvious that Matthew's sixty-one verses cannot be
derived from Mark's five. Yet, as the parallel texts and underlining
above clearly show, practically everything in Mark's five verses is
found, but at various points, in Matthew's sixty-one. Mark xiii. 33 f.
gives a parallel to Matt. xxv. 13 and then to the immediately following
Matthaean simile of the absent householder; Mark's hesitation between 'authority' and 'work' may show that the influence of
Matt. xxiv. 45 is present, along with Matt. xxv. 16 'he worked with
them'. As regards the doorkeeper (Mark xiii. 34), the late Professor
C. H. Turner 'cannot help suspecting' a reference here to St Peter,
who according to Matthew was entrusted with the keys of the
divine Kingdom; in that case we may suppose the further influence
of Matt. xxiv. 45 ff., where the major-domo, who—like a doorkeeper,
though for other reasons—would carry keys, is doubtless pre-
eminently St Peter or one wielding his authority. Most of the other
parallels require no special comment, but I have suggested that
Mark's final clause takes account of the extension of the picture
to a universal judgement at Matt. xxv. 1–32.

Quite clearly, Mark's five verses, found as they are in a context
exactly corresponding to Matthew's sixty-one verses, and having
connexions of thought or language or both with almost every
paragraph of Matthew's long passage, have a literary connexion
with that passage. But it would be preposterous to suggest that
St Matthew accidentally or deliberately worked practically the total
contents of Mark's five verses, in tiny fragments, into his own freely
soaring and monumental structure; the more so, as the ideas con-
veyed by the 'fragments' are often integral to the contexts in which
they are found in Matthew. We are driven to the alternative and
natural supposition, that Mark has hastily telescoped Matthew's

sixty-one verses into the brief finale of a chapter which no doubt was felt to be already too long (Bishop Rawlinson seems to suspect a fusion of matter in Mark's five verses).

And there is one detail, not immediately apparent, which very strongly confirms and guarantees the truth of our supposition. In *v.* 34 Mark appears to compare 'the Son of Man' (last mentioned at *v.* 26) to a man 'on his travels' (ἀπόδημος), who leaves the members of his household with their several tasks, and bids the 'doorkeeper' to 'watch'. 'Watch ye therefore; for you know not when the master of the house is returning, whether late in the evening or at midnight or at cockcrow or in the early morning; lest coming on a sudden he find you sleeping.'

A moment's reflexion will suffice to show that there is something odd about this comparison. A man who goes away from home for a period long enough to make necessary a special assignment of household tasks will not leave instructions that a watch is to be kept up through all the nights against his return. Nor will he blame his household if they are found sleeping at midnight. He will probably arrange to return by daylight; he will give due notice of his approach, and if not he will not want to find his servants on the watch for him (like idle slaves or misbehaving schoolboys), but to see them at the tasks assigned to them.

Who is it that does choose an hour of the night for his unlooked-for arrival? It is of course a thief. And an examination of Matt. xxiv. 42–4, xxv. 14–30 alongside the Marcan passage shows that the oddity in Mark's simile is due to the fact that *he has fused the Thief in the Night with the Absent Master of the Talents parable*, with perhaps some influence from the simile of the major-domo. As Matthew says: If the master of the house had known *at what watch* (cf. Mark's four watches) the *thief* was coming, he would have kept awake (during that particular watch, of course; it is assumed that no one can keep awake all and every night).[1] But as regards the Absent Master of the House, it is true that the day and hour (not necessarily a night-hour) of his return are uncertain (Matt. xxiv. 50);

[1] Take Matt. xxiv. 42 as the last verse of the preceding paragraph—not (as Huck prints it) as the first verse of the Thief in the Night simile. As, unfortunately, one does not know at what watch the thief is coming, one does not keep awake for him; but one tries to be *ready* for him (*v.* 44).

but the major-domo is blamed, not for failing to watch for him, but for abusing his authority and position. Similarly, the Absent Master of the Talents parable comes back not specifically at night, but after 'much time', and proceeds not to rebuke his slaves for failing to keep watch for him, but to take account of their dealings during his absence with the monies entrusted to them.

This analysis and comparison makes it certain that we are justified in supposing that Mark xiii. 33–7 is a telescoped abbreviation of the teaching found in Matt. xxiv. 37–xxv. 46. And, to review the whole matter of Mark xiii as compared with the parallel discourse in Matthew, it is clear that at least one of the authors has built up his version of the discourse by conflation. There is nothing to show that Matthew has done this, and everything suggests that his version is an organic, not a synthetic, whole (contrast Luke's synthetic discourses, where the joints are visible and the connexions tend to be verbal and external, not internal to the development of a single thought-sequence). It is certain, on the other hand, that Mark has employed conflation, for Mark xiii. 9–13 does not belong to its present context, and *v.* 10 is intrusive in this paragraph itself. We have, besides, found a series of other indications that Mark is secondary, and nothing but considerations extraneous to the literary problem presented by these two versions of the same discourse could justify us in denying that while Matthew here shows no sign of having edited a source such as Mark, Mark on the other hand is dependent on a source or sources indistinguishable from Matthew.

III

We may now turn to the discourse containing the parables of the Kingdom, Matt. xiii; cf. Mark iv. 1–34.

In both Gospels this discourse is described as spoken from a boat to an audience collected on the sea-shore. In both it is interrupted by the description of a conversation with the disciples (Matthew) or 'those in his entourage along with the Twelve' (Mark), which includes an explanation of the parable of the Sower. After this explanation Mark has five verses of sayings which at first sight would seem to be still addressed to this small audience; the parallels to these sayings in Matthew are not found in the chapter of parables but are scattered about in various parts of that Gospel. Next Mark has the parable of the farm-land bearing fruit of itself, which is not found in Matthew at all; Matthew at this point has the parable of the Tares (om. Mark), after which both Gospels have the parable of the Mustard-seed, to which Matthew, but not Mark, appends the parable of the Leaven. It is quite clear that the Mustard-seed and the Leaven are a pair of 'twin' parables. Note that in Matthew the 'man' who planted the Mustard-seed has the same prominence as the 'woman' who put in the leaven. They correspond to the 'man' who sowed good seed in the parable of the Tares, and to the Sower in the first parable of the series. The 'man' of the Tares parable is interpreted at *v.* 37 as a figure of the Son of Man. Mark has obscured the significance of this 'man' in the Mustard-seed parable. At this point both evangelists appear to be bringing the discourse to an end, with the remark that our Lord (on this occasion?) spoke nothing but parables to the crowds. When, therefore, Matthew next proceeds to give our Lord's explanation of the Tares parable, followed by the parables of the Hidden Treasure, the Pearl of Great Price, and the Net, and then concludes by the saying about Things New and Old, does it not seem obvious that he has (*a*) copied Mark, (*b*) added an appendix after taking from Mark the natural finale to the section? Against this easy hypothesis there are grave objections:

Matt. xiii. 3, 34	Mark iv. 2, 33 f.
καὶ ἐλάλησεν αὐτοῖς πολλὰ ἐν παρα-βολαῖς λέγων....	καὶ ἐδίδασκεν αὐτοὺς ἐν παραβολαῖς πολλά, καὶ ἔλεγεν αὐτοῖς ἐν τῇ διδαχῇ αὐτοῦ....
34. ταῦτα πάντα ἐλάλησεν ὁ Ἰησοῦς ἐν παραβολαῖς τοῖς ὄχλοις καὶ χωρὶς παραβολῆς οὐδὲν ἐλάλει αὐτοῖς.	33. καὶ τοιαύταις παραβολαῖς πολλαῖς ἐλάλει αὐτοῖς τὸν λόγον, καθὼς ἠδύναντο ἀκούειν· 34. χωρὶς δὲ παραβολῆς οὐκ ἐλάλει αὐτοῖς, κατ᾽ ἰδίαν δὲ τοῖς ἰδίοις μαθηταῖς ἐπέλυεν πάντα.

We have met Mark's phrase ἐν τῇ διδαχῇ before (xii. 38), and on that occurrence it appeared to mean 'among the things He taught on that occasion'. It was used to introduce an excerpt from a long discourse which St Mark (or his authority) knew, but which he did not propose to reproduce in full. There is a presumption that this is also its meaning in our present passage, and this presumption is very strongly confirmed by the difference between Matthew's 'all these things spake Jesus in *parables* to the crowds' (*v.* 34) and

Mark's 'and with *many such parables* He spake the word to them' (*v.* 33). The point would not perhaps be obvious if we had not Matthew to compare with Mark, but as we have Matthew's words, and *as we know from the identity of context that there is a literary connexion between the two Gospels here,* we can clearly see how the words 'with many such' (contrasted with Matthew's 'all these things') emphasize and reassert the implication of ἐν τῇ διδαχῇ: 'He spoke many such parables, of which I have given you some illustrative examples.' In other words, Mark knows and states that he is excerpting. Well then, what other parables, belonging to this discourse, were found in the source from which Mark's discourse is an excerpt? We at once notice that Matthew has the Tares and the Leaven (both omitted by Mark) and, a little later in the same chapter, the Hidden Treasure, the Pearl of Great Price, and the Net; of which the last-named is the twin of the Tares, just as the Leaven is the twin of the Mustard-seed which Mark does reproduce. We naturally conclude that these are the missing parables, and this conclusion is borne out by the absence of ἐν τῇ διδαχῇ from Matt. xiii. 3 and the presence of 'all these things' in *v.* 34 in contrast with Mark's 'with many such'. It would be pure paradox to maintain that in these two phrases Mark is original, and that in the omission of the one and the difference of 'all these things' from the other Matthew is secondary. For it should be observed that all Matthew's seven parables are parables of the Kingdom, and that if we can suppose Mark's peculiar parable (the Land producing fruit of itself) to be the missing twin of the Sower, we have four pairs of parables, of which Mark gives one and a half pairs, and Matthew three and a half, each pair illustrating different aspects of the single immensely rich and dynamic idea of the Kingdom which is at once eschatological (as the Jews had expected) and developmental (which they had not expected).

If we insist, despite this evidence, on the priority of Mark and the secondariness of Matthew, we shall be bound to conclude that (*a*) Mark here derives from some source other than Matthew; (*b*) St Matthew had a copy of Mark's source and recognized that Mark here was an excerpt from it; (*c*) St Matthew substituted Mark's source for Mark's own text; (*d*) he carefully removed Mark's ἐν τῇ διδαχῇ and changed 'with many such' to 'all these things' in consequence of this substitution; but (*e*) he did not take the trouble to fit in the parables of the Treasure, the Pearl and the Net before copying Mark's conclusion to the discourse! Truly, a strange combination of luck, meticulous care and casualness. Once again it should be observed that the dogma of Mark's priority leads us into critical absurdities of the first water.[1]

A close examination of the wording of the two Gospels in this section gives a minute but valuable point in confirmation of the hypothesis that Mark is excerpting from Matthew. At Matt. xiii. 3, 10, 13, 14 αὐτοῖς is used of the crowds, as indeed throughout the parables section xiii. 1–52. Although the disciples are directly addressed in the paragraphs xiii. 10–23, there is no real ambiguity, because in the conversation with them it has been made abundantly clear that the audience of the parables are 'the crowds'. The matter is finally cleared up by v. 34 τοῖς ὄχλοις...αὐτοῖς.

But in Mark iv. 13 (and apparently v. 21) αὐτοῖς means the disciples. At its next occurrence, therefore (v. 33), we should naturally take it as still referring to them, and Mark does nothing to enlighten us, although on closer examination it proves to refer to the crowds; we have to make an awkward mental adjustment to this effect when we read v. 34b ('but in private he explained everything to his disciples'). The ambiguity would seem to be an unnoticed result of St Mark's alterations, omissions and additions to his source. It is less likely that St Matthew noticed the ambiguity in Mark and rewrote his source so as to exclude it.

We have been dealing mainly with St Mark's omissions from Matt. xiii. But further confirmation of his dependence on Matthew can be derived from a comparison of Mark iv. 21–5 with the parallels to the several parts of this little paragraph at Matt. v. 15, etc.

Bishop Rawlinson, on this passage of Mark (which he describes as a 'catena of short sayings'), observes: 'The sayings collected in this paragraph occur scattered in various contexts in Matthew and

[1] For another example of Mark excerpting and indicating that he is doing so, cf. Mark xii. 1 ἤρξατο αὐτοῖς ἐν παραβολαῖς [plural] λαλεῖν followed by only one parable. Matthew has the same parable, followed by the Wedding-Feast and the Wedding-Garment, which Streeter thought was probably two parables under a single heading (unless the heading of the second one has accidentally dropped out of the text); *The Four Gospels*, p. 243 n. 2. Is it to be supposed that Matthew, noticing Mark's plural 'in parables', dipped into his lucky bag and produced one or two more parables to make it true?

Matthew

v. 15. οὐδὲ καίουσιν λύχνον καὶ τιθέασιν αὐτὸν ὑπὸ τὸν μόδιον, ἀλλ' ἐπὶ τὴν λυχνίαν καὶ λάμπει πᾶσιν τοῖς ἐν τῇ οἰκίᾳ.

x. 26. οὐδὲν γάρ ἐστιν κεκαλυμμένον ὃ οὐκ ἀποκαλυφθήσεται, καὶ κρυπτὸν ὃ οὐ γνωσθήσεται.

xiii. 9. ὁ ἔχων ὦτα ἀκουέτω.

vii. 2. (ἐν ᾧ γὰρ κρίματι κρίνετε κριθήσεσθε καὶ) ἐν ᾧ μέτρῳ μετρεῖτε μετρηθήσεται ὑμῖν.

vi. 33. (ζητεῖτε δὲ πρῶτον τὴν βασιλείαν καὶ τὴν δικαιοσύνην αὐτοῦ) καὶ ταῦτα πάντα προστεθήσεται ὑμῖν.

xiii. 12. ὅστις γὰρ ἔχει δοθήσεται αὐτῷ καὶ περισσευθήσεται· ὅστις δὲ οὐκ ἔχει, καὶ ὃ ἔχει ἀρθήσεται ἀπ' αὐτοῦ.

Mark iv. 21-5

καὶ ἔλεγεν αὐτοῖς ὅτι μήτι ἔρχεται ὁ λύχνος ἵνα ὑπὸ τὸν μόδιον τεθῇ ἢ ὑπὸ τὴν κλίνην; οὐχ ἵνα ἐπὶ τὴν λυχνίαν τεθῇ;

22. οὐ γάρ ἔστιν τι κρυπτόν, ἐὰν μὴ ἵνα φανερωθῇ· οὐδὲ ἐγένετο ἀπόκρυφον, ἀλλ' ἵνα ἔλθῃ εἰς φανερόν.

23. εἴ τις ἔχει ὦτα ἀκούειν, ἀκουέτω.

24. καὶ ἔλεγεν αὐτοῖς· βλέπετε τί ἀκούετε. ἐν ᾧ μέτρῳ μετρεῖτε μετρηθήσεται ὑμῖν

καὶ προστεθήσεται ὑμῖν.

25. ὃς γὰρ ἔχει δοθήσεται αὐτῷ· καὶ ὃς οὐκ ἔχει, καὶ ὃ ἔχει ἀρθήσεται ἀπ' αὐτοῦ.

Luke.... They were probably therefore contained in "Q"; Mark may either have derived them from "Q^R" or from general Church tradition.' He adds that the Matthaean contexts seem generally more appropriate than the Marcan. Indeed, that ἐν ᾧ μέτρῳ κτλ. belongs with the former half of Matt. vii. 2 is obvious. Especially to be noted are the words added to this saying in Mark: καὶ προστεθήσεται ὑμῖν. These words are found in Matthew, but three verses earlier than vii. 2, and in this Matthaean context they are integral to the sense. We cannot suppose a coincidence (προστίθημι occurs nowhere else in Mark, and at only one other place in Matthew; and note the reverential passive to avoid the use of the divine Name), and it is inevitable to conclude that St Mark has taken them from Matt. vi. 33 and added them to his loan of Matt. vii. 2b. The only escape from this conclusion is to remove these words altogether from the text of Mark; there is some MS. authority for such procedure, but the omission is probably due to homœoteleuton. Once again we see that Mark is not original, but derivative from either Matthew or some source (but we have shown the baselessness of the Q hypothesis) to which Matthew also had access.

We may add these further considerations: (a) At iv. 2, where he is slightly modifying Matthew's phraseology in order to indicate that he will only give an excerpt from the teaching available, St Mark uses the words καὶ ἔλεγεν. The same phrase is used at Mark ii. 27, where it interrupts our Lord's words quite unnecessarily, but at a point where St Mark—if secondary—has broken away from Matthew by omission (cf. Matt. xii. 5–7). It recurs at iv. 21, again as an unnecessary interruption of our Lord's words, but again at a point of divergence from Matthew; at iv. 24, to help to knit together the patchwork of that paragraph; and at iv. 13, vi. 10, vii. 9 (and 27, though this is a normal case), in each case marking a divergence from Matthew, and at iv. 9, where the divergence is very slight. (Its use at, for example, vi. 4 and viii. 21 is the normal usage, the previous speaker not having been our Lord.) It looks as though the use of this phrase is an editorial mannerism when normal connexion has been broken through St Mark deserting his source.

(*b*) In Matt. xiii. 10–13 our Lord is asked by the disciples why he addresses the crowds in parables. He replies that it is because they lack, what the disciples already possess, the grace of a 'knowledge' (understanding? the verb, γινώσκειν, seems to suggest a more appreciative knowledge than εἰδέναι) of the 'mysteries of the kingdom', such that further clear teaching can profitably be offered to them—'whoso hath, to him shall be given'. The crowds, hitherto, have seen and heard what the disciples have seen and heard, but without spiritual insight into its significance. Hence, it is implied, our Lord's *clear* teaching will in future be reserved for the disciples; and the condition of the unconverted crowds is illustrated by a quotation from Isaias (vi. 9 f.). No one can fail to realize that this presents us with a turning-point in the preaching of the Gospel, a point which, it may be felt, is inevitable when a new teaching is offered to the world; a minority of the public to which it is addressed has shown itself less incapable than the rest of understanding and accepting the whole paradoxical new message, and it would be useless to persist in casting pearls before swine, lest they trample them with their feet and turn and rend the teacher. (It is, perhaps, worth noticing that in the previous chapter the Pharisees are described as having thrown down the gauntlet by declaring that our Lord's exorcisms were done by diabolic power; and our Lord has pointed out his disciples as taking the place of the dearest family relations in his esteem; while the parable of the Sower, at the opening of our chapter, has drawn the contrast between those really converted to the new teaching and the rest.) It was probably becoming dangerous for our Lord to make his full claims too public.

Mark's corresponding paragraph is very different. To begin with, the disciples 'ask our Lord the parables', and it is not easy to understand what this means; St Luke took it, it would seem, as a request for explanation, and therefore substitutes the singular: they asked him 'what this parable might be'. It seems doubtful whether St Matthew could have derived his own quite different question from Mark's. And our Lord's reply in Mark, *unless expounded in the light of Matthew's version*, would seem to amount to a blunt statement that (for no reason given) our Lord intends to disclose the truth to his intimates but deliberately to cloak it from the crowds, *in order that* they may see and yet not see, hear and yet not hear, for fear lest they should be converted and forgiven!

Two questions suggest themselves. First, which evangelist probably gives a more complete impression of our Lord's mind here? To me, it seems indefinitely more probable that our Lord recognized the imperceptiveness of the multitude as a fact and adapted his teaching methods to it, than that he deliberately sought to produce it because he did not want the multitude to be forgiven. Secondly, which account is more likely to have been derived from the other? It is not easy to believe that Matthew's perfectly sensible and profound version was evolved from Mark's very disconcerting verses: (1) By a not very obvious glossing of the question in Mark *v.* 10 a theme is given to the paragraph, so necessary that Bishop Rawlinson suggests that we should regard Mark's paragraph as 'patchwork'; (2) Mark iv. 25 must have been lifted from its Marcan context (poor enough) and inserted with utter naturalness so as to explain the spiritual law to which our Lord here appeals—how fortunate for St Matthew that Mark's word δοθήσεται harmonized so perfectly with the δέδοται of the new context! (3) It was again a stroke of genius to substitute Matt. xiii. 13 for Mark iv. 12, and then, by insertion of the quotation from Isaias, to utilize the last words of that same verse of Mark, thus removing the 'scandal' of Mark's text and at the same time bringing in Matthew's favourite appeal to prophecy. On the other hand, it is easy to see how, if Mark derives from Matthew, the drift of the paragraph was changed by mistaking Matthew's ὅτι (*v.* 11, meaning 'because') for a case of ὅτι *recitantis*. Then, in abbreviating the passage, as Mark regularly abbreviates discourse, the Old Testament quotation was, as usual, omitted, *except the concluding phrase* μήποτε... ἐπιστρέψωσιν καὶ ἰάσομαι αὐτούς, of which the last two words were changed to ἀφεθῇ αὐτοῖς.

It is interesting to observe that, if Mark's version would have been unwelcome to St Matthew, still more so must it have been to St Luke, captivated as he was by the tender merciful love of the Redeemer. Yet all that St Luke succeeds in doing to tone down the harshness of Mark is to omit the last clause of Mark's *v*. 12. I venture to suggest that that is how an editor might have been expected to deal with Mark, but that what St Matthew is supposed to have done is beyond the power of genius.

(*c*) But the hypothesis of Matthew's dependence here on Mark has further to face the question, whence did St Matthew obtain his next two, perfectly placed and perfectly worded, verses ('Blessed are your eyes', etc.)? Did he invent them? Such a suggestion would, of course, be a counsel of despair (the passage is quoted by C. F. Burney (*op. cit.* p. 145) as an example of *kina* rhythm in our Lord's utterances). But who can fail to see that they belong inevitably to their present context, and that it is preposterous to suppose that they ever came into existence out of it, to be discovered by St Matthew and used to this superlative effect?

> Therefore I speak to them in parables:
> Because seeing they see not:
> And hearing they hear not,
> Nor do they understand [cf. the quotation from Isaias].....
> But blessed are *your* eyes, because they see [cf. line 2]:
> And your ears because they hear [cf. line 3].
> Verily I say unto you, that many prophets and just men desired
>   to see the things you see
> And did not see them [cf. lines 2 and 5]:
> And to hear what you hear
> And did not hear them [cf. lines 4 and 6].

Matthew at once proceeds:

> *You* therefore, hear the parable of the Sower.....

The truth is that the whole of Matt. xiii. 10–17 is a paragraph of the highest organic unity, and that Mark iv. 10–12 is quite plainly produced, by a process of omission and rather awkward alteration, from a source indistinguishable from Matthew.

We may now sum up the evidence pointing to the secondary character of Mark iv. 1-34: (1) St Mark gives indications, both before and after the discourse, that his version is only an excerpt; Bishop Rawlinson says that St Mark was probably drawing upon 'some already existing collection of our Lord's parables'. (2) Mark has the Mustard-seed parable without its twin, the Leaven parable; but Matthew has the Mustard-seed parable along with its twin, and in a form (emphasizing the kinship of the pair) that is not preserved in Mark. (3) The parables in Matt. xiii, both those that are found also in Mark and those that are not, are homogeneous. (4) The ambiguity of Mark's αὐτοῖς is explained if he was copying Matthew. (5) Mark iv. 21-5 is a catena of short sayings, all of which are paralleled in various parts of Matthew, and the Matthaean contexts are usually superior to the Marcan; the phrase καὶ προστεθήσεται αὐτοῖς is especially tell-tale. (6) St Mark's repeated καὶ ἔλεγεν seems to be due to editorial divergences from his source. (7) Matt. xiii. 10-17 is a highly unitary paragraph, not explicable by derivation from Mark; but the parallel paragraph in Mark is easily explained if its source was Matthew.

The cumulative effect of these seven pieces of evidence must be pronounced to be very powerful. It may be stated with confidence that Mark here is not the simple transcript of the words of an oral teacher depending simply on his own recollections of our Lord's discourse; and that there is nothing here that militates against the supposition that Matthew's version of the discourse was a source of Mark's.

IV

Matt. xviii. 1-4 is a single paragraph, in which our Lord replies to the ambitions of his disciples by giving them an object-lesson in humility, with a child as the illustration of the theme. Verses 5 and 6 proceed to inculcate the Christian attitude towards children, a subject which, with one interruption, is carried on to v. 14, after which it gives place to that of man's forgiveness of man.

Mark ix. 33-42 begins with an instruction on Christian leadership. Then the same incident of the child as that used to inculcate humility in Matthew is used to give point to the first part of the instruction on the right attitude towards children. This subject is interrupted

(iv)   Matt. xviii. 1–6

(Cf. xvii. 24 and xvii. 25.)

ἐν ἐκείνῃ τῇ ὥρᾳ προσῆλθον οἱ μαθηταὶ τῷ 'Ιησοῦ λέγοντες· τίς ἄρα μείζων ἐστὶν ἐν τῇ βασιλείᾳ τῶν οὐρανῶν;

(Cf. xx. 26 f. and Mark x. 43 f.)

2. καὶ προσκαλεσάμενος παιδίον ἔστησεν αὐτὸ ἐν μέσῳ αὐτῶν. 3. καὶ εἶπεν· ἀμὴν λέγω ὑμῖν, ἐὰν μὴ στραφῆτε καὶ γένησθε ὡς τὰ παιδία, οὐ μὴ εἰσέλθητε εἰς τὴν βασιλείαν τῶν οὐρανῶν. 4. ὅστις οὖν ταπεινώσει ἑαυτὸν ὡς τὸ παιδίον τοῦτο, οὗτός ἐστιν ὁ μείζων ἐν τῇ βασιλείᾳ τῶν οὐρανῶν. 5. καὶ ὃς ἐὰν δέξηται ἐν παιδίον τοιοῦτο ἐπὶ τῷ ὀνόματί μου, ἐμὲ δέχεται. (Cf. x. 40.)

(Cf. x. 42.)

6. ὃς δ' ἂν σκανδαλίσῃ ἕνα τῶν μικρῶν τούτων τῶν πιστευόντων εἰς ἐμέ, συμφέρει αὐτῷ, κτλ.

Mark ix. 33–42

καὶ ἦλθον εἰς Καφαρναούμ, καὶ ἐν τῇ οἰκίᾳ γενόμενος ἐπηρώτα αὐτούς· τί ἐν τῇ ὁδῷ διελογίζεσθε; 34. οἱ δὲ ἐσιώπων· πρὸς ἀλλήλους γὰρ διελέχθησαν ἐν τῇ ὁδῷ τίς μείζων. 35. καὶ καθίσας ἐφώνησεν τοὺς δώδεκα καὶ λέγει αὐτοῖς· εἴ τις θέλει πρῶτος εἶναι, ἔσται πάντων ἔσχατος καὶ πάντων διάκονος. 36. καὶ λαβὼν παιδίον ἔστησεν αὐτὸ ἐν μέσῳ αὐτῶν, καὶ ἐναγκαλισάμενος αὐτὸ εἶπεν αὐτοῖς· (Cf. x. 15.)

37. ὃς ἂν ἓν τῶν παιδίων τούτων δέξηται ἐπὶ τῷ ὀνόματί μου, ἐμὲ δέχεται· καὶ ὃς ἂν ἐμὲ δέχηται, οὐκ ἐμὲ δέχεται ἀλλὰ τὸν ἀποστείλαντά με. 38. ἔφη αὐτῷ ὁ 'Ιωάννης· διδάσκαλε, εἴδομέν τινα ἐν τῷ ὀνόματί σου ἐκβάλλοντα δαιμόνια, ὃς οὐκ ἀκολουθεῖ ἡμῖν, καὶ ἐκωλύομεν αὐτόν, ὅτι οὐκ ἠκολούθει ἡμῖν. 39. ὁ δὲ 'Ιησοῦς εἶπεν· μὴ κωλύετε αὐτόν. οὐδεὶς γάρ ἐστιν ὃς ποιήσει δύναμιν ἐπὶ τῷ ὀνόματί μου καὶ δυνήσεται ταχὺ κακολογῆσαί με· 40. ὃς γὰρ οὐκ ἔστιν καθ' ἡμῶν, ὑπὲρ ἡμῶν ἐστιν. 41. ὃς γὰρ ἂν ποτίσῃ ὑμᾶς ποτήριον ὕδατος ἐν ὀνόματί μου, ὅτι Χριστοῦ ἐστε, ἀμὴν λέγω ὑμῖν ὅτι οὐ μὴ ἀπολέσῃ τὸν μισθὸν αὐτοῦ. 42. καὶ ὃς ἂν σκανδαλίσῃ ἕνα τῶν μικρῶν τούτων τῶν πιστευόντων, καλόν ἐστιν αὐτῷ μᾶλλον κτλ.

by the discussion of the exorcist 'who followed not after us', after which we have one more verse on the subject of children. It is important to realize that Mark's text gives no ground for a connexion between the disciples' ambitious discussion and the episode of the child in our Lord's arms. The following considerations make it practically certain that in this section Mark is to be held dependent on Matthew:

(1) Mark ix. 33 has two place-references ('into Capernaum' and 'in the house', both of which occur in the *previous* episode in

Matthew (xvii. 24f.) in which St Peter is told by our Lord to pay the Temple-tribute 'for me and thee'. It is perhaps more likely that Mark, omitting this episode, has borrowed its place-references, than that Matthew, inserting it, has worked into it the place-references of the next episode in Mark. For Mark's probable procedure we may compare that of Luke xx. 39f., where, omitting Mark's episode of the Great Commandment question, he nevertheless borrows from Mark xii. 32a and 34 to construct a needed conclusion to his own previous episode.

(2) In Mark ix. 33 our Lord asks, 'What were you arguing about on the way?' This seems all right at first, because they had been 'journeying through Galilee' (v. 30). But we note that a very similar situation arises at Matt. xx. 17–28 (cf. Mark x. 32–45), where again they are 'on the way', again our Lord prophesies His passion and resurrection (cf. Matt. xvii. 22f. and Mark ix. 30–2), and again the ambitions of (two of) the disciples lead to a lesson in humility. It may be suggested that St Mark, having omitted the Temple-tribute episode that gave rise to the discussion on precedence in Matt. xviii, has turned in thought to this second episode to give a 'setting' for the discussion in Mark ix.

(3) In that later episode (Matt. xx. 25; cf. Mark x. 42) the 'ten' are apparently indignant among themselves with John and James, and our Lord 'summons' them to receive His teaching on humility. So also in Mark ix. 35 (om. Matthew) our Lord 'calls' the 'twelve' to receive the same teaching, though the summons is out of place, because the disciples are already there.

(4) Both the foregoing points link up with the fact that Mark ix. 35b is a quite different reply to the precedence question from that of Matt. xviii. 3. The reply given in Mark is, in fact, a doublet-twin of Mark x. 43b, 44 (cf. Matt. xx. 26b, 27). It is notorious that St Matthew does not mind doublets, so, if he is secondary, why did he not follow Mark here? But if Mark is secondary, we observe how, after omitting the Temple-tribute incident with its apparent glorification of St Peter above the 'eleven', the evangelist has given us here a lesson in humility for St Peter, the 'first' (Matt. x. 2) of the apostles; in Matthew the corresponding lesson is one for the disciples in general. The combination of these three points strongly suggests that Mark here represents a conflation of the two incidents

so carefully distinguished in Matthew. To suppose that St Matthew is secondary and has bleached out the elements intruded from the later episode is to credit him with a finesse of critical and editorial ingenuity that is almost beyond belief.

(5) Similarly, it is to credit St Matthew with too much ingenuity to suppose that, having found the irrelevant child in Mark ix. 36—a lucky find, for Bishop Rawlinson appears to think that the child's connexion with its Marcan context is purely verbal—he managed to turn it into a lesson on humility. Whereas, of course, if St Mark is secondary, he had no use for the child for this purpose, the lesson having been given already in *v.* 35; so in Mark the child is closely attached to the saying about receiving such a child in Christ's name.

(6) And again, it would have been too ingenious in St Matthew to have selected from Mark x. 15 just the right words to accompany the object-lesson, and then (despite his willingness to admit doublets) to omit this verse when he came to copy Mark x. 13–16 in context (Matt. xix. 13–15). In point of fact, Mark x. 15 is not necessary to its context, and that it has been inserted there from Matt. xviii. 3 is shown by its peculiar wording: '*Whoso does not receive* the kingdom of God', etc. (cf. Matt. xviii. 5 '*Whoso receives* one such child', and the parallel in Mark *ad loc.*).

(7) Had Matthew been secondary, the author would not have felt an objection to producing a doublet with x. 40 by copying Mark ix. 37*b*. We shall find Mark borrowing from the passage Matt. x. 40–2 a little lower down.

(8) Mark ix. 38–41 is inserted *editorially*, the connecting link, as Bishop Rawlinson points out, being purely verbal. Turner gave this as an example of Marcan parenthesis; but it is, in that case, a parenthesis that is irrelevant to its context.

(9) Matt. xviii. 5 f. are rightly placed in immediate sequence, being so sharply contrasted; and they are wrongly separated in Mark. Quite clearly, the Matthaean collocation coincides with the 'original', before Mark inserted his 'parenthesis'.

(10) The contrast in Matthew between 'Who is greater *in the kingdom of heaven*' (om. Mark) and 'you shall not enter into the kingdom of heaven', together with the *inclusio* provided by Matthew's concluding verse, 'this man is greater in the kingdom of heaven', points to Matthew's priority: on asking who is greater in

the kingdom, the disciples are told that without humility they will
not even *enter* it, and that humility spells greatness in it. Mark has
spoiled all this.

(11) A comparison of Mark ix. 41 ('Whoso gives you to drink
a cup of water in my name, because you are Christ's, verily I say
unto you, that he will not lose his reward') with Matt. x. 42 ('And
whoso gives *one of these little ones* to drink a cup of cold water only,
in the name of a disciple, verily I say unto you that he will not lose
his reward') may at first suggest that the Marcan verse is the source
of the Matthaean. For 'one of these little ones' seems quite irrelevant
to its context in the Mission Charge, and it might be thought that
it was picked up from Mark ix. 42 in the process of borrowing
Mark's previous verse. But it is interesting to observe that Bishop
Rawlinson considers that the Matthaean verse is in more appropriate
context than the Marcan and probably gives 'the more original form
of the saying'; he quotes Lagrange's remark that the phraseology
'because you are Christ's' is Pauline, the word Christ without the
article being used nowhere else in the Synoptic Gospels or in Acts
as a proper name, and suggests that it is the gloss of 'some early
copyist'—but we cannot but remember Mark's Pauline use of the
phrase 'the Gospel' (for example, i. 15). In view of these opinions
of a Two-Documentarian, the following considerations are probably
decisive against Matthew's dependence in this verse on Mark: (*a*) if
Matthew were copying Mark, it would be stupid of him to change
Mark's 'you' into 'one of these little ones', for 'you' would suit
the Matthaean context and 'one of these little ones', as we have
pointed out, does not. St Mark, on the other hand, copying Matthew,
will have changed 'one of these little ones' to 'you' to fit the passage
to which the verse is appended in Mark. (*b*) Mark's verse is nevertheless poorly connected with the preceding passage. (*c*) We shall
show reason to believe that Matthew has frequent self-quotations or
'cross-references', creating doublets: now in Matthew's simile of
the Sheep and the Goats, the 'sheep' are said to have '*given the
Son of Man to drink*', inasmuch as they 'did it to *one* of the *least*
of *these my brethren*' (xxv. 40), while the goats are said not to have
done so, inasmuch as they 'did it not to *one* of *these least* ones'
(*v*. 45); 'least', in Greek as in English, is the superlative of 'little'.
Matt. x. 42 is thus a 'cross-reference' to Matt. xxv. 40, and the

THE ORIGINALITY OF ST MATTHEW

irrelevance of the phrase 'one of these little ones' is explained. Yet it was perhaps this phrase that served to remind Mark of the Matthaean verse in Mark ix.

(12) We have finally to ask ourselves whether an editor could have achieved the ultimate felicity of combining his new creation (Matt. xviii. 1–4) with his previously interpolated episode (xvii. 24–7) by the simple addition of the word ἄρα in the question 'who is greater?' borrowed from Mark ix. 34. This one word makes up in Matthew for the absence of the references to a dispute 'on the way' which we saw reason to regard as a Marcan loan from the episode of the Sons of Zebedee.

It may be worth while to pursue our investigations a little further in the immediate sequels to these parallel passages in Matthew and Mark:

Matt. xviii. 5–9

καὶ ὃς ἐὰν δέξηται ἓν παιδίον τοιοῦτο ἐπὶ τῷ ὀνόματί μου, ἐμὲ δέχεται. 6. ὃς δ' ἂν σκανδαλίσῃ ἕνα τῶν μικρῶν τούτων τῶν πιστευόντων εἰς ἐμέ, συμφέρει αὐτῷ ἵνα κρεμασθῇ μύλος ὀνικὸς περὶ τὸν τράχηλον αὐτοῦ καὶ καταποντισθῇ ἐν τῷ πελάγει τῆς θαλάσσης. 7. οὐαὶ τῷ κόσμῳ ἀπὸ τῶν σκανδάλων· ἀνάγκη γάρ ἐστιν ἐλθεῖν τὰ σκάνδαλα, πλὴν οὐαὶ τῷ ἀνθρώπῳ δι' οὗ τὸ σκάνδαλον ἔρχεται. 8. εἰ δὲ ἡ χείρ σου ἢ ὁ πούς σου σκανδαλίζει σε, ἔκκοψον αὐτὸν καὶ βάλε ἀπό σου· καλόν σοί ἐστιν εἰσελθεῖν εἰς τὴν ζωὴν κυλλὸν ἢ χωλόν, ἢ δύο χεῖρας ἢ δύο πόδας ἔχοντα βληθῆναι εἰς τὸ πῦρ τὸ αἰώνιον.

9. καὶ εἰ ὁ ὀφθαλμός σου σκανδαλίζει σε, ἔξελε αὐτὸν καὶ βάλε ἀπὸ σοῦ· καλόν σοί ἐστιν μονόφθαλμον εἰς τὴν ζωὴν εἰσελθεῖν ἢ δύο ὀφθαλμοὺς ἔχοντα βληθῆναι εἰς τὴν γέενναν τοῦ πυρός.

Mark ix. 42–8

καὶ ὃς ἂν σκανδαλίσῃ ἕνα τῶν μικρῶν τούτων τῶν πιστευόντων, καλόν ἐστιν αὐτῷ μᾶλλον εἰ περίκειται μύλος ὀνικὸς περὶ τὸν τράχηλον αὐτοῦ καὶ βέβληται εἰς τὴν θάλασσαν.

43. καὶ ἐὰν σκανδαλίσῃ σε ἡ χείρ σου, ἀπόκοψον αὐτήν· καλόν ἐστίν σε κυλλὸν εἰσελθεῖν εἰς τὴν ζωήν, ἢ τὰς δύο χεῖρας ἔχοντα ἀπελθεῖν εἰς τὴν γέενναν, εἰς τὸ πῦρ τὸ ἄσβεστον. [44] 45. καὶ ἐὰν ὁ πούς σου σκανδαλίζῃ σε, ἀπόκοψον αὐτόν· καλόν ἐστίν σε εἰσελθεῖν εἰς τὴν ζωὴν χωλόν, ἢ τοὺς δύο πόδας ἔχοντα βληθῆναι εἰς τὴν γέενναν. [46] 47. καὶ ἐὰν ὁ ὀφθαλμός σου σκανδαλίζῃ σε, ἔκβαλε αὐτόν· καλόν σέ ἐστιν μονόφθαλμον εἰσελθεῖν εἰς τὴν βασιλείαν τοῦ θεοῦ, ἢ δύο ὀφθαλμοὺς ἔχοντα βληθῆναι εἰς τὴν γέενναν, 48. ὅπου ὁ σκώληξ αὐτῶν οὐ τελευτᾷ καὶ τὸ πῦρ οὐ σβέννυται.

We have already suggested that the immediate collocation of Matt. v. 5 with the preceding verse must be considered original, and

98

that the separation of these two verses in Mark by the parenthesis about the exorcist cannot be original. Nothing can be proved from the presence of *v.* 7 in Matthew, and the absence of a corresponding verse in Mark.

Matt. *vv.* 8 f. form a doublet with v. 29 f.; but in that passage of the Sermon on the Mount the 'right eye' is mentioned first, followed by the 'right hand'; there is no mention of the foot. The Sermon passage is in perfect context, and in correct order for that context, as it follows immediately on the statement that πᾶς ὁ βλέπων γυναῖκα πρὸς τὸ ἐπιθυμῆσαι ἤδη ἐμοίχευσεν αὐτὴν ἐν τῇ καρδίᾳ αὐτοῦ. But xviii. 8 f. is not well connected with what precedes; for our Lord has been speaking of scandal given to *others*, whereas these verses refer to scandal given to oneself. The probable explanation of the doublet (see the chapter on doublets, pp. 138 ff. *infra*) is, as often in Matthew, that the author shares the ancient inconvenience of not being able to subjoin cross-references in footnotes. He therefore employs the simple device of appending in the text itself the passage to which he wishes to call his readers' attention. It will be observed that the omission of xviii. 8 f. leaves a perfect connexion between *vv.* 6 f. and 10 ff.

If this is the correct explanation of the doublet (and one suspecst that it would have been offered long ago if critics had not been obsessed by the dogma of Mark's priority), it is manifest that Mark has, as elsewhere, omitted part of Matthew's text but preserved the 'footnote', which in Mark no longer performs its function of a cross-reference, the original passage from the Sermon on the Mount not being preserved in the Second Gospel. (Mark's final quotation, *v.* 48, is one that might have occurred to any Jew or Christian familiar with the Old Testament. It does not affect the structure of Mark's passage.)

The notion that Matt. xviii. 8 f. comes from Mark, and Matt. v. 29 f. from another source (for example, Q or Streeter's 'M') is untenable, unless it is conceded that Mark ix. 43, 45, 47 are themselves derived from the conjectural source; the wording of the two Matthaean passages is far too similar to allow of derivation from two independent documents.

Mark ix. 49 f. are without parallel in the Matthaean context. Verse 49 seems to be a reference to Leviticus ii. 13, and to owe its place here to the mention of 'fire' in *v.* 48. In its turn, *v.* 49, with its verb ἁλισθήσεται, gives a verbal link for the attachment of *v.* 50*a*, a half verse to which a parallel occurs at Matt. v. 13, where of course the saying is in perfect context—Mark appears, as often, to be extracting a snippet from a section of his source, which, as a whole, he did not intend to utilize. The word 'salt' in this half verse gives a link for *v.* 50*b*, which may be a brief résumé of the gist of Matt. xviii. 15–35 (on the duty of forgiveness of one's fellow-men).

In Matthew the passage on scandal is immediately followed by *v.* xviii. 10 ὁρᾶτε μὴ καταφρονήσητε ἑνὸς τῶν μικρῶν τούτων, κτλ. As we have observed, this gives a perfect connexion with xviii. 6f., the intervening verses being probably in the nature of a 'footnote'.

Once again, therefore, the study of a section of discourse in Matthew alongside of the shorter parallel section of Mark has brought to light a series of converging indications that the Marcan section depends on a source, and that if this source is not Matthew it must in all probability have been in St Matthew's hands and been substituted by him in his own Gospel for the section of Mark which was before his eyes.

V

Matthew (xxi. 23–7) and Mark (xi. 27–33) both proceed from the conversation about the withered fig-tree to the question of the Chief Priests and Elders (and scribes, adds Mark) about the authority on which our Lord bases his actions, and to his refusal to answer this question. Matthew then gives our Lord's story of the Obedient and Disobedient Sons, the parable of the Vineyard and that of the Wedding of the King's Son and the Wedding-garment. Mark has the parable of the Vineyard only; after which it goes straight on to the question about the Imperial Tribute, which in Matthew follows the Wedding-garment.

Matthew tells us that the question about authority was addressed to our Lord while he was teaching, which explains ταῦτα ποιεῖς in the question. Mark does not mention that our Lord was teaching and the meaning of ταῦτα ποιεῖς is thus left vague.

The complete relevance of the story of the Obedient and Disobedient Sons in this context is obvious, the previous conversation having already suggested the contrast between official Judaism and the ordinary people in their attitude to St John the Baptist. It would be surprising if Matthew found himself able to add such an apt fragment from an unknown source to the Marcan text.

Mark xii. 1 begins ἤρξατο αὐτοῖς ἐν παραβολαῖς λαλεῖν, but despite this plural only one parable follows. As Matthew has in the same context the story of the Two Sons and the parable of the Wedding as well as that of the Vineyard, we find in Matthew the explanation of Mark's plural. It is a strain on one's credibility to prefer the other hypothesis: that (a) Mark used the plural loosely (meaning 'parabolically'),[1] (b) St Matthew noticed the plural and was able to extract from an unknown source some further parables to make it true. We may note that St Luke certainly noticed that the plural raised false hopes, and in consequence substituted the singular 'this parable' (Luke xx. 9).

Mark's discourse ends at xii. 12 with the words 'and leaving Him they went away'. This phrase does not occur in Matthew till xxii. 22. This is not the only occasion when Mark appears to omit a part of Matthew and to round off the discourse, thus abbreviated, with a finale found somewhat later in Matthew. The alternative hypothesis, that St Matthew held these words from Mark in reserve till he had completed his interpolated matter, is perhaps less probable.

Loisy remarked that there is no sequence of ideas in Mark from our Lord's refusal to state his authority to the parable of the Vineyard. In Matthew there intervene the story of the Two Sons and its application. This gives the missing connexion. The reference therein to St John the Baptist links up with the paragraph on authority, and the implication that the officials of Judaism have refused to enter the Kingdom leads on to the Vineyard parable, which in its turn implies that God will transfer that Kingdom to others. If Matthew interpolated the story of the Two Sons, he has done so with an extraordinarily felicitous result.

[1] The same phrase is used at Matt. xxii. 1, where it is followed only by the Wedding of the King's Son and the Wedding-garment. Streeter (*The Four Gospels*, p. 243 n. 2) suggests that Matthew here gives under a single heading what were originally a pair of parables; this would explain Matthew's plural παραβολαῖς. In Mark iii. 23 the plural refers to the various small similes of the paragraph it introduces. Elsewhere in the Synoptic Gospels the distinction between παραβολή and παραβολαί is carefully observed. Outside these Gospels the word does not occur in the New Testament, except twice, in the singular, in Hebrews. In Ps. lxxviii. 2 the plural may refer to the two periods of the history of Israel's redemption described, in the inverse order of their occurrence, in the rest of the Psalm.

VI

Matt. ix. 35–x. 18

ix. 35. καὶ περιῆγεν ὁ Ἰησοῦς τὰς πόλεις πάσας καὶ τὰς κώμας, διδάσκων ἐν ταῖς συναγωγαῖς αὐτῶν, κτλ.

x. 1. καὶ προσκαλεσάμενος τοὺς δώδεκα μαθητὰς αὐτοῦ ἔδωκεν αὐτοῖς ἐξουσίαν πνευμάτων ἀκαθάρτων ὥστε ἐκβάλλειν αὐτὰ καὶ θεραπεύειν πᾶσαν νόσον καὶ πᾶσαν μαλακίαν.

(Cf. x. 5, 7.)

(Cf. x. 8.)

2. τῶν δὲ δώδεκα ἀποστόλων τὰ ὀνόματά ἐστι ταῦτα· πρῶτος Σίμων ὁ λεγόμενος Πέτρος καὶ Ἀνδρέας ὁ ἀδελφὸς αὐτοῦ, καὶ Ἰάκωβος ὁ τοῦ Ζεβεδαίου καὶ Ἰωάννης ὁ ἀδελφὸς αὐτοῦ, κτλ. 5. τούτους τοὺς δώδεκα ἀπέστειλεν ὁ Ἰησοῦς παραγγείλας αὐτοῖς λέγων.... 7. πορευόμενοι δὲ κηρύσσετε λέγοντες.... 8. ...δαιμόνια ἐκβάλλετε· δωρεὰν ἐλάβετε, δωρεὰν δότε. 9. μὴ κτήσησθε χρυσὸν μηδὲ ἄργυρον μηδὲ χαλκὸν εἰς τὰς ζώνας ὑμῶν, 10. μὴ πήραν εἰς ὁδὸν μηδὲ δύο χιτῶνας μηδὲ ὑποδήματα μηδὲ ῥάβδον· ἄξιος γὰρ ὁ ἐργάτης τῆς τροφῆς αὐτοῦ. 11. εἰς ἣν δ᾿ ἂν πόλιν ἢ κώμην εἰσέλθητε ἐξετάσατε τίς ἐν αὐτῇ ἄξιός ἐστιν, κἀκεῖ μείνατε ἕως ἂν ἐξέλθητε. 12. εἰσερχόμενοι δὲ εἰς τὴν οἰκίαν ἀσπάσασθε αὐτήν. 13. καὶ ἐὰν μὲν ᾖ ἡ οἰκία ἀξία, ἐλθάτω ἡ εἰρήνη ὑμῶν ἐπ᾿ αὐτήν· ἐὰν δὲ μὴ ᾖ ἀξία, ἡ εἰρήνη ὑμῶν πρὸς ὑμᾶς ἐπιστραφήτω. 14. καὶ ὃς ἂν μὴ δέξηται ὑμᾶς μηδὲ ἀκούσῃ τοὺς λόγους ὑμῶν, ἐξερχόμενοι ἔξω τῆς οἰκίας ἢ τῆς πόλεως ἐκείνης ἐκτινάξατε τὸν κονιορτὸν ἐκ τῶν ποδῶν ὑμῶν.... 18. καὶ ἐπὶ ἡγεμόνας δὲ καὶ βασιλεῖς ἀχθήσεσθε ἕνεκεν ἐμοῦ, εἰς μαρτύριον αὐτοῖς καὶ τοῖς ἔθνεσιν.

Mark vi. 6b, 7; iii. 14–19; vi. 8–11

vi. 6b. καὶ περιῆγεν τὰς κώμας κύκλῳ διδάσκων.

7. καὶ προσκαλεῖται τοὺς δώδεκα καὶ ἤρξατο αὐτοὺς ἀποστέλλειν δύο δύο, καὶ ἐδίδου αὐτοῖς ἐξουσίαν τῶν πνευμάτων τῶν ἀκαθάρτων.

iii. 14. καὶ ἐποίησεν δώδεκα ἵνα ὦσιν μετ᾿ αὐτοῦ καὶ ἵνα ἀποστέλλῃ αὐτοὺς κηρύσσειν 15. καὶ ἔχειν ἐξουσίαν ἐκβάλλειν τὰ δαιμόνια. 16. καὶ ἐποίησεν τοὺς δώδεκα καὶ ἐπέθηκεν ὄνομα τῷ Σίμωνι Πέτρον· 17. καὶ Ἰάκωβον τὸν τοῦ Ζεβεδαίου καὶ Ἰωάννην τὸν ἀδελφὸν τοῦ Ἰακώβου, καὶ ἐπέθηκεν αὐτοῖς ὀνόματα Βοανηργές, ὅ ἐστιν υἱοὶ βροντῆς, κτλ.

(Cf. iii. 14.)
(Cf. vi. 8.)
(Cf. iii. 14.)

vi. 8. καὶ παρήγγειλεν αὐτοῖς ἵνα μηδὲν αἴρωσιν εἰς ὁδὸν εἰ μὴ ῥάβδον μόνον, μὴ ἄρτον, μὴ πήραν, μὴ εἰς τὴν ζώνην χαλκόν, 9. ἀλλὰ ὑποδεδεμένους σανδάλια, καὶ μὴ ἐνδύσησθε δύο χιτῶνας. 10. καὶ ἔλεγεν αὐτοῖς· ὅπου ἐὰν εἰσέλθητε εἰς οἰκίαν ἐκεῖ μένετε ἕως ἂν ἐξέλθητε ἐκεῖθεν.

11. καὶ ὃς ἂν τόπος μὴ δέξηται ὑμᾶς μηδὲ ἀκούσωσιν ὑμῶν, ἐκπορευόμενοι ἐκεῖθεν ἐκτινάξατε τὸν χοῦν τὸν ὑποκάτω τῶν ποδῶν ὑμῶν

εἰς μαρτύριον αὐτοῖς.

Of the seven sections of discourse in Matthew mentioned on p. 72 we have now discussed the five that have parallels in corresponding contexts of Mark. The Sermon on the Mount has only odd verses paralleled here and there in Mark. Matt. ix. 37–x. 42 has no parallel in corresponding Marcan context, but parts of it are paralleled out of context at Mark vi. 7, iii. 14–19, vi. 8–11 and xiii. 9–13. We have already discussed Mark xiii. 9–13 in connexion with Matt. xxiv, xxv (pp. 79ff. *supra*). It remains to consider the remaining Marcan parallels.

It will be remembered that Matt. x. 9–15 is given by Streeter as an example of 'the almost meticulous care with which Matthew conflates Mark and Q' (*The Four Gospels*, p. 248). Indeed, it is obvious that (apart from the apparent discrepancy over the staff and a possible one over the sandals) there is nothing in the Marcan parallel that is not in Matthew, though Matthew has a good deal that is not in Mark. We have tried to show, in the opening chapters of this book, that Q is a complete illusion, and if that is so we cannot say that Matthew's additional matter here is derived from that source. As far as this passage taken by itself goes, we are at perfect liberty to regard Matthew as the source of Mark. And given this liberty, there is no doubt that that is the hypothesis suggested by the internal evidence:

(*a*) For where, if not in their present context, can the parts of Matthew's section absent from Mark be supposed to have had their original existence? 'The labourer is worthy of his hire. . . . Seek out who is worthy. . . . Greet the house and if it is worthy let your peace come upon it; but if it is not worthy, let your peace return to you.' They belong inseparably to their present context.

(*b*) And if we suppose that nevertheless these sayings did have an independent existence somewhere, it is incredible that they would have fitted *so exactly* into the Marcan passage and that Matthew could have discovered how so to fit them, that there is no sign of a join and that they complete Mark's meaning perfectly. Note that the 'labourer' points back to Matt. ix. 37f. (no parallel in Mark), and that Matt. x. 12f. is so thoroughly Semitic that it reads like a too literal translation from Aramaic (a Greek might well be unaware that a religious greeting would be in the form '*Peace* be to this house', and hence might not see the significance of the saying about peace resting on the worthy house and returning from the unworthy one. It has been suggested that Matthew's imperatives may be misunderstandings of Semitic futures as jussives).

(c) Mark has got into trouble with his rendering of the passage by beginning to turn (Matthew's) direct prohibitions into indirect speech; unable to keep up the effort he relapses into direct speech without warning at the end of *v*. 9, after having perpetrated an accusative *pendens* in ὑποδεδεμένους. We are asked to believe, on the contrary, that St Mark produced this syntactical curiosity in free composition, and that St Matthew was able to straighten it out into his own lucid version.

(d) Bishop Rawlinson appears to regard Mark's version of the instructions with regard to staff and sandals as a modification of the original, whether accidental or due to consideration for the circumstances of missionaries beyond the Galilaean limits envisaged in the discourse as originally delivered. Here again, therefore, it is easier to derive Mark from Matthew than *vice versa*.

(e) Mark concludes with the words εἰς μαρτύριον αὐτοῖς. Elsewhere in the New Testament this phrase means 'so that witness may be borne to them on behalf of' the Christian message. But here it must mean 'to bear witness against them before God'.[1] As, however, the phrase occurs a few verses lower down in Matthew (x. 18) with its proper meaning, it is probable that, as elsewhere, Mark has omitted part of his source and sought a finale to his abbreviated discourse from among the omitted verses.

(f) It will be observed that Mark has parallels to Matt. x. 1 at both vi. 7 and iii. 14. The latter is not a close parallel, but it links up curiously with the language of Matt. x. 5, 7, 8, and (like Matt. x. 1) it immediately precedes the (appointment and) list of the Twelve. It is far more likely that Mark has used the same passage of Matthew twice over, than that Matthew has unnecessarily conflated two passages of Mark, working into the words attributed to our Lord Himself the words ἀποστέλλειν, κηρύσσειν, ἐκβάλλειν τὰ δαιμόνια from Mark's narrative clause of purpose.

Bishop Rawlinson supposes Mark's version of the Mission Charge to represent a 'brief summary' of a Roman tradition of the Charge (Q^R) parallel to Q's version. But to do justice to the evidence in paragraphs (a) to (e) above, it would be necessary to say either that this Roman 'tradition' was indistinguishable from that preserved

---

[1] St Luke apparently saw the difficulty, and therefore substituted μαρτύριον ἐπ᾽ αὐτούς (ix. 5).

in Matthew, or that it had modified the original discourse exactly on the lines on which we suggest that Mark has modified Matthew. We should further have to suppose that Matthew had once again turned from Mark to the original of which Mark's is a shortened and corrupted version.

The Matthaean list of apostles, unlike Mark's, is in six pairs. The evidence of Acts and of Mark vi. 7 shows that the apostles did habitually go forth in pairs (hence, perhaps, Matt. x. 11 f. a singular house, but plural visitors, ὑμῶν and ὑμᾶς, not σοῦ and σε). Has Matthew deliberately 'archaized' his list by the arrangement in pairs, or has Mark destroyed Matthew's delicate indication of the original practice?

We have pointed out, when discussing Luke's dependence on Matthew (p. 17 supra), that Matt. ix. 35–x. 42 is profoundly homogeneous in content and in literary form, with numerous echoes, not only of one 'Marcan' section in another 'Marcan' section, or of one 'non-Marcan' section in another 'non-Marcan' section, but of a 'Marcan' in a 'non-Marcan' section and vice versa. Yet, if St Matthew took his Marcan sections from Mark, he must either have invented(!) the non-Marcan material or derived it from some other source, which must have been very 'Jewish' in outlook and presumably very primitive. The unity of the resultant whole on the latter supposition becomes an insoluble mystery. What could be more 'Jewish', primitive and authentic, or truer to the original Semitic rhythms, than Matt. x. 5–8, with its parallelism, its reference to 'the ways of the Gentiles', the cities of the Samaritans, the lost sheep (cf. ix. 36) and 'the house of Israel', and its restriction of the apostles' work to Jewish territory? As regards the general structure, note how our Lord goes to 'cities and villages' (ix. 35), preaching the Gospel of the Kingdom and 'healing every sickness and weakness', and finding the 'harvest' abundant (v. 37) sends out the Twelve to (Jewish) 'cities and villages' (x. 11) to 'preach' the proximity of the 'kingdom' of Heaven, and to 'cure' those who are ill, etc. On arriving at one of these, they are to make their way to a 'house' (v. 11); and, if rejected, they leave that 'house' or 'city' (v. 14; note the quite logical change of order). Compared with this magnificent composition Mark vi. 6–13 reads rather like a clumsy piece of excerpting and abbreviation; note, for instance, how the missionaries are taken straight to a 'house', but leave a 'place'.

It may be suggested that the claim of this section of Matthew to be original, and to be the source of its parallels in Mark, would probably have been much more widely recognized, had not the Q hypothesis been wrongly accepted, with the inevitable consequence that Matthew seems to be incorporating here Marcan elements and elements of Q found in Luke x. 4–12. We see how (*a*) the dogma of Marcan priority drives scholars to the acceptance of the Q hypothesis, and (*b*) acceptance of the Q hypothesis anchors them more firmly in the dogma of Marcan priority. On the other hand, the refutation of either the Q hypothesis or the dogma of Marcan priority rapidly undermines the other element in the double error.

CHAPTER VII

STREETER AND BURNEY ON MARK'S USE OF Q

We have seen that on several occasions Bishop Rawlinson, who is of course a Two-Documentarian, appears to think that Mark is dependent upon Q^R, the Roman version—whether written or oral—of the tradition of our Lord's sayings supposed to be enshrined—in its Antiochene form—in the conjectural document usually designated as Q. From an examination of his deeply interesting commentary on Mark I have collected the following references to Q, Q^R or other traditional sources:

(1) Mark i. 2. He thinks that this verse is not genuine, but that if it is St Mark derived it from the Q tradition.

(2) The Temptation of our Lord. Mark 'perhaps presupposes' the Q account of the Temptations; that our Lord was fasting, though not mentioned in Mark as it is in Matthew, is probably presupposed by the statement that the angels ministered to Him.

(3) Mark iii. 22–30, the Beelzebub Controversy, is probably derived from Q^R.

(4) Mark iv. St Mark is probably drawing upon some existing collection of our Lord's parables.

(5) In particular, the sayings in iv. 21–5 may have been derived from (various contexts of?) Q^R.

(6) Mark vi. 7–13, the Mission Charge, 'no doubt represents a brief summary' of the account in Q^R.

(7) Mark viii. 15 contains a saying which came to St Mark from the tradition—'perhaps from Q^R'.

(8) Mark viii. 34–ix. 1. Most if not all of these sayings were probably derived from Q^R, and Matt. x. 38, 39, 33 seem more original than Mark viii. 34, 35, 38. 'For the Gospel's sake' in Mark viii. 35 (absent from the parallel passage in Matthew) is added by 'Mark the missionary'.

(9) Mark ix. 33–7. In this 'catena of sayings' Bishop Rawlinson seems to think that Mark depends on Q^R (ix. 41–50 is also described

as a 'catena of sayings', though here we are not told whether they are derived from Q^R or not).

(10) Mark x. 30. 'It seems likely that the original "Q" form of the saying is given in Matt. xix. 29', while 'for the Gospel's sake' (Mark v. 29, om. Matthew) is probably an editorial addition on St Mark's part. Matt. xix. 28 (om. Mark) is probably in correct Q context; and this would seem, though Bishop Rawlinson does not say so, to imply that St Matthew has in this passage substituted the 'original' Q for Mark, recognized by him as an inferior reproduction of the original.

(11) Mark x. 35–40 may have originally formed the sequel to the saying in Q, Matt. xix. 28.

(12) And in the same connexion Bishop Rawlinson mentions Bacon's suggestion that the reference to baptism (Mark x. 38, om. Matthew in the parallel passage) is an editorial addition.

(13) Mark xii. 38–40. Here Mark appears 'to be summarizing from memory' from 'the long discourse against Pharisaism which apparently stood in "Q", and which Matthew and Luke (especially the former) reproduce at fuller length'. This of course will mean that Matthew will have recognized the extract from Q and substituted for it the original Q discourse.

(14) Mark xiii may owe its present arrangement, setting and adaptation to editing.

(15) In particular, Mark xiii. 9–13 probably stood in Q.

(16) Mark xiii. 33–7 looks as though it contains reminiscence of the Talents parable or that of the Pounds (Luke xix. 11–27).

These sixteen references to nine of the first thirteen chapters of Mark, and to the possible influence on the Marcan document of 'tradition', usually the doubly conjectural written or oral source Q^R, are most interesting. Bishop Rawlinson summarizes his own position on p. 111 of the *Commentary*. After speaking of those who 'regard the Marcan narrative as being a report, virtually at first hand, of the vividly remembered story of St Peter', he there says: 'The view taken in this commentary is that the Evangelist's materials came to him from tradition, but that the arrangement of them was largely his own.' It will be remembered that one of the points on which Streeter laid most stress, in his 'fourth head' of evidence supposed to indicate Mark's priority, was that the difference between Mark's style and that of the other two Synoptists is the difference which always exists between the spoken and the written word; Mark reads like the transcript of the words of 'an impromptu speaker' (*The Four Gospels*, p. 163). This at first seems to militate strongly against the supposition that Mark was dependent on Matthew, but if so eminent a Two-Documentarian as Bishop Rawlinson has felt bound to concede Mark's dependence on 'tradition', part of which tradition he is quite prepared to regard as documentary, then we can at once retort that the tradition may have been none other than Matthew itself.

One of the most acute essays in criticism in *Oxford Studies in the Synoptic Problem* was contributed by B. H. Streeter under the title 'St Mark's Knowledge and Use of Q'. Assuming the truth of the Two-Document hypothesis Streeter there infers, from a study of the records of the Preaching of St John the Baptist, the Temptation, the Beelzebub controversy, and the Mission Charge, and of other passages, that St Mark knew Q and quoted from it occasionally, though probably only from memory. After examining eight cases of such alleged use by St Mark of Q he sums up as follows (p. 176): 'The *cumulative* effect of these instances is irresistible, and must establish beyond reasonable doubt that Mark was familiar with Q.' Professor Sanday in his 'Introductory Essay' to the volume accepts this conclusion in the following words (p. xvi): 'It is not without reluctance that I have come round to the conclusion advocated by Mr Streeter in Essay V, that St Mark already possessed a knowledge of Q....I have for some time had before my mind arguments similar to those put forward by Mr Streeter, and in the form in which he states them they seem to compel assent.'

In *The Four Gospels*, however, Streeter withdraws from this position. He there (p. 188) argues that Mark's representation of the Temptation is very ('so wholly') different from that of Q; that Q's record of the voice from heaven at our Lord's baptism is contained in the Western reading of Luke *ad loc.*: 'Thou art My beloved Son, this day have I begotten Thee', and is therefore different from the Marcan record; that the details given in Mark of St John the Baptist's dress and food 'look authentic, but there is no reason to suppose they stood in Q'; and in general that Q is more faithfully preserved in Luke than in Matthew, while Mark's divergences from *Luke* in the passages where Mark and Q 'overlap' are more striking than the resemblances; that in Mark the Mustard-seed parable is a 'twin' of the Seed Growing Secretly, whereas in Q it is a twin of the Leaven; and finally that the sayings about 'taking up the cross' and 'denying Christ on earth', since they occur twice over in Matthew and Luke, must *certainly* (my italics) have been found by them in two distinct sources, and the Q version of them is considerably different from the Marcan. Streeter also records Professor Dodd's remark that Mark iii. 28, iv. 22 and vi. 8 diverge from the Q version in ways that 'might be explained as divergent translations of Aramaic'.

A careful reading of the important pages 187–91 of *The Four Gospels* will disclose that it was probably, above all, the virtual identification of Q with the *Lucan* form of the Q passages that persuaded Streeter to cast doubt upon the position, with regard to Mark's supposed use of Q, which he put forward in *Oxford Studies*, and which Sanday accepted. This argument of course falls to the ground once it is realized that Luke depends, in his Q passages, directly upon Matthew; and even for a Two-Documentarian it involves a paradoxical neglect of the careful studies by Harnack in *The Sayings of Jesus*. It will therefore be interesting to see how far the arguments adduced by Streeter in 1911 in favour of Mark's dependence on Q will tell validly in favour of Mark's dependence on Matthew, Q's residuary legatee; and whether in some cases they are not stronger in favour of this dependence than they were in favour of dependence on Q. In the following review we shall in places strengthen Streeter's case with the help of considerations not mentioned by him.

(1) The first case examined by Streeter is Mark i. 7f. (cf. Matt. iii. 7–12), the Preaching of St John the Baptist. His argument, transposed to fit the fact that Luke depends directly on Matthew (a transposition which we shall make in every case), runs as follows (*Oxford Studies*, pp. 167f.): Matthew's parallel contains a message of St John (repentance, the wrath to come even upon Abraham's children, the axe at the root of the tree, the threshing-floor) in addition to the mere announcement of 'One coming after', which is all that Mark gives. Mark i. 7f. occurs almost word for word in

Matt. iii. 11, but it would seem that Matthew derived this verse not from Mark but from the same source whence he derived the preceding and following verses (i.e. Matt. iii. 7–10 and iii. 12). For *the subject of the relative in Matt. iii. 12 is contained in this verse, iii. 11, which he has in common with Mark.* Matt. iii. 12 'has no meaning apart from the preceding verse' and therefore the preceding verse belongs inseparably with it and cannot have been borrowed by Matthew from Mark, who has nothing to correspond with Matt. iii. 12. Streeter concludes that Matt. iii. 7–12 is one connected whole, of which Mark i. 7f. is a mutilated fragment.

Streeter's case here is weakened by our rejection of the Q hypothesis, for the agreements of Matt. iii. 11 and Luke iii. 16 against Mark i. 7f. were a further, converging, argument for the derivation of the whole passage from Q. But the argument, in the form given to it above, is still not without force. The Matthew passage is one of that large number in which Matthew's supposed 'additions to Mark' cohere completely with the 'Marcan' elements and *cannot be reasonably supposed to have had any existence apart from them.*

It will be observed that Streeter's argument here is in no way touched by the considerations brought forward in his subsequent retractation in *The Four Gospels* of the opinion that Mark used Q.

Streeter further draws attention to the fact that in Mark i. 2, St Mark (alone of the evangelists) prefixes to the quotation of Isaias, promised in *v.* 1 and given in *v.* 3, a quotation from Malachi (iii. 1):

Matt. iii. 1–3	Mark i. 1–3
ἐν δὲ ταῖς ἡμέραις ἐκείναις παραγίνεται	ἀρχὴ τοῦ εὐαγγελίου 'Ιησοῦ Χριστοῦ·
'Ιωάννης ὁ βαπτιστὴς κηρύσσων ἐν τῇ	
ἐρήμῳ τῆς 'Ιουδαίας 2. λέγων· μετα-	
νοεῖτε· ἤγγικεν γὰρ ἡ βασιλεία τῶν	
οὐρανῶν. 3. οὗτος γάρ ἐστιν ὁ ῥηθεὶς	2. καθὼς γέγραπται ἐν τῷ
διὰ 'Ησαΐου τοῦ προφήτου λέγοντος·	'Ησαΐᾳ τῷ προφήτῃ· ἰδοὺ ἐγὼ ἀπο-
	στέλλω τὸν ἄγγελόν μου πρὸ προσώ-
(Cf. xi. 10.)	που σου, ὃς κατασκευάσει τὴν ὁδόν σου·
φωνὴ βοῶντος ἐν τῇ ἐρήμῳ, κτλ.	3. φωνὴ βοῶντος ἐν τῇ ἐρήμῳ, κτλ.

This quotation of Malachi occurs (in the same translation, which differs from LXX and in fact appears to 'conflate' Mal. iii. 1 with Exod. xxiii. 20) at Matt. xi. 10 (no parallel in Mark) in a passage to which it is integral; its removal from this paragraph of Matthew would ruin the rhetorical and logical sequence. 'It looks', says Streeter, 'as if Mark's double quotation [in i. 2f.] is a conflation of the two quotations applied to John in two different contexts of Q', or, as we should say, of Matthew. It would not be reasonable to maintain that Matthew, copying Mark, noticed that the quotation did not come from Isaias, and therefore omitted it when reproducing Mark i. 1–3, but finding that his Aramaic source for Matt. xi. 7–14 included this quotation from Malachi, turned back to Mark for the exact translation of it, conflation with Exodus and all. As we have seen, Rawlinson elects to regard the verse as not authentic in Mark; and he can point out that it is omitted by both St Matthew and St Luke, who, on the Two-Document hypothesis, are independent copiers of Mark. His view is that the verse is original in the Q passage Matt. xi. 10 (that is, in our view, original in *Matthew*) and that its presence in our copies of Mark is due to copying of Matthew. (Lagrange also chooses to regard the verse as only doubtfully authentic in Mark, but he may be influenced by non-critical considerations here.) As there is no manuscript authority for omitting the verse in Mark it should be retained as authentic, and as one of the many examples showing St Mark's knowledge of Matthaean passages which, as a whole, he omitted.

(2) 'Mark's brief allusion to the Temptation [i. 12f.] is less original than the longer account' in Matt. iv. 1–11 (Streeter, p. 168). 'An original tradition is always detailed and picturesque', though on this point Form Critics would not agree, nor should we, 'and would hardly record as does Mark a temptation to do nothing in particular.' It is perhaps a stronger argument, that the tradition of the temptations as described in Matt. iv. 3–10 cannot be supposed to have been floating about without a framework or context. Why, then, should Matthew have torn it out of the context in which he found it and insert it, by a process of invisible mending, into Mark's brief account?

In *The Four Gospels* (pp. 187 ff.) Streeter says that 'if we did not unwittingly read into Mark's account what is so familiar to us from the other two Gospels' we should interpret Matthew's 'And the angels ministered to him' as meaning that our Lord was continuously fed by angels, as once Elijah was by ravens, Mark making no mention of a fast. The question at once arises: Did our Lord fast, or did he not? As Streeter attributes the detailed Temptation story to Q (for it is found in Luke in almost identical terms), we presume that he would agree that he *did*, the first temptation being to supply bodily needs by a miracle. But if so, can Mark be supposed to be unaware of the fact and to believe that, precisely to the contrary, our Lord was fed all through the forty days by a miracle? If not, we shall agree with Bishop Rawlinson that Mark's statement that 'angels ministered to him' probably presupposes the fast which Mark does not mention, and in consequence we shall hold that Mark is probably abbreviating a received tradition, and in fact is abbreviating that account of the Temptation that is found in Matthew. Otherwise, it must be attributed to St Matthew's habitual good fortune that Mark's account (accidentally?) gave him exactly the desired finale ('the angels ministered to Him') to a story of a fast faithfully maintained.

(3) The next case is the Beelzebub Controversy, Matt. xii. 22–32, Mark iii. 22–30; cf. Luke xi. 14–23. I propose to deal with this in my own way, indicating Streeter's treatment as occasion may arise:

We gather from Matthew (om. Mark) that the Pharisaic blasphemy was evoked by the crowds' suggestion that our Lord, as having performed the exorcism of xii. 22, was 'the son of David', that is, the Messiah. Matt. *vv.* 27, 28 and 30 also have no parallel in Mark. Streeter (in *Oxford Studies*) says that Matt. *vv.* 27 f. are indubitably 'original in their context', for they have no point except as a reply to the challenge in xii. 24, Mark iii. 22. 'Although therefore the verse' containing this challenge 'is found exactly in Mark [iii. 22] it must have occurred also in Q.' It will further be observed that Matt. *v.* 28 'But if I by the Spirit of God cast out demons' (om. Mark) explains the reference in Matt. xii. 31 f. *and in Mark iii.* 28 f. to blasphemy against the *Holy Spirit.* And, added Streeter, 'the curious phrase Mark iii. 28, τοῖς υἱοῖς τῶν ἀνθρώπων, here only in N.T., is perhaps due to a hazy reminiscence of the τὸν υἱὸν τοῦ ἀνθρώπου' of the half of Matt. xii. 32 which Mark omits. The omission of this half verse by Mark is easily explained by its contents; its *addition* by Matthew to the text as found in Mark would be extraordinary.

We have pointed out earlier in this volume (pp. 11 f.) the internal coherence of this discourse in Matthew. Can anyone believe, for instance, that the source that contained Matt. xii. 24, 27, 28 (assuming, for the sake of argument, that Matthew here depends on a source) did not also contain Matt. xii. 25 f., which is parallel to Mark iii. 23–5? And we note how the notion of punishment for sinful speech is carried on in νν. 34–7 (om. Mark).

Matt. xii. 22–32

τότε προσηνέχθη αὐτῷ δαιμονιζόμενος τυφλὸς καὶ κωφός· καὶ ἐθεράπευσεν αὐτόν, ὥστε τὸν κωφὸν λαλεῖν καὶ βλέπειν. 23. καὶ ἐξίσταντο πάντες οἱ ὄχλοι καὶ ἔλεγον· μήτι οὗτός ἐστιν ὁ υἱὸς Δαυείδ; 24. οἱ δὲ Φαρισαῖοι ἀκούσαντες εἶπον· οὗτος οὐκ ἐκβάλλει τὰ δαιμόνια εἰ μὴ ἐν τῷ Βεελζεβοὺλ ἄρχοντι τῶν δαιμονίων. 25. εἰδὼς δὲ τὰς ἐνθυμήσεις αὐτῶν εἶπεν αὐτοῖς·

πᾶσα βασιλεία μερισθεῖσα καθ᾽ ἑαυτῆς ἐρημοῦται, καὶ πᾶσα πόλις ἢ οἰκία μερισθεῖσα καθ᾽ ἑαυτῆς οὐ σταθήσεται. 26. καὶ εἰ ὁ σατανᾶς τὸν σατανᾶν ἐκβάλλει, ἐφ᾽ ἑαυτὸν ἐμερίσθη· πῶς οὖν σταθήσεται ἡ βασιλεία αὐτοῦ; 27. καὶ εἰ ἐγὼ ἐν Βεελζεβοὺλ ἐκβάλλω τὰ δαιμόνια, οἱ υἱοὶ ὑμῶν ἐν τίνι ἐκβάλλουσιν; διὰ τοῦτο αὐτοὶ κριταὶ ἔσονται ὑμῶν. 28. εἰ δὲ ἐν πνεύματι θεοῦ ἐγὼ ἐκβάλλω τὰ δαιμόνια, ἄρα ἔφθασεν ἐφ᾽ ὑμᾶς ἡ βασιλεία τοῦ θεοῦ. 29. ἢ πῶς δύναταί τις εἰσελθεῖν εἰς τὴν οἰκίαν τοῦ ἰσχυροῦ καὶ τὰ σκεύη αὐτοῦ ἁρπάσαι, ἐὰν μὴ πρῶτον δήσῃ τὸν ἰσχυρόν, καὶ τότε τὴν οἰκίαν αὐτοῦ διαρπάσῃ; 30. ὁ μὴ ὢν μετ᾽ ἐμοῦ κατ᾽ ἐμοῦ ἐστιν, καὶ ὁ μὴ συνάγων μετ᾽ ἐμοῦ σκορπίζει. 31. διὰ τοῦτο λέγω ὑμῖν, πᾶσα ἁμαρτία καὶ βλασφημία ἀφεθήσεται τοῖς ἀνθρώποις, ἡ δὲ τοῦ πνεύματος βλασφημία οὐκ ἀφεθήσεται. 32. καὶ ὃς ἐὰν εἴπῃ λόγον κατὰ τοῦ υἱοῦ τοῦ ἀνθρώπου, ἀφεθήσεται αὐτῷ· ὃς δ᾽ ἂν εἴπῃ κατὰ τοῦ πνεύματος τοῦ ἁγίου, οὐκ ἀφεθήσεται αὐτῷ οὔτε ἐν τούτῳ τῷ αἰῶνι οὔτε ἐν τῷ μέλλοντι.

Mark iii. 22–30

καὶ οἱ γραμματεῖς οἱ ἀπὸ Ἱεροσολύμων καταβάντες ἔλεγον ὅτι Βεελζεβοὺλ ἔχει, καὶ ὅτι ἐν τῷ ἄρχοντι τῶν δαιμονίων ἐκβάλλει τὰ δαιμόνια. 23. καὶ προσκαλεσάμενος αὐτοὺς ἐν παραβολαῖς ἔλεγεν αὐτοῖς· πῶς δύναται σατανᾶς σατανᾶν ἐκβάλλειν; 24. καὶ ἐὰν βασιλεία ἐφ᾽ ἑαυτὴν μερισθῇ, οὐ δύναται στῆναι ἡ βασιλεία ἐκείνη. 25. καὶ ἐὰν οἰκία ἐφ᾽ ἑαυτὴν μερισθῇ, οὐ δυνήσεται ἡ οἰκία ἐκείνη σταθῆναι. 26. καὶ εἰ ὁ σατανᾶς ἀνέστη ἐφ᾽ ἑαυτόν, ἐμερίσθη καὶ οὐ δύναται στῆναι ἀλλὰ τέλος ἔχει.

27. ἀλλ᾽ οὐ δύναται οὐδεὶς εἰς τὴν οἰκίαν τοῦ ἰσχυροῦ εἰσελθὼν τὰ σκεύη αὐτοῦ διαρπάσαι, ἐὰν μὴ πρῶτον τὸν ἰσχυρὸν δήσῃ, καὶ τότε τὴν οἰκίαν αὐτοῦ διαρπάσει.

28. ἀμὴν λέγω ὑμῖν ὅτι πάντα ἀφεθήσεται τοῖς υἱοῖς τῶν ἀνθρώπων τὰ ἁμαρτήματα καὶ αἱ βλασφημίαι, ὅσα ἂν βλασφημήσωσιν·

29. ὃς δ᾽ ἂν βλασφημήσῃ εἰς τὸ πνεῦμα τὸ ἅγιον, οὐκ ἔχει ἄφεσιν εἰς τὸν αἰῶνα, ἀλλὰ ἔνοχος ἔσται αἰωνίου ἁμαρτήματος. 30. ὅτι ἔλεγον· πνεῦμα ἀκάθαρτον ἔχει.

(4) Mark iv. 21–5 has been discussed above (pp. 88 f.), and (5) Mark iv. 30–2 is discussed on p. 86. The former passage is said by Streeter (*Oxford Studies*, p. 171) to consist of 'five sayings having no internal connexion with one another' and he agrees with us that their contexts in Matthew as a rule seem 'more original' than the context in Mark. As regards Streeter's suggestion in *The Four Gospels* that in Mark the parable of the Seed Growing Secretly is a 'twin' of the Mustard-seed parable, we have already (p. 87) pointed out that the former may be a twin of the Sower parable. Streeter's suggestion is that in Mark and Q we have two pairs (Seed Growing Secretly with Mustard-seed; Mustard-seed with Leaven) 'which have descended along quite independent lines of tradition' (*The Four Gospels*, p. 190). This would seem to imply that you make two parables into 'twins' by appending one to the other. But that is not so. Parables are 'twins' if in form and content they recall each other, and twinship is a matter of birth not environment. The Mustard-seed and the Leaven parables satisfy this criterion and must have been spoken originally by our Lord *as twins*. If the Parable of the Seed Growing Secretly had the required parallelism of form and content with the Mustard-seed (but it has not) we should have not two pairs of twins but one set of triplets.

(6) is the Mission Charge (Matt. x. 1, 7–16*a*, Mark vi. 7–11) which we have discussed above (pp. 102 ff.). Streeter (*Oxford Studies*, p. 175) argues that Matt. x. 13 implies something equivalent to Mark vi. 10 (cf. Matt. x. 11) indicating entrance of the house.

(7) Matt. xviii. 6–9 (cf. Mark ix. 42–50), on Scandal, has been discussed above, pp. 98 f. Streeter (*loc. cit.* p. 175) says that Matt. xviii. 7 ('Woe to the world', etc.) 'is explained by the connected saying "it is better for him that a millstone"', etc., apart from which it has little meaning. Mark ix. 42 reproduces only one of these sayings, 'again breaking up an original pair'. Regarding Matt. xviii. 8f. and its doublet-twin Matt. v. 29f., he says that the natural explanation of the doublet is that in one case Matthew copies Mark, and in the other case Q. It must be stated emphatically that this is *not* the natural explanation, for the close similarity of the two passages is hardly consistent with diverse provenance. We have already argued that at xviii. 8f. Matthew is *quoting his own passage in the Sermon on the Mount,* and if that is so Mark's dependence on

Matthew is of course proved.[1] Streeter thinks that Mark ix. 50 καλὸν τὸ ἅλα comes from Q, 'because it looks more original than Matthew's ὑμεῖς ἐστε τὸ ἅλα τῆς γῆς'. But as Q never existed we cannot follow him here.

(8) Mark xii. 38–40, the Denunciation of the Scribes, 'looks like a reminiscence of the long denunciation' in Matt. xxiii. 1–36. We examined this case in some detail (pp. 73 ff.), and concluded that St Mark was excerpting from the parallel passage in Matthew, with some alteration in view of the ignorance of Gentile Christians of special features of Palestinian Judaism. In *The Four Gospels* Streeter does not review this instance of Mark's alleged 'dependence on Q'.

It must be emphasized that for Streeter the arguments adducible for Mark's dependence on Q in the above instances had an added strength from the fact that the parallels in Luke, with agreements with Matthew against Mark, are naturally taken by him as showing that the passages, including often such verses as are also paralleled in Mark, come from Q, and therefore existed in their integrity before Matthew copied Mark. This confirmation of the argument by appeal to Luke is no longer possible, now that the reasons for believing in Q's existence have been shown to be insufficient. On the other hand, the disappearance of Q from the argument destroys Streeter's contention in *The Four Gospels* that the original form of the Q passages is to be found in Luke, which enabled him to emphasize the differences between the Marcan and Q versions. The 'cumulative effect' of the eight instances remains considerable, and it may be suggested that upholders of the priority of Mark should try to discover a comparable set of passages in which Matthew should show his dependence on Mark.

We have already had occasion to refer to the late Professor Burney's pioneer work, *The Poetry of Our Lord*, published in 1925 after the author's untimely death, and described on its title-page as 'An Examination of the Formal Elements of Hebrew Poetry in the Discourses of Jesus Christ'. In his Preface Burney suggests that the 'formal connexion of much of our Lord's teaching with the Hebrew poetry of the Old Testament' may be a help in determining

---

[1] For a general discussion of the doublets in Matthew, see chapter IX below.

whether or not we have in the Gospels 'something approaching to, if not actually representing, the *ipsissima verba* of His teaching'. The book is a first essay, many of its findings probably demand revision or fail to produce conviction, but it is hard to resist the conclusion that Burney, who was one of the leading Hebraists of his day, was on the track of real Semitic rhythms, implied again and again by the Greek of our Lord's discourses in the Gospels, which can at least help us in the attempt to decide which of two or three versions of a saying or paragraph is likely to be closer to the Aramaic original. Reference was made on p. 81 *supra* to one striking fact, tending to confirm the validity of Burney's technique: he separated out from Mark xiii, as being rhythmically out of harmony with its context, a paragraph (*vv.* 9–13) which he subsequently found to have its parallel in quite a different context in Matthew (x. 17–21).[1]

Burney accepted the ordinary Two-Document hypothesis, and it is interesting to see what, from his own point of view, he has to say on the question of 'Mark's knowledge and use of "Q"'. He observes in his Preface (p. 8): 'Evidence adduced in the present volume should go far to prove' that Mark knew and used Q. 'Such a conclusion emerges first through comparison of certain antithetically parallel sayings of our Lord as given by Mark and by the other Gospels, from which it appears that a characteristic clear-cut form of antithesis, preserved by these latter and attested by numerous parallels, has been to some extent lost in Mark through the addition of new matter. The inference is that the other Synoptists cannot, in these passages, have been drawing from Mark, but that both they and Mark were dependent upon a common source (Q), to which they have adhered more faithfully than he.' It will be noted that (*a*) with this hypothesis of the dependence of Mark as well as

---

[1] Strictly speaking, it is not necessary, for the purpose to which it is proposed here to apply Burney's findings, to hold that the Semitic parallelism goes back to our Lord's own oral teaching. Our argument takes the following form: (*a*) this parallelism is not found in all the sayings of our Lord as preserved to us in the Gospels, but examples of it are found in all four Gospels, and more in Matthew than in Mark or Luke. (*b*) As Matthew and Mark sometimes both have the parallelism in the same saying, it is probable that where Matthew has it *and Mark lacks it*, the Matthaean version is the more original. For if Matthew was responsible for giving Semitic poetic form to Greek prose material borrowed from Mark, to what influence are we to attribute the Semitic verse form in those passages where Mark also exhibits it?

Matthew and Luke on the same document (Q) in passages where all three are running parallel, criticism threatens to return to the despairing notion of an Ur-Evangelium as the common source of all three Synoptic Gospels; (b) but once we admit, as was argued in the first four chapters of the present work, that Q is a myth and that Luke depends directly on Matthew in his Q passages and on Mark in his Marcan passages, then Burney's conclusion must be revised; the considerations adduced by him, if their validity is accepted, 'go far to prove' that Mark used Matthew. (It may further be observed that Burney's explanation involves the improbable sequence: (a) Mark used Q; (b) Matthew, copying Mark, recognized Mark's distorted reproductions of Q and, turning to the original Q, substituted the correct form of the sayings as found there.)

Besides the case of Mark xiii. 9–13, already considered, Burney refers to Matt. xvi. 25 (cf. Mark viii. 35):

(1)	Matthew	Mark
	ὃς γὰρ ἂν θέλη τὴν ψυχὴν αὐτοῦ σῶσαι, ἀπολέσει αὐτήν· ὃς δ' ἂν ἀπολέση τὴν ψυχὴν αὐτοῦ ἕνεκεν ἐμοῦ, εὑρήσει αὐτήν.	ὃς γὰρ ἐὰν θέλη τὴν ψυχὴν αὐτοῦ σῶσαι, ἀπολέσει αὐτήν· ὃς δ' ἂν ἀπολέση τὴν ψυχὴν αὐτοῦ ἕνεκεν ἐμοῦ καὶ τοῦ εὐαγγελίου, σώσει αὐτήν.

The verse in Matthew is given by Burney as an example of 'Antithetical Parallelism'. He points out that καὶ τοῦ εὐαγγελίου in Mark 'clearly overweights the clause' and goes on (p. 74 n. 4): 'As, then, it is improbable that both Matthew and Luke should have improved upon the form of Mark's parallelism by excision of the words καὶ τοῦ εὐαγγελίου, we must infer that they depended upon a source of information superior to Mark, that is, probably Q; in other words, the passage is an indication that Mark knew and used Q [or, as we should say, Matthew], and in this case has glossed it to the detriment of the parallelistic form of the antithesis.'

Quite apart from the rhythmical argument, Mark's use here of 'the Gospel', *tout court*, is noteworthy. In four of the remaining six occurrences of the phrase in Mark it is used in the same absolute way: i. 15, 'believe in the Gospel' (om. Matthew; no parallel in Luke), though as 'the Gospel of God' has been mentioned in the previous verse this case is not so significant; x. 29, 'for My sake and for the sake of the Gospel' (Matthew: 'for My sake', om. 'and the Gospel's'); xiii. 10, 'to all the nations first must the Gospel be preached'

(Matthew: 'the Gospel of the Kingdom'); xiv. 9, 'wherever the Gospel is preached' (Matthew: 'this Gospel', no parallel in Luke). Matthew never uses 'the Gospel' without qualification, although, as we have seen, Mark has it thus five times *where Matthew lacks it*. The word does not occur in Luke or John; in Acts it occurs twice (once, on the lips of St Peter, absolutely, xv. 7). The absolute use is common in St Paul. Elsewhere in the New Testament the word occurs only at I Pet. iv. 17 ('the Gospel of God') and Rev. xiv. 6 ('an angel...having an eternal Gospel'). The 'absolute' use must be considered a later development from the qualified use, and is specially characteristic, in the New Testament, of St Paul. Matthew's failure to present this usage in passages parallel to Mark's instances of it gives an effect of greater primitivity, and we naturally conclude that the Marcan usage, in our passage as elsewhere, represents an adaptation of our Lord's words to the needs of the early Church. Thus we have here an independent argument to confirm Burney's conclusion on rhythmical grounds that the Marcan text here is secondary as compared with the Matthaean. It may be mentioned in passing that the suggestion has been mooted that the words in Mark viii. 35 are an 'early gloss'; but their genuineness is confirmed by the other four occurrences in Mark.

<table>
<tr><td>(2) Matt. xix. 26</td><td>Mark x. 27</td></tr>
</table>

(2) Matt. xix. 26

παρὰ ἀνθρώποις τοῦτο ἀδύνατόν ἐστιν, παρὰ δὲ θεῷ δυνατὰ πάντα.

Mark x. 27

παρὰ ἀνθρώποις ἀδύνατον, ἀλλ' οὐ παρὰ θεῷ· πάντα γὰρ δυνατὰ παρὰ τῷ θεῷ.

Burney comments (p. 75 n. 1): 'The insertion [in Mark] of "But not with God", which is really redundant by the side of the following line, has the effect of marring the sharpness of the antithesis. Clearly the addition is a gloss.' Yes, but, as in the next instance below, a gloss by Mark on Matthew's text.

(3) Matt. xxvi. 11

πάντοτε γὰρ τοὺς πτωχοὺς ἔχετε μεθ' ἑαυτῶν, ἐμὲ δὲ οὐ πάντοτε ἔχετε.

Mark xiv. 7

πάντοτε γὰρ τοὺς πτωχοὺς ἔχετε μεθ' ἑαυτῶν καὶ ὅταν θέλητε δύνασθε εὖ ποιῆσαι, ἐμὲ δὲ οὐ πάντοτε ἔχετε.

Burney (p. 76 n. 1): 'The sharp and telling antithesis of Matthew...is destroyed in Mark by the insertion after the first *stichos* of the words, "And whenever ye will ye can do (them) good". This must be thought to be a gloss adding a correct, but unnecessary, explanation of the implication of the first clause.'

It will be noticed that two verses later we have an instance of Mark's 'the Gospel' used absolutely (for Matthew's 'this Gospel').

(4) Matt. xvi. 4

γενεὰ πονηρὰ καὶ μοιχαλὶς σημεῖον ἐπιζητεῖ, καὶ σημεῖον οὐ δοθήσεται αὐτῇ εἰ μὴ τὸ σημεῖον 'Ιωνᾶ.

Mark viii. 12

τί ἡ γενεὰ αὕτη ζητεῖ σημεῖον; ἀμὴν λέγω ὑμῖν, εἰ δοθήσεται τῇ γενεᾷ ταύτῃ σημεῖον.

Burney quotes the verse from Matthew as an example of 'Step-Parallelism', and remarks that 'Mark phrases somewhat differently'. Mark's version, in fact, destroys the rhythm.

(5) Matt. vi. 14f.

ἐὰν γὰρ ἀφῆτε τοῖς ἀνθρώποις τὰ παραπτώματα αὐτῶν, ἀφήσει καὶ ὑμῖν ὁ πατὴρ ὑμῶν ὁ οὐράνιος· 15. ἐὰν δὲ μὴ ἀφῆτε τοῖς ἀνθρώποις [their trespasses][1] οὐδὲ ὁ πατὴρ ὑμῶν ἀφήσει τὰ παραπτώματα ὑμῶν.

Mark xi. 25

ἀφίετε εἴ τι ἔχετε κατά τινος, ἵνα καὶ ὁ πατὴρ ὑμῶν ὁ ἐν τοῖς οὐρανοῖς ἀφῇ ὑμῖν τὰ παραπτώματα ὑμῶν.

Burney (p. 107) quotes the passage from Matthew as a quatrain with ac, bd parallelism. He does not discuss the Marcan verse in relation to it. We show below that Mark gives numerous indications of his dependence on Matthew here. But he has rewritten Matthew in prose form.

(6) Matt. x. 8–16; cf. Mark vi. 8–11. Here Burney claims that a four-beat rhythm is more clearly observable in Mark and in the Lucan parallel ix. 3–5 than in Matthew. But he accepts Matt. x. 8 (om. Mark) and *v.* 16 (om. Mark). He also 'restores' *oratio recta* in Mark vi. 8 (the parallel in Matthew is already in *oratio recta*), rejects ἔλεγεν αὐτοῖς (Mark vi. 10, lacking in Matthew), and inserts Matthew's ἀσπάσασθε αὐτήν. He also rejects Mark's εἰς μαρτύριον αὐτοῖς (*v.* 11). Thus his attempts to find rhythm in Mark here frequently drive him back to Matthew. It is interesting to compare the results of his procedure with our analysis of the passage, from a different point of view, on pp. 102 ff. We cannot accept Burney's view that Matthew and Mark have here independently of each other, and both imperfectly, reproduced Q, but must hold that Matthew has imperfectly reproduced the Aramaic rhythms, which in some

[1] Om. Huck. But there is strong MS. authority for the reading, which completes the rhythm.

places have been still further blurred by Mark, though occasionally (but presumably by accident) Mark's version seems more rhythmical than Matthew's.

(7) Matt. ix. 15–17 (cf. Mark ii. 19–22), the Children of the Bride-chamber, etc. This passage is given by Burney as an example of *kina* rhythm. He says: 'Here we follow the text of Matthew, which, as judged by the rhythmical standard, is certainly superior to that of Mark. Note that in Mark ii. 19 the placing of the infinitive νηστεύειν after the temporal clause…is less natural in a Semitic language than is the position of πενθεῖν in Matthew…. In Mark ii. 20 the addition of ἐν ἐκείνῃ τῇ ἡμέρᾳ…throws out the rhythm…. In Matt. ix. 16 οὐδεὶς δὲ ἐπιβάλλει ἐπίβλημα ῥάκους ἀγνάφου, κτλ. gives the original Semitic order of words rather than Mark ii. 21, οὐδεὶς ἐπίβλημα ῥάκους ἀγνάφου ἐπιβάλλει, κτλ. In Mark ii. 21 εἰ δὲ μή, αἴρει τὸ πλήρωμα ἀπ' αὐτοῦ τὸ καινὸν τοῦ παλαιοῦ is more awkward than Matthew's simple and rhythmical αἴρει γὰρ τὸ πλήρωμα αὐτοῦ ἀπὸ τοῦ ἱματίου, and has the air of an unnecessary attempt at explanation.' He adds that Mark ii. 19*b* (om. Matthew) is perfectly rhythmical, but may be of the nature of an explanatory addition.

(8) Matt. xvi. 24–7 (cf. Mark viii. 34–8), the Cross of Disciple-ship. 'Here again,' says Burney (p. 142 n. 1), 'if our rhythmical scheme is right, Matthew represents the nearest approximation to the original', though he points to a few details in which he thinks Mark's version is superior to Matthew's.

In attempting to assess the value of Burney's testimony to the superiority in rhythmical form of so much of Matthew over Mark, there are some points to be observed. (*a*) There are some instances in which, on rhythmical grounds, he prefers Mark to Matthew; besides those already mentioned, I have noticed Mark iv. 30 (regarded by Burney as a couplet of synonymous parallelism, not found in Matthew), vii. 8 (an alleged case of antithetical parallelism, om. Matthew), viii. 17f. But (*b*) the reconstruction of the original rhythms from the Greek is bound to be somewhat tentative, and individual cases can rarely be relied upon. (*c*) Where, however, the argument from rhythm coincides with other considerations, as in Mark xiii. 9–13 and in paragraphs (1), (5) and (6) above, it is strengthened by their concurrence, and in turn strengthens them.

(*d*) It is the cumulative effect of Burney's instances of Matthaean superiority that is impressive. [And it may prove difficult to confine the inference, that Matthew's superior style is not evolved from Mark's crudity, to cases where Burney's criterion is directly applicable. The full force of the evidence is only measured when it is recognized that Q is an inadmissible hypothesis. Once this is realized, no one can fail to see the grave difficulties that Burney's findings will produce for those who persist in maintaining Mark's priority. They will be compelled either to dismiss the whole idea of Semitic poetic or quasi-poetic rhythms, when applied to our Lord's discourses, as so much moonshine;[1] or to maintain that the author of Matthew, writing in Greek, has restored the broken rhythms found by him in the Greek Mark. An uncomfortable dilemma.

This chapter has shown that three distinguished scholars, all of the Two-Document persuasion, have, each following his own line, come to recognize that Mark is not always original and that Matthew does in places preserve a more primitive version of their common material. As has been pointed out, this means that *either* St Mark copied Matthew, *or* St Matthew (*a*) frequently recognized that Mark was giving a secondary version of a passage of which St Matthew possessed a more original version in a source unknown to us; and (*b*) *inserted the version from the unknown source into the Marcan context*. This is the same result as that to which we were driven in our examination of the Great Discourses, and there can be no question that the hypothesis of Marcan dependence on Matthew is the one that is critically preferable.

The present chapter has extended the area of Matthaean originality considerably beyond the Great Discourses, to cover, for example, the Teaching of St John the Baptist, the Temptation of our Lord, the Beelzebub Controversy, the Teaching on Riches and the Kingdom of God, the Anointing at Bethany, and the Question of Fasting (Matt. ix. 15–17). It is already noticeable that the limits of the Q passages have been overstepped, and in the following chapters we shall find that the area threatens to expand so far as to become indistinguishable from that of Matthew as a whole.

[1] And Burney held that these rhythms could be detected not only in the Synoptic discourses but in some Johannine ones also.

CHAPTER VIII

MISCELLANEOUS PASSAGES

In the present chapter it is proposed to examine certain other passages where Mark seems, more or less plainly, to be secondary to Matthew. The order of Mark's Gospel will be followed, omitting the instances already investigated. Our previous results justify us in expecting that Mark will from time to time disclose his editorial activity. Specially significant are cases (2), (8) and (13) below.

(1) Matt. iv. 17	Mark i. 14f.
(Cf. iv. 12.)	μετὰ δὲ τὸ παραδοθῆναι τὸν Ἰωάννην ἦλθεν ὁ Ἰησοῦς εἰς τὴν Γαλιλαίαν, κηρύσσων τὸ εὐαγγέλιον τοῦ θεοῦ,
ἀπὸ τότε ἤρξατο ὁ Ἰησοῦς κηρύσσειν καὶ λέγειν· μετανοεῖτε· ἤγγικεν γὰρ ἡ βασιλεία τῶν οὐρανῶν.	15. ὅτι πεπλήρωται ὁ καιρὸς καὶ ἤγγικεν ἡ βασιλεία τοῦ θεοῦ· μετανοεῖτε καὶ πιστεύετε ἐν τῷ εὐαγγελίῳ.

We have seen that Mark's phrase τὸ εὐαγγέλιον, used absolutely (v. 15), is probably a usage that developed after our Lord's Ascension (p. 119). Similarly τὸ εὐαγγέλιον τοῦ θεοῦ (v. 14) is a phrase that links Mark up with I Peter (iv. 17) and St Paul (six times). Just as Matthew's τὸ εὐαγγέλιον τοῦτο is more primitive than τὸ εὐαγγέλιον (for it does not exclude the idea of other sorts of 'Good news'), so also τὸ εὐαγγέλιον τῆς βασιλείας sounds more primitive than τὸ εὐαγγέλιον τοῦ θεοῦ; it is first found at Matt. iv. 23, obviously referring back to iv. 17, and therefore only on the way to becoming a technical term, which Mark's τὸ εὐαγγέλιον already is.

In view of this, it is interesting to note that πεπλήρωται ὁ καιρός (Mark, om. Matthew) is curiously like Gal. iv. 4 ὅτε δὲ ἦλθεν τὸ πλήρωμα τοῦ χρόνου, Eph. i. 9 τὸ πλήρωμα τῶν καιρῶν, Luke xxi. 24 ἄχρι οὗ πληρωθῶσιν καιροὶ ἐθνῶν, John vii. 8 ὁ ἐμὸς καιρὸς οὔπω πεπλήρωται, Acts ix. 23 ὡς δὲ ἐπληροῦντο ἡμέραι ἱκαναί; cf. vii. 23, 30.

Again πιστεύειν ἐν τῷ εὐαγγελίῳ—belief, not in a person (as, for example, Matt. xviii. 6, xxvii. 42), but in the Christian revelation—

perhaps gives the atmosphere of the early Church rather than of our Lord's personal language.[1]

Thus in the first formulation of our Lord's message, there is an accumulation of small indications, impressive when taken together, that Mark may reflect a period subsequent to our Lord's own lifetime. Matthew's short statement of the same message is unimpeachably primitive,[2] and it would be a happy accident indeed if, in copying Mark, he had managed to omit from his source precisely those features of the two verses that seem, to the eyes of a modern critic, to show the influence of later development. Such an achievement would be comparable to that of purging Mark ix. 33–7 of just those traits which suggest that it has been influenced by the somewhat similar incident at Mark x. 32–45. A criticism that can accept such consequences of its theory is strangely complacent.

(2) At Mark i. 21 we encounter the 'first discrepancy in order between Mark and Matthew, and the first passage in Mark that has no parallel in Matthew (Mark i. 21–8, our Lord teaching in the Synagogue of Capernaum and performing a miracle of exorcism there). The miracle invites comparison with Matt. viii. 29–32 (cf. Mark v. 1–13), the possessed person(s) at Gerasa.

It was suggested by Streeter (*The Four Gospels*, p. 170) that, in the passage from which we have quoted, Matthew has combined the Gerasene demoniac of Mark v. 1–13 with the demoniac of Mark i. 21–8, thus presenting us with *two Gerasene demoniacs*. But to transfer a demoniac from the synagogue at Capernaum to the 'territory of the Gadarenes' and the tombs there would, it may be suspected, be beyond the limits of what St Matthew would consider legitimate editing—and in any case, why should he do it? There was nothing to compel him to preserve both the miracles. Streeter's explanation is not much helped by his further suggestion that Matthew has *twice over* (Matt. ix. 27–31 and xx. 29–34) combined the blind man of Bethsaida (Mark viii. 22–6) with Bartimaeus (Mark x. 46–52); and it is in fact a *tour de force*. But on the theory of Marcan priority

[1] Cf. Mark ix. 42, where one MS. tradition has τῶν πιστευόντων, absolutely. But there is also good MS. authority for the addition of εἰς ἐμέ, which may, however, be a cross-harmonization with Matthew *ad loc.*

[2] On the contrast 'Kingdom of the heavens' (Matthew) and 'Kingdom of God' (Mark) see chapter x *infra*. It is a further very striking indication of Matthew's originality.

Mark (A) i. 23–6	Matt. viii. 28–32	Mark (B) v. 2–13
...ἦν...ἄνθρωπος ἐν πνεύ- ματι ἀκαθάρτῳ καὶ ἀνέκραξεν 24. λέγων·	...ὑπήντησαν αὐτῷ δύο δαι- μονιζόμενοι.... 29. καὶ ἰδοὺ ἔκραξαν λέγοντες·	...ὑπήντησεν αὐτῷ...ἄν- θρωπος ἐν πνεύματι ἀκα- θάρτῳ.... 6. καὶ ἰδὼν τὸν Ἰησοῦν...προσεκύνησεν αὐτῷ, 7. καὶ κράξας φωνῇ μεγάλῃ
τί ἡμῖν καὶ σοί, Ἰησοῦ Ναζαρηνέ; ἦλθες ἀπολέσαι ἡμᾶς· οἴδαμέν σε τίς εἶ, ὁ ἅγιος τοῦ θεοῦ. 25. καὶ ἐπετίμησεν αὐτῷ ὁ Ἰησοῦς· φιμώθητι καὶ	τί ἡμῖν καὶ σοί, υἱὲ τοῦ θεοῦ; ἦλθες ὧδε πρὸ καιροῦ βασανίσαι ἡμᾶς;...	λέγει· τί ἐμοὶ καὶ σοί, Ἰησοῦ, υἱὲ τοῦ θεοῦ τοῦ ὑψίστου; ὁρκίζω σε τὸν θεόν, μή με βασανίσῃς. 8. Ἔλεγεν γὰρ αὐτῷ· ἔξελθε τὸ πνεῦμα τὸ ἀκάθαρτον ἐκ τοῦ ἀνθρώ-
ἔξελθε ἐξ αὐτοῦ. 26. ...καὶ...τὸ πνεῦμα τὸ ἀκάθαρτον...φωνῆσαν φωνῇ μεγάλῃ ἐξῆλθεν ἐξ αὐτοῦ.	32. ...οἱ δὲ ἐξελθόντες ἀπῆλ- θον, κτλ.	που.... 13. ...καὶ ἐξελθόντα τὰ πνεύματα τὰ ἀκάθαρτα εἰσῆλθον, κτλ.

(Full underlining: Mark A and Matthew. Dotted underlining: Mark B and Matthew.)

he was driven to adopt it, because of the verbal links between Mark i. 24, Matt. viii. 29 (cf. Mark v. 7). These links he explains as due to Matthew having conflated the two verses of Mark—though even if he had wanted to conflate the miracles, there was no need for him to conflate the wording of the two stories. We have discussed Matthew's supposed weakness for ingenious and futile conflation of sources in chapter I *supra*, and have pointed out that the natural critical explanation of such phenomena as are found here (document A connected with document B; document B connected with document C) is that *the document showing relationship with each of the other two is the intermediary between them*. And in the case before us, since Matthew is the intermediary between two *Marcan* passages (that is, passages both in the same document), there is only *one* natural solution:

Matthew

Mark (A)   Mark (B)

There is one feature in this instance that corroborates the natural critical solution: in Mark i. 24 the single demoniac says: τί ἡμῖν καὶ σοί;...ἦλθες ἀπολέσαι ἡμᾶς· οἴδαμέν σε, κτλ. Why plural, when the speaker is singular? The reason is that Matt. viii. 29 reads the plural—because *two* demoniacs are there speaking.

It would seem, therefore, that so far from Matthew having combined two disparate demoniac stories from Mark, Mark, on the contrary, left for once to tell a story of which he could not find even the framework in Matthew, has nevertheless drawn upon a demoniac story in Matthew (or on his recollection of that story) to help him out in the telling of his own incident.[1]

And this same passage of Mark is indebted to Matthew in another respect. Since the summary description of our Lord's message at i. 15, the only information Mark has given us relates to the call of Saints Peter, Andrew, James and John. He now goes on (i. 21f.): καὶ εἰσπορεύονται εἰς Καφαρναούμ· καὶ εὐθὺς τοῖς σάββασιν ἐδίδασκεν εἰς τὴν συναγωγήν. καὶ ἐξεπλήσσοντο ἐπὶ τῇ διδαχῇ αὐτοῦ· ἦν γὰρ διδάσκων αὐτοὺς ὡς ἐξουσίαν ἔχων, καὶ οὐχ ὡς οἱ γραμματεῖς. The underlined words (with the addition of οἱ ὄχλοι after the first, and of αὐτῶν after the last, word) occur also at Matt. vii. 28f. at the end of the Sermon on the Mount (a discourse from which Mark borrows only odd verses here and there, in various parts of his Gospel). Either Matthew took the words from Mark or *vice versa*, since coincidence is ruled out by the exactness of the similarity, taken together with the fact that we know that one of the two evangelists had the work of the other before him as a source.

But the words are perfectly placed in Matthew. The preceding Sermon is a marvellous example of our Lord's *authoritative* teaching, above all in the repeated 'Ye have heard that it was said...but I say unto you'. The comment 'they were astonished', etc., is analogous to Mark i. 27, Matt. viii. 27, ix. 8 ('they glorified God who had given such *authority* unto men')—*it is a terminal comment on the reaction of the audience to our Lord's self-manifestation.*

In Mark the words are preceded by no such sample of his teaching as would explain this reaction. They are indeed *followed* by an echo at i. 27 (in the same incident): 'And all were astonished, so that they enquired, saying: What is this? *A new teaching with authority*; He even commands the unclean spirits and they obey Him.' Now from the point of view of Form-Criticism a miracle-story, in its

---

[1] It may be objected: If Mark used Matthew, why has he turned the two Gadarene demoniacs into one? And how is it that his own story of that exorcism is so much fuller than Matthew's? The reader is referred to chapter XI *infra*, where explanations of these facts are offered.

most primitive shape, should be *simple*, short, and proceeding straight to its end. If it includes discussion of some controversial issue, the discussion should arise out of the situation requiring the miracle, and should lead up to the miracle, as in the story of the Man with a Withered Hand, Matt. xii. 9–14. But in our passage, Mark i. 21–8, it is plain that *v.* 22 with its echo in *v.* 27 has imparted a *double current* to the story, making it serve the two *parallel* purposes of relating a miracle and drawing attention to the impression created by our Lord's teaching. The 'astonishment' of the witnesses in i. 27 ought logically to be at the exorcism, not at the teaching. *Remove i. 22 and its echo in i. 27 and you have a straightforward miracle-story true to type.*[1]

Now it is of course quite true that we need not suppose that Mark is dependent on a source just because he 'spoils' the simplicity, the presumably primitive form, of one of his own stories. What is past belief is that St Matthew should have found and salvaged—from an incident in Mark which, as a whole, he did not use—a sentence which (*a*) spoils the simplicity of Mark's story, but (*b*) can be used by him without alteration (except the addition of 'the crowds' and a possessive pronoun) to give the perfect *finale* to his own Great Sermon. The theory of Marcan priority involves supposing that, whereas at Matt. iv. 17 and xviii. 1–6 the author purified of alien elements two passages of Mark which he then proceeded to incorporate in his own Gospel, here he has purified a Marcan story, not in order to utilize the story but to utilize the intrusive element.

We thus have a combination of clues: the plural of Mark i. 24 and the intrusiveness of Mark i. 22, both explained by reference to Matthew, and criticism is not really at liberty to withhold its verdict.

[1] The above analysis receives an interesting confirmation from a footnote on p. 69 of Professor R. H. Lightfoot's Bampton Lectures, *History and Interpretation in the Gospels*: 'It seems probable' that the section Mark i. 21–7 'is composite, i.e. that verses 21 and 22 and the words "a new teaching with authority"...have been combined with an independent story of an expulsion of a demon.' The Form Critics are often right in suspecting editorial work in Mark, but their dogmatic adherence to the Two-Document hypothesis has prevented them from observing the natural and obvious explanation of this phenomenon. Professor Lightfoot adds that Mark i. 28 is 'an "additional conclusion"...; it breaks the immediate connexion between i. 21–7 and i. 29 ff., the sections being linked by their common reference to the synagogue'. Is it necessary to point out that, as noted in the text above, i. 28 is borrowed from Matt. iv. 24?

127

If, after this, we compare Matt. iv. 24 (om. Mark *ad loc.*) with Mark i. 28, the last verse of the paragraph we have been studying, we shall have no difficulty in deciding that Mark is secondary here also, though taken by itself the case might be explained either way.

How did it all happen? If we assume that Mark is dependent on Matthew, the answer is as follows: Having followed Matt. iv. 18–22 closely in Mark i. 16–20, St Mark sees ahead of him in Matthew (*a*) a general summary of the 'movement' consequent upon our Lord's self-manifestation (iv. 23–5), and (*b*) the Sermon on the Mount (v–vii), which he intends to omit.[1] He decides to substitute for the general statement about the movement a collection of miracle-stories, one of which is peculiar to himself (the others are in Matt. viii. 14–17), and a 'peculiar incident' (Mark i. 35–8) which looks as though it came from St Peter himself. But he takes care in his first miracle-story at least to refer to the impression created by our Lord's teaching, and in describing this impression, as well as in details of his narration, he helps himself from passages of Matthew, mainly occurring in his 'long omission' from that Gospel (Matt. iv. 23–vii. 29).

(3) Matt. ix. 23 (cf. Mark v. 38), from the Raising of Jairus's daughter. Matthew says: καὶ ἐλθὼν ʼΙησοῦς εἰς τὴν οἰκίαν τοῦ ἄρχοντος καὶ ἰδὼν τοὺς αὐλητὰς καὶ τὸν ὄχλον θορυβούμενον ἔλεγεν —that is, he assumes that his readers know the mourning customs of the Jews. St Mark, writing for those who may be expected not to know, says: θεωρεῖ θόρυβον καὶ κλαίοντας καὶ ἀλαλάζοντας πολλά —the difference is significant, and Matthew is the more primitive. We remember how πλατύνουσιν τὰ φυλακτήρια καὶ μηκύνουσιν τὰ κράσπεδα is changed in Mark to περιπατεῖν ἐν στολαῖς (p. 74 *supra*).

(4) Matt. xiii. 55 (at Nazareth): 'Is not this the carpenter's son?'; cf. Mark vi. 3: 'Is not this the carpenter?' Matthew gives the words actually, it may be presumed, used by the people of Nazareth, who of course regarded our Lord as the son of Joseph. St Matthew can safely reproduce this saying, as he has told us at the beginning of his Gospel that Joseph was not our Lord's father. Mark has not related our Lord's birth, and therefore changes Matthew's words

---

[1] For an explanation of Mark's reduction of the teaching element in his Gospel, see p. 169 *infra*. It is little more of a difficulty for us than for those who, like Bishop Rawlinson, regard Mark as indebted to tradition.

here. It is not so likely that St Matthew has deliberately changed Mark's 'carpenter' to 'son of the carpenter', thus *introducing* a difficulty. (Luke iv. 22, 'Is not this the son of Joseph?' is in a different context; we should therefore suppose (as usual in such cases) that Luke is not there dependent on Mark. He may depend (by reminiscence?) on Matthew.)

(5) Matt. xv. 1–20 (cf. Mark vii. 1–23), the Controversy about Unwashen Hands. (*a*) Mark vii. 3 f. is a long parenthesis, breaking the construction, an explanation about Jewish purification usages for Mark's Gentile readers. There is nothing corresponding to it in Matthew (though Matt. *v*. 2 probably provided Mark *v*. 3's 'tradition of the elders'); yet Marcan priorists hold that Matthew is a Gospel originally written in Greek, later in date than Mark, and dependent on it. The more primitive text is presumably the one without a commentary. (*b*) In Matthew the Pharisees' question, 'Why do your disciples transgress the tradition of the elders? For they do not wash their hands when they eat bread', is at once followed by the direct and pointed retort: (But He said to them) 'Why do you also transgress the commandment of God by reason of your tradition? For God', etc. The retort occurs also, in a less pointed form, in Mark *v*. 9, but it is there separated from the Pharisees' question by *vv*. 6–8 = Matt. *vv*. 7–9. One or other of the evangelists has altered the order of his source here, and it is obviously easier to suppose that Mark has spoiled the effect of the repartee than that Matthew has created the effect by alteration of Mark's order and wording. (*c*) Bishop Rawlinson thinks that 'the discussion in the present section' of Mark 'appears composite, and shows signs of editing'. He finds the original nucleus in *vv*. 1, 2, 5, 14, 15, and sees editorial links at *vv*. 6, 9, 14, 17, 18, 20; *vv*. 3 f. he regards as an interpolated editorial note. It will at once be observed that *vv*. 3 f. are, in our view, an interpolation by St Mark into a passage borrowed from Matthew. The 'editorial links' at *vv*. 6, 9 and 20 come at points where Mark diverges from, or reverts to, or changes the order of, Matthew. The 'links' at *vv*. 14 and 17–18, or their equivalents, are found also in Matthew. But it should be emphasized that at least Matt. *vv*. 2–6 seem to belong inseparably to their context, and cannot be supposed to have existed outside it, and the 'link' at Matt. *v*. 10 is therefore original. A case might be put

forward for regarding Matt. *vv.* 12–14 as an addition, but Lagrange says 'it must be recognized on the contrary that' this little paragraph 'reproduces a very vivid note, quite in conformity with the purpose of pursuing the Pharisaic spirit everywhere'. In fact, it is only when we read the text, not of Matthew but of Mark, that the suggestion of composition of various fragments arises forcibly, and this is mainly due to Mark's alterations of Matthew. Note that Matt. *v.* 11 states the aphorism in a much more pointed and 'enigmatic' way than Mark *v.* 15, and that Matthew has been able to retain the reference to 'mouth' in the explanation. Note also the effect of *inclusio* given by Matt. *vv.* 6*b* (cf. *v.* 3) and 20*b* (cf. *v.* 2*b*). On the mention of 'Peter' at Matt. *v.* 15, Lagrange comments: 'His intervention is not an invention of St Matthew, who shows little interest in concrete details. Mark's silence is explained as in the other cases; in his oral teaching Peter did not put himself forward.' Finally, if either of the evangelists has given a more radical statement of the principles held to justify the early Church's attitude to the Law, it is not St Matthew but St Mark, and the law of historical entropy will therefore, to that extent, pronounce in favour of Matthew's greater originality.

(6) Matt. xv. 21–8 (cf. Mark vii. 24–30), the Gentile mother of a demoniac. An instance which cannot be reconciled with the theory of Mark's priority. The opening scene of Matthew's version is entirely absent from Mark's. The woman is described as a Chananaean, in terms of the Old Testament opposition between Israel and Chanaan, whereas Mark reflects the 'political divisions of the territory' (Lagrange). The derivation of Mark's version from Matthew, with the help of the recollections of an eyewitness, is simple. No one, addressing himself to a Gentile Christian Church after about A.D. 50, could fail to feel the difficulties suggested by Matthew's version. In Matt. *v.* 23 our Lord, so far from showing mercy, does not even reply to the poor woman's request. The disciples seem more charitable than their Master, and even when they ask him to deal with the case, he replies that he has no mission to Gentiles. In *v.* 26 he seems to tell the woman herself that what she asks for is not permissible, and the description of the Gentiles as κυνάρια is at first sight rather shocking. What is St Mark, or the oral reproducer of Matthew to whom he is indebted for additional details, to do?

He omits the whole of the first scene. He changes 'it is not per-missible' to 'it is not good (or seemly)', and he inserts the clause which changes the whole feeling of the passage: 'Let the children *first* be fed.' To argue, on the other hand, that St Matthew, writing, as the Marcan priorists commonly suppose, about A.D. 70 or later, St Matthew, with his clear understanding of the universal mission of the Christian Church (cf. xxiv. 14, xxviii. 19), has substituted his own version in preference to Mark's, is not only to disregard the law of historical entropy: it is critically quite inadmissible.

(7) Matt. xvi. 1–4 (cf. Mark viii. 11–13), Request for a Sign from Heaven. The question of dependence is here linked up with a question of the right reading in Matthew. This important case is reserved for treatment in the chapter on Matthaean Doublets.

(8) Matt. xvi. 13–23 (cf. Mark viii. 27–33), Thou art the Christ: thou art Peter. The two accounts are closely parallel up to and including St Peter's confession of faith, though Matthew has 'son of man' for 'me' (Mark *v.* 27) and gives Jeremias (om. Mark) as one of the Old Testament figures with which popular opinion identified our Lord—neither of them very natural 'additions' for a Greek editor to make, whereas Mark's omission of them is natural if he is copying Matthew. It is often thought that Matthew's addition of 'the Son of the living God', in St Peter's confession, shows Mark's greater originality; but St Mark was aware (i. 1) that our Lord was the Son of God, and that He claimed to be such (xiii. 32), and in view of the various passages where his presentation is influenced by post-Resurrection developments it is doubtful whether he would have been sensitive to the notion that Messiahship did not at first connote Sonship to the disciples. The omission is just as likely to have been casual, especially as Mark lacks the next three verses of Matthew. Both accounts are also closely parallel for the end of the story (Matt. *vv.* 20–3, Mark *vv.* 30–3), though Mark has 'and He spake the word openly' (om. Matthew), while Matthew has, beyond Mark, 'God be kind to thee, sir; this shall not happen to thee' and 'thou art a scandal to me'.

But between *vv.* 16 and 20 Matthew has the famous 'Thou art Peter' passage (om. Mark). Is this an insertion into a paragraph borrowed almost verbatim from Mark, or did its context belong to it from the first, so that Mark's paragraph must be borrowed from

Matthew with omission of the central section? The dogma of Marcan priority has, it seems to me, blinded the eyes of the critics to certain vital facts here. Attention is drawn to the following list of balancing or contrasted items in Matthew's paragraph; those which are found also in Mark are underlined twice, that not in Mark but occurring in the parts of Matthew's paragraph which, as a whole, are paralleled in Mark is underlined once:

15. ὑμεῖς δὲ τίνα με λέγετε εἶναι;	Cf. 18. κἀγὼ δέ σοι λέγω ὅτι σὺ εἶ....
16. ἀποκριθεὶς δὲ Σίμων Πέτρος εἶπεν	Cf. 17. ἀποκριθεὶς δὲ ὁ Ἰησοῦς εἶπεν αὐτῷ.
σὺ εἶ ὁ Χριστός....	Cf. 18. σὺ εἶ Πέτρος.
17. ὅτι σάρξ καὶ αἷμα οὐκ ἀπεκάλυψέν σοι ἀλλ᾽ ὁ πατήρ μου ὁ ἐν τοῖς οὐρανοῖς.	Cf. 23. ὅτι οὐ φρονεῖς τὰ τοῦ θεοῦ ἀλλὰ τὰ τῶν ἀνθρώπων.
18. ἐπὶ ταύτῃ τῇ πέτρᾳ οἰκοδομήσω μου τὴν ἐκκλησίαν.	Cf. 22. σκάνδαλον εἶ ἐμοῦ.
17. μακάριος εἶ.	Cf. 22. ὕπαγε, ὀπίσω μου, σατανᾶ.

Two facts emerge from a consideration of these parallelisms or contrasts. (a) Matt. xvi. 15–23 appears to be a highly elaborated aesthetic structure with a series of careful and deliberate interior balances; (b) in each case, except one, Mark has one of the contrasted items, but *in no case has he more than one.* Sometimes the item which is present in Mark precedes, in Matthew, the balancing item that is lacking in Mark; sometimes the item lacking in Mark precedes, in Matthew, the item paralleled in Mark.

Can anyone believe that St Matthew found the passage as it stands in Mark, with no hint of this elaborate pattern in it, saw nevertheless that it was patient of such a pattern, and in fact produced this pattern by inserting (a) 'thou art a stumbling-stone to me' at Matt. xvi. 23; (b) Matt. *vv.* 17–19—a passage so profoundly Semitic in content and rhythm as to suggest strongly that it was translated directly from the Aramaic?[1] The more one contemplates this solution the more incredible, I venture to suggest, it must appear; you cannot transform one jigsaw puzzle into another by

[1] Cf. Bultmann, *Geschichte der synoptischen Tradition* (1931), pp. 147 ff. Burney (*op. cit.* p. 117) translates the passage (including 'And I say unto thee') into Aramaic, in three tristichs of four-beat rhythm.

the addition of a few pieces in the middle—unless indeed the original puzzle was made intentionally for such treatment. Observe the supreme audacity of inserting the 'Thou art Peter' section just before St Peter receives a stinging rebuke for his 'too human' thoughts.

There is only one alternative. If the above solution is incredible, it remains that St Mark has copied the passage from Matthew, omitting from it the promise of a tremendous privilege to St Peter. For a possible explanation of this omission, the reader is referred to chapter XI *infra*.

(9) Matt. xix. 16–30 (cf. Mark x. 17–31), Riches and Eternal Life. The incident with which this section opens is usually regarded as a strong indication of Mark's priority, the view being held that Matthew has changed the initial question and answer of Mark, because they might give scandal. There is some uncertainty about the original text of Matthew, and it is also questionable whether the early Christian writers found anything shocking in the Marcan text (see Lagrange *ad loc.*). If Matthew had wanted to change the Marcan version, he could have found an easier way of doing so (by simple omission of our Lord's comment on the man's mode of speech), and there is thus some difficulty in deriving either version of the question and answer from the other. If it were not for the complication introduced into the general problem of Matthew's relations with Mark, one would in this case be tempted to suppose that one or other had misunderstood an Aramaic record of the words exchanged on the occasion in question.

It is interesting to note that Matthew, with 'What do I still lack?'... If thou dost wish to be *perfect*', etc., has the real gradation which the story seems to demand (for it is indeed a hard doctrine that a man cannot enter into 'life' by 'keeping the commandments'). Moreover, Matthew's 'Keep the commandments'. 'Which?', says he. 'And Jesus said', etc., is a wonderfully clever improvement of style, if Mark is the source. On the other hand, Mark's 'None is good save one, God' looks suspiciously like an explanation of the enigmatic remark in Matthew 'One is good' (om. God, if the reading is right).

We have pointed out above (p. 108) that Bishop Rawlinson thinks that Matt. xix. 28 (om. Mark) is probably in correct Q context;

that is, is original here. Note the emphasis on 'We have left all things.... You who have followed me'—this comes out more clearly in the Greek, where the pronouns are not needed except for emphasis. Then the generalization 'And everyone who', etc., has its full meaning.

(10) Matt. xix. 30 πολλοὶ δὲ ἔσονται πρῶτοι ἔσχατοι καὶ ἔσχατοι πρῶτοι should begin the following section, with the parable of the Labourers in the Vineyard, as is shown by the Semitic *inclusio* produced by Matt. xx. 16 (at the end of the parable): οὕτως ἔσονται οἱ ἔσχατοι πρῶτοι καὶ οἱ πρῶτοι ἔσχατοι. Mark (x. 31) betrays his secondariness by copying Matt. xix. 30 but omitting the parable and the repetition of the saying.

(11) Matt. xx. 20–8 (cf. Mark x. 35–45), the (mother of) the sons of Zebedee. It is usually assumed, by Marcan priorists, that Matthew has attributed the request to the mother in order to spare the reputation of the sons; a falsification that we may hope the evangelist would have eschewed. If St Mark copies Matthew he has given the substantial truth, as Matthew, by stating that the Ten were angry not with the mother but with the sons, enables us to infer that the mother was their spokeswoman. Bishop Rawlinson refers to B. W. Bacon's opinion that the reference to 'baptism' (Mark *vv.* 38f., om. Matthew) is an editorial addition in Mark.

(12) Mark xi. 25, after the teaching on faith consequent upon the withering of the fig-tree; without parallel in this context in Matthew,

Matt. vi. 14	Mark xi. 25	Matthew
ἐὰν γὰρ ἀφῆτε τοῖς ἀνθρώποις τὰ παραπτώματα αὐτῶν, ἀφήσει καὶ ὑμῖν ὁ πατὴρ ὑμῶν ὁ οὐράνιος.	καὶ ὅταν στήκετε προσευχόμενοι, ἀφίετε εἴ τι ἔχετε κατά τινος, ἵνα καὶ ὁ πατὴρ ὑμῶν ὁ ἐν τοῖς οὐρανοῖς ἀφῇ ὑμῖν τὰ παραπτώματα ὑμῶν.	vi. 9. πάτερ ἡμῶν ὁ ἐν τοῖς οὐρανοῖς. vi. 5. καὶ ὅταν προσεύχησθε, οὐκ ἔσεσθε ὡς οἱ ὑποκριταί· ὅτι φιλοῦσιν ἐν ταῖς συναγωγαῖς καὶ ἐν ταῖς γωνίαις τῶν πλατειῶν ἑστῶτες προσεύχεσθαι. v. 23. ἐὰν οὖν προσφέρῃς τὸ δῶρόν σου ἐπὶ τὸ θυσιαστήριον κἀκεῖ μνησθῇς ὅτι ὁ ἀδελφός σου ἔχει τι κατὰ σοῦ, 24. ἄφες ἐκεῖ τὸ δῶρόν σου ἔμπροσθεν τοῦ θυσιαστηρίου, καὶ ὕπαγε πρῶτον διαλλάγηθι τῷ ἀδελφῷ σου, κτλ.

but a parallel occurs at Matt. vi. 14. With a view to studying the problem of this verse of Mark, it will be convenient to have before our eyes both Matt. vi. 14 and also certain other extracts from the Sermon on the Mount.

Mark xi. 20–4 runs closely parallel to Matt. xxi. 20–2. In Matthew the disciples 'marvelled' at the sudden withering of the fig-tree; in Mark St Peter draws attention to the fact that it is withered. In both, our Lord draws from the occurrence a lesson on faith and believing prayer, and on their efficacy. Matthew's version of the discourse ends here, but Mark adds the verse now under consideration, and so provides a powerful argument in favour of his own dependence on Matthew.

(a) The connexion of this verse with Matt. vi. 14 can hardly be doubted. This is the only occasion in Mark on which God is described as Father in Heaven (it will be remembered that the title 'heavenly Father' is peculiar among the evangelists to Matthew; so is 'Father in heaven' except for this Marcan passage. Luke has 'Father from heaven' once). Bishop Rawlinson therefore suggests that the verse is connected with the 'Our Father' as known in Rome, though we have no other evidence that the prayer was known in Rome so early, or at any time except through knowledge of Matthew or Luke. But this suggestion fails to take account of the fact that the verse is connected with the 'Our Father' *and with the context of that prayer in Matthew*. For Matt. vi. 14 is the immediate sequel of the 'Our Father'. And Mark has paraphrased Matt. vi. 14, *keeping the tell-tale* ἀφιέναι ὑμῖν τὰ παραπτώματα *and the intensifying* καί, but *substituting* 'Your Father in heaven' (cf. 'Our Father in heaven', the opening words of the prayer itself in Matt. vi. 9) *for* '*your heavenly Father*'. Even if it were considered likely that the 'Our Father' itself had found its way to Rome apart from Matthew, there is no probability that it travelled about with its corollary, unless Bishop Rawlinson is prepared to appeal to Q^R as the source of the 'Our Father' and to argue that the corollary was attached to it in that alleged source. But then, as usual, Q^R has nothing to distinguish it from Matthew.

(b) It is unnatural that the injunction to forgive should be applied to the time 'when you stand praying'. We should expect to be taught to forgive at all times, not only when we pray formally.

Mark is no doubt under the influence of Matt. vi. 5, only a few verses before vi. 9 and 14: '*When* you pray...they love to pray standing....'

(*c*) He further remembers Matt. v. 23, where the situation is envisaged of a man in act to offer sacrifice, who then (when he is actually standing at the altar) remembers that 'a brother *has something against him*'—Matthew's verse is made entirely reasonable (as Mark's is not) by the words 'and there *remember*'; we have to imagine a man who has forgotten the quarrel until that moment, but Mark does not suggest this special circumstance. That Mark has Matthew's passage in mind is made certain by his use of the phrase 'if *you have anything against* anyone'. For the phrase ἔχειν τι κατά *c.gen. occurs nowhere in the New Testament* except in this verse of Mark and Matt. v. 23. Ἔχειν τι is in fact an Aramaism (Lagrange on Matt. v. 23). It should further be noted that Mark's plural is due to the context in which he has placed this piece of teaching, but is not really suitable to the clause 'when you stand praying' and to 'if you have anything against anyone' (singular).

Wellhausen had rightly suspected a connexion between Matt. v. 23 and Mark xi. 25, but, hypnotized by the dogma of Marcan priority, had supposed, absurdly enough, that St Matthew derived his verse from Mark's. The links connecting Mark's verse also with Matt. vi. 5, 9, 14 make it obvious that the connexion is in the inverse direction.

(*d*) Mark's verse has no internal connexion of meaning with the discourse to which it is appended; the discourse would be complete without it, and it is in this pure form that we find it in Matthew. It is clear that St Mark, influenced by the word 'pray' (Mark xi. 24) and the idea of a prayer qualified by faith, was moved to add the associated, but not logically implied, idea of a prayer qualified by a state of charity towards one's neighbour; an associated idea, but not relevant to the context.

The case for Mark's priority could hardly be more gravely damaged by a single verse than it is by this one. Although St Mark did not reproduce the whole, or any considerable portion, of the Sermon on the Mount, he here clearly shows his knowledge of it, a knowledge which seems to extend at least from Matt. v. 23 to vi. 14.

(13) Matt. xxii. 34–40 (cf. Mark xii. 28–34), the Precept of Charity. The greater originality of Matthew, so far as the accounts

run parallel, can hardly be disputed. ⌈Note the Semitic use of the positive ('great') for the superlative in Matthew's version of the lawyer's question.⌉And note that Matthew, with the words ʻin the Law' (*v.* 36), locates the question firmly in the atmosphere of Judaism. Mark's text of the quotation from Deut. vi. 5 looks like a conflation of Matthew's rendering of the Hebrew (ἐν and three members) with that of the LXX (ἐξ and three members). ⌈Again, Matthew's 'the second is like unto it' is not easily derivable from Mark's 'the second is this'. And Matt. *v.* 40 is plainly Semitic and original. ⌋

Rawlinson has two interesting comments. He says that the words 'and no man durst after that ask him any question' (Mark *v.* 34*b*) might at first sight appear to be more in place after the last controversy between our Lord and His opponents, and Mark has represented the conversation in this paragraph as non-controversial; 'it is likely enough that, here as elsewhere, the arrangement of Mark's materials is due to the Evangelist'—it will be noted that the words in question do not occur at this point in Matthew, but after the following question about 'David's Son', after which our Lord proceeds not to discuss but to denounce.⌉ Rawlinson also points out that Mark alone gives the opening affirmation of monotheism (from Deut. vi. 4), 'a doctrine which the Church in a Gentile atmosphere could by no means afford to take for granted'; this then will be a Marcan editorial addition to the more primitive, because more Judaic, Matthaean record. ⌋

The passages considered in this chapter are found in eight of the first twelve chapters of Mark. Added to the passages mentioned or discussed in our two previous chapters, they constitute a list of secondary features in Mark which omits none of Mark's first thirteen chapters, and it thus appears more and more clearly that we cannot satisfy the evidence by the hypothesis that Mark was dependent on a Q^R or other traditional source which Matthew, copying Mark, had at hand and used to improve what he found in Mark. In the next chapter we shall examine a characteristic of Matthew's own composition which, if our explanation of it is correct, makes Mark's dependence on Matthew certain.

CHAPTER IX

DOUBLETS IN MATTHEW

Hawkins writes (*Horae Synopticae*, 1st ed., p. 64): 'The "doublets", or repetitions of the same or closely similar sentences in the same Gospel, are of great value in supplying hints as to the sources and composition of the Gospels.' And it is indeed obvious that a saying of our Lord might be preserved independently in two documents, perhaps in diverse contexts, and that the author of a third document, using these two documents as his sources, might copy it from each, thus producing a 'doublet'. Doublets may therefore be due to compilation from different sources, but students of Homer will agree that this is not necessarily their explanation. Matthew's doublets do not prove his dependence on Mark. It will be argued below that the correct explanation of a large proportion of them provides a peremptory argument for Mark's dependence on Matthew. [Hawkins collected ten pairs of doublets in Luke; he collected twenty-two from Matthew, and this difference may suggest that in Matthew a different cause has been in operation to produce them.] The following examination makes it probable that they are in some cases due to St Matthew's habit of repeating himself; that he is, in fact, employing, in some of them, a device for cross-reference, the custom of using footnotes not being found in antiquity. We may follow Hawkins's list:

(1) Matt. v. 29f. and xviii. 8f. We had occasion to discuss this doublet in chapter VI (p. 99 *supra*). It was there pointed out that its first member is in perfect context, while the second is not. The second member can be removed without injury to the context, with which it is indeed verbally linked, since both relate to scandal; but whereas the context refers to scandalizing others, the doublet-member refers to scandal given to oneself. The wording of the two members of the doublet is too closely similar to give grounds for thinking that they are from different sources. [The alternative explanation, that St Matthew is repeating himself, seems more probable, and would no doubt have been suggested and accepted long ago but

DOUBLETS IN MATTHEW

for the supposition that the second member is from Mark. If the
hypothesis of self-repetition is correct, v. 29f. is the original, and
xviii. 8f. is the cross-reference.

(2) Matt. v. 32

ἐγὼ δὲ λέγω ὑμῖν ὅτι πᾶς ὁ ἀπολύων
τὴν γυναῖκα αὐτοῦ παρεκτὸς λόγου
πορνείας ποιεῖ αὐτὴν μοιχευθῆναι, καὶ
ὃς ἐὰν ἀπολελυμένην γαμήσῃ, μοιχᾶται.

Matt. xix. 9

λέγω δὲ ὑμῖν ὅτι ὃς ἂν ἀπολύσῃ
τὴν γυναῖκα αὐτοῦ μὴ ἐπὶ πορνείᾳ καὶ
γαμήσῃ ἄλλην μοιχᾶται [καὶ ὁ ἀπολελυμένην γαμήσας μοιχᾶται].

The similarities between the two passages are obvious. The most
striking difference (assuming that the omission of the last clause of
xix. 9 in an important number of manuscripts is due to homoeote-
leuton) is that v. 32 deals exclusively with the consequences of
divorce as regards the woman, while xix. 9 adds the point that the
divorced man is not free to remarry. v. 32 is required by its context.
xix. 9 is not necessary to its context; indeed it is added after the
paragraph has been rounded off, with Semitic *inclusio*, by the words
'but from the beginning it was not so'(cf. v. 4, 'He who made them
from the beginning made them male and female'). It would therefore
seem that v. 32 is original, and that xix. 9 is secondary and a cross-
reference. Note that λέγω δὲ ὑμῖν (xix. 9) is an echo of ἐγὼ δὲ
λέγω ὑμῖν (v. 32), which is the regular formula of reply to ἐρρέθη δέ
(v. 31).

(3) Matt. vii. 16–20

ἀπὸ τῶν καρπῶν αὐτῶν ἐπιγνώσεσθε
αὐτούς· μήτι συλλέγουσιν ἀπὸ ἀκαν-
θῶν σταφυλὰς ἢ ἀπὸ τριβόλων σῦκα;
17. οὕτω πᾶν δένδρον ἀγαθὸν καρποὺς
καλοὺς ποιεῖ, τὸ δὲ σαπρὸν δένδρον
καρποὺς πονηροὺς ποιεῖ. 18. οὐ δύναται
δένδρον ἀγαθὸν καρποὺς πονηροὺς
ἐνεγκεῖν, οὐδὲ δένδρον σαπρὸν καρποὺς
καλοὺς ποιεῖν. 19. πᾶν δένδρον μὴ
ποιοῦν καρπὸν καλὸν ἐκκόπτεται καὶ
εἰς πῦρ βάλλεται. 20. ἄραγε ἀπὸ τῶν
καρπῶν αὐτῶν ἐπιγνώσεσθε αὐτούς.

Matt. xii. 33

ἢ ποιήσατε τὸ δένδρον καλὸν καὶ τὸν
καρπὸν αὐτοῦ καλόν, ἢ ποιήσατε τὸ
δένδρον σαπρὸν καὶ τὸν καρπὸν αὐτοῦ
σαπρόν· ἐκ γὰρ τοῦ καρποῦ τὸ δένδρον
γινώσκεται.

Matt. vii. 16–20 is required by its context, since it gives the means to
detect false prophets (v. 15) and mediates to the next paragraph on
effective discipleship. xii. 33, on the other hand, is superfluous to
its context. And whereas the former passage is complete with its

139

comparisons with briars and thistles, and is rounded off by Semitic *inclusio*, xii. 33 reads like a brief abstract. Hawkins suggests that St Matthew has adapted both passages from a single passage of Q; as we reject the Q hypothesis we shall naturally say rather that xii. 33 is an adaptation of vii. 16–20.

(4)   Matt. x. 15

ἀμὴν λέγω ὑμῖν, ἀνεκτότερον ἔσται γῇ Σοδόμων καὶ Γομόρρων ἐν ἡμέρᾳ κρίσεως ἢ τῇ πόλει ἐκείνῃ.

Matt. xi. 24

πλὴν λέγω ὑμῖν ὅτι γῇ Σοδόμων ἀνεκτότερον ἔσται ἐν ἡμέρᾳ κρίσεως ἢ σοί.

xi. 24 is integral to its context, echoing as it does *v.* 22. x. 15 is well placed but could be removed without serious loss. It is perhaps worth noticing that Burney (*op. cit.* p. 122), in giving the section Mark vi. 8–11 (cf. Matt. x. 8–16) as an example of four-beat rhythm, leaves out Matt. x. 15 but not the succeeding verse. We may therefore be justified in concluding that x. 15 is a cross-reference to xi. 24, or rather an editorial adaptation of that verse. Plurality of sources is not a probable explanation of the doublet.

(5) and (6) Matt. x. 22; cf. xxiv. 9*b*, 13. We have dealt with the contexts of these passages above (pp. 79 ff.), and have pointed out that the simple theory of Marcan priority breaks down badly in its attempt to deal with them and their relation to Mark xiii. 9–13. Mark is here dependent on Matt. x. 17–22 (or on Matthew's source for that passage, as Burney would say). Unless our Lord is Himself responsible for the Matthaean doublet, it is natural to suppose that in ch. xxiv St Matthew has abridged and adapted the passage given in ch. x.

(7) and (8)   Matt. x. 38f.

καὶ ὃς οὐ λαμβάνει τὸν σταυρὸν αὐτοῦ καὶ ἀκολουθεῖ ὀπίσω μου, οὐκ ἔστιν μου ἄξιος. 39. ὁ εὑρὼν τὴν ψυχὴν αὐτοῦ ἀπολέσει αὐτήν, καὶ ὁ ἀπολέσας τὴν ψυχὴν αὐτοῦ ἕνεκεν ἐμοῦ εὑρήσει αὐτήν.

Matt. xvi. 24f.

εἴ τις θέλει ὀπίσω μου ἐλθεῖν, ἀπαρνησάσθω ἑαυτὸν καὶ ἀράτω τὸν σταυρὸν αὐτοῦ καὶ ἀκολουθείτω μοι. 25. ὃς γὰρ ἐὰν θέλῃ τὴν ψυχὴν αὐτοῦ σῶσαι, ἀπολέσει αὐτήν· ὃς δ' ἂν ἀπολέσῃ τὴν ψυχὴν αὐτοῦ ἕνεκεν ἐμοῦ, εὑρήσει αὐτήν.

Each of these passages seems to belong integrally to its context, so that derivation from different sources does not explain the doublet, which may well have its origin in our Lord's own repetition of a fundamental yet very difficult Christian principle. The close similarity of language is perhaps a further argument against diversity of sources. (The absence of exact parallelism in xvi. 25 might suggest that this verse at least is an editorial repetition of x. 39; but its genuineness in the present context is probably guaranteed by ν. 26.)

(9) and (18) Matt. xii. 38 f.

τότε ἀπεκρίθησαν αὐτῷ τινες τῶν γραμματέων καὶ Φαρισαίων λέγοντες· διδάσκαλε, θέλομεν ἀπὸ σοῦ σημεῖον ἰδεῖν. 39. ὁ δὲ ἀποκριθεὶς εἶπεν αὐτοῖς·

γενεὰ πονηρὰ καὶ μοιχαλὶς σημεῖον ἐπιζητεῖ, καὶ σημεῖον οὐ δοθήσεται αὐτῇ εἰ μὴ τὸ σημεῖον ᾿Ιωνᾶ τοῦ προφήτου, κτλ.

Matt. xvi. 1–4

καὶ προσελθόντες οἱ Φαρισαῖοι καὶ Σαδδουκαῖοι πειράζοντες ἐπηρώτων αὐτὸν σημεῖον ἐκ τοῦ οὐρανοῦ ἐπιδεῖξαι αὐτοῖς. 2. ὁ δὲ ἀποκριθεὶς εἶπεν αὐτοῖς· [ὀψίας γενομένης λέγετε· εὐδία, πυρράζει γὰρ ὁ οὐρανός· 3. καὶ πρωΐ· σήμερον χειμών, πυρράζει γὰρ στυγνάζων ὁ οὐρανός. τὸ μὲν πρόσωπον τοῦ οὐρανοῦ γινώσκετε διακρίνειν, τὰ δὲ σημεῖα τῶν καιρῶν οὐ δύνασθε;] 4. γενεὰ πονηρὰ καὶ μοιχαλὶς σημεῖον ἐπιζητεῖ, καὶ σημεῖον οὐ δοθήσεται αὐτῇ εἰ μὴ τὸ σημεῖον ᾿Ιωνᾶ. καὶ καταλιπὼν αὐτοὺς ἀπῆλθεν.

The study of this doublet is complicated by a problem of textual criticism. Matt. xvi. 2*b*, 3 are omitted in B (Neutral), 13, 124 (fam. 13), 157, Sy^sc, Arm, Sa, Bo (some MSS.), etc., and Origen shows no sign of knowing them. The passage is in consequence regarded as an interpolation, or as only doubtfully authentic, by, for example, Hort, Tischendorf, von Soden, Huck.

But it is in all probability authentic. (*a*) Its origin, if interpolated, is inexplicable. Nothing, says Lagrange, could explain the addition by a copyist of this penetrating and delicately ironical observation. The *same sign* (redness in the sky) foretells at one time fine weather, and at another time rain. The Pharisees and Sadducees have the perspicacity to interpret it correctly at these different times—yet they cannot interpret 'the signs of the times'! (*b*) It is probably the source of Luke xii. 54 f. (*c*) It links up with ν. 1, 'a sign *from heaven*' —the request in Matt. xii. 38 is merely for 'a sign'. (*d*) ὀψίας γενομένης is characteristically Matthaean; there are six other occurrences of the phrase in Matthew; five in Mark, all probably borrowed from Matthew (at Mark iv. 35 the phrase probably comes from Matt. viii. 16); no other example in the New Testament (Luke xii. 54 has ἐπὶ δυσμῶν). (*e*) οἱ καιροί (plural, with definite article) occurs once elsewhere in Matthew, twice in St Paul, not elsewhere in the New Testament. (*f*) The passage would seem to have been omitted in the Neutral text because (Lagrange suggests) its meteorology does not correspond with Egyptian climatic conditions. (*g*) If it is omitted as unauthentic we are left with a Matthaean paragraph which is a sheer and otiose 'repeat' of xii. 38f. If, however, the passage is authentic, then Matt. xvi. 4 is a cross-reference to Matt. xii. 39, where the mention of Jonah is explained by the following verses (Jonah is omitted from Mark viii. 12, parallel to Matt. xvi. 4), and the doublet comes into line with others in Matthew—an editorial device, not an indication of diversity of sources. It will be noticed that Matt. xii. 39 and xvi. 4 are absolutely identical, except for the addition of 'the prophet' in the former verse—a strong argument against diversity of sources.

(10) Matt. xiii. 12

ὅστις γὰρ ἔχει δοθήσεται αὐτῷ καὶ περισσευθήσεται. ὅστις δὲ οὐκ ἔχει, καὶ ὃ ἔχει ἀρθήσεται ἀπ' αὐτοῦ.

Matt. xxv. 29

τῷ γὰρ ἔχοντι παντὶ δοθήσεται καὶ περισσευθήσεται. τοῦ δὲ μὴ ἔχοντος καὶ ὃ ἔχει ἀρθήσεται ἀπ' αὐτοῦ.

The first member of this doublet is in irreproachable context. Having taught in plain language, and having produced an effect on the disciples but not on the crowds, our Lord has now begun to speak in parables, because the crowds have not, like the disciples, had the grace to understand his previous plain teaching. The disciples 'have' a certain comprehension already, and they will receive more; but the crowds lack that comprehension, and will therefore be deprived of the plain teaching which they had been receiving outwardly but not inwardly. Matt. xxv. 29 is unnecessary to its context; and it would be hard to say (if its originality were admitted) whether it is a comment by our Lord or part of the speech of the 'lord' in the parable. Obviously it is a cross-reference to xiii. 12. Derivation from different sources is made improbable by the close similarity of language.

(11) Matt. xvii. 20

ἀμὴν γὰρ λέγω ὑμῖν, ἐὰν ἔχητε πίστιν ὡς κόκκον σινάπεως, ἐρεῖτε τῷ ὄρει τούτῳ Μετάβα ἔνθεν ἐκεῖ, καὶ μεταβήσεται, καὶ οὐδὲν ἀδυνατήσει ὑμῖν.

Matt. xxi. 21

ἀμὴν λέγω ὑμῖν, ἐὰν ἔχητε πίστιν καὶ μὴ διακριθῆτε, οὐ μόνον τὸ τῆς συκῆς ποιήσετε, ἀλλὰ κἂν τῷ ὄρει τούτῳ εἴπητε Ἄρθητι καὶ βλήθητι εἰς τὴν θάλασσαν, γενήσεται.

Derivation from different sources is again improbable, owing to the close similarity of the two passages. But xxi. 21 can hardly be treated as an editorial addition, for *v.* 22 by itself seems an inadequate climax to the paragraph, and οὐ μόνον τὸ τῆς συκῆς ποιήσετε, ἀλλὰ κἂν τῷ ὄρει τούτῳ, κτλ. explains why the simile of the mountain was used; it is a splendid rhetorical παρὰ προσδοκίαν. It is possible that xvii. 20 is a utilization of xxi. 21, bereft, of course, of the fig-tree, to round off a paragraph. The mustard-seed may be a reminiscence of the parable of the Mustard-seed with its lesson of mighty results from apparently small causes.

(12) Matt. xix. 30 and xx. 16, 'Many that are first will be last', etc. These form a typical Semitic *inclusio* for the parable of the Labourers in the Vineyard, and are not therefore a characteristic doublet. Hawkins's suggestion that one comes from Q, the other (presumably) from Mark is an unfortunate lapse of critical judgement, for which the dogma of Marcan priority must be held responsible.

(13) Matt. xx. 26 f.

οὐχ οὕτως ἔσται ἐν ὑμῖν· ἀλλ' ὃς ἂν θέλῃ ἐν ὑμῖν μέγας γενέσθαι ἔσται ὑμῶν διάκονος, 27. καὶ ὃς ἂν θέλῃ ἐν ὑμῖν εἶναι πρῶτος ἔσται ὑμῶν δοῦλος.

Matt. xxiii. 11

ὁ δὲ μείζων ὑμῶν ἔσται ὑμῶν διάκονος.

The first member of this pair is necessary to its context. The second is not necessary and is probably an editorial cross-reference. Burney (*op. cit.* p. 89) quotes xxiii. 5–10 as an illustration of synthetic parallelism; and the rhythmical passage would be aptly rounded off with *v.* 12 if *v.* 11 were omitted.

(14) Matt. xxiv. 42 and xxv. 13 are possibly an example of Semitic *inclusio*.

(15) Matt. iv. 23 and ix. 35 are summaries of our Lord's Galilaean ministry, almost identical in wording, though ix. 35 omits ἐν τῷ λαῷ, the last words of iv. 23, just as xvi. 4 omits the last words of xii. 39 (τοῦ προφήτου). There are parallels in Mark at i. 39 and vi. 6b, and these are far more probably brief borrowings from Matthew than the germs out of which St Matthew produced his two practically identical long verses:

Matt. iv. 23

καὶ περιῆγεν ἐν ὅλῃ τῇ Γαλιλαίᾳ, διδάσκων ἐν ταῖς συναγωγαῖς αὐτῶν καὶ κηρύσσων τὸ εὐαγγέλιον τῆς βασιλείας καὶ θεραπεύων πᾶσαν νόσον καὶ πᾶσαν μαλακίαν ἐν τῷ λαῷ.

Mark i. 39

καὶ ἦλθεν κηρύσσων εἰς τὰς συναγωγὰς αὐτῶν εἰς ὅλην τὴν Γαλιλαίαν καὶ τὰ δαιμόνια ἐκβάλλων.

Matt. ix. 35

καὶ περιῆγεν ὁ Ἰησοῦς τὰς πόλεις πάσας
καὶ τὰς κώμας, διδάσκων ἐν ταῖς συναγωγαῖς αὐτῶν καὶ κηρύσσων τὸ εὐαγγέλιον τῆς βασιλείας καὶ θεραπεύων
πᾶσαν νόσον καὶ πᾶσαν μαλακίαν.

Mark vi. 6b

καὶ περιῆγεν τὰς κώμας κύκλῳ διδάσκων.

(16) Matt. ix. 27–31 (two blind men healed in the house at Capernaum) and xx. 29–34, the two blind men near Jericho. This is hardly a doublet in the strict sense, but two stories, somewhat similar, in which St Matthew uses similar language for the similar features. There are also great differences between the stories, and the suggestion that St Matthew twice related the same incident (or incidents; since it has also been suggested that he conflates Mark's blind man of Bethseda with Bartimaeus) is not probable. Lagrange, however, thinks that 'Have mercy on us, Son of David' in the account of the former incident is borrowed from the latter.

(17) Matt. ix. 32–4 and xii. 22–4. No comment seems to be called for, except that if there were two incidents, St Matthew has as usual economized by describing similar facts in similar language.

(18) See no. (9) above. Matthaean economy.

(19) Matt. iii. 2 and iv. 17 describe the messages of St John the Baptist and our Lord in identical terms. Diversity of sources would of course be an absurd suggestion. It is another example of Matthaean economy, but useful inasmuch as it emphasized the continuity of the two missions.

(20) Matt. iii. 10 and vii. 19. It is just possible that vii. 19 is a cross-reference to iii. 10, as it is really intrusive in its context. Diversity of sources is excluded. (It is also just possible that iii. 8 has affected the wording of xii. 33, which is itself a cross-reference to vii. 16–18.)

(21) Matt. ix. 13 and xii. 7; our Lord uses the same Old Testament quotation. He probably did use it more than once.

(22) Matt. xvi. 19 and xviii. 18; binding and loosing on earth and in heaven. Both passages are appropriate to their contexts, and no one will suggest diversity of sources.

It will be seen that in no case does the evidence suggest that a Matthaean doublet is due to the use of Mark and another source.

On the contrary, diversity of sources is usually rendered improbable by close similarity or virtual identity of wording in the two members of the doublet, and the cumulative effect is to suggest that the doublets are due to the same editorial characteristics that lead to Matthaean repetition of formulae. In seven cases (nos. (1), (2), (3), (9), (10), (13) and (20)) the evidence suggests, sometimes very forcibly, that the one member of the doublet is an editorial cross-reference to the other; one member in each case being loosely inserted into, or more often appended to, its context, which would usually read as well or better without it. Nos. (4), (5) and (6), (7) and (8), (11), (21), (22) may be instances of our Lord repeating Himself, though in some of these cases we have suggested Matthaean editorial repetition. Nos. (12) and (14) are probably instances of Semitic *inclusio*. Nos. (15)–(19) we have provisionally attributed to St Matthew's economical habit of self-repetition.

We now give a list of the Matthaean doublets of which Mark has at least one member:

(1) Mark has the second member.

(2) Mark has the second member.

(5) and (6) Mark has one member, in position parallel to Matthew's second, but its real parallel, as we have seen, is Matthew's first member.

(7) Mark has the second member.

(8) Mark has the second member.

(9) and (18) Mark has the second member.

(10) Mark has the first member.

(11) Mark has the second member.

(12) Mark has the first member.

(13) Mark has the first member.

(14) Mark has the first member.

(15) Mark has what look like brief reproductions of both members.

(16) Mark has the second member.

(19) Mark has the second member.

It will be observed that in no less than five of these cases (nos. (1), (2), (9), (10), (13)) we have seen reason to believe that Matthew's doublet is due to editorial cross-reference. And in three of these (nos. (1), (2), (9)) Mark has the *second* member, that is, the reference-note, not the original occurrence. If our results are correct, this is of course demonstrative evidence that Mark is secondary and dependent on Matthew. No. (9) is particularly interesting, since St Mark seems there to have taken the reference-note but to have omitted the saying to which it was appended in Matthew.

Turning to the other cases where Mark has one member or both, Mark's parallel in nos. (5) and (6) has been shown to be an insertion into an alien context. Our investigation of doublets has given no guidance, as regards priority, in nos. (7) and (8), (10), (11), (14). The argument seems slightly in favour of Matthew's priority in nos. (12), (15), (18) and (19). On no. (14) see pp. 83 ff. *supra*.

This leaves no. (16). It may be suspected that Mark x. 46–52, which is parallel to Matt. xx. 29–34, has a reminiscence of Matt. ix. 27–31 κατὰ τὴν πίστιν ὑμῶν γενηθήτω ὑμῖν in *v.* 52 ὕπαγε, ἡ πίστις σου σέσωκέν σε (om. Matt. xx. 34). There has been no mention, but only the implication, of faith in the earlier part of the Marcan passage, but in Matthew our Lord's saying echoes the earlier question and answer, 'Do you believe that I can...?' Yes, sir.'

The Matthaean doublets are sometimes supposed to be a strong argument in favour of Mark's priority. The truth is that they provide a very powerful argument for Mark's dependence, and this argument, cogent in any case when taken in combination with the results obtained in earlier chapters of this study, would be decisive even in isolation if the longer reading in Matt. xvi. 1–4 were certain and not only very probable.[1]

Note. In chapter VI we argued that Matt. x. 42 is an editorial adaptation from xxv. 37 ff. We have here something that fails to qualify for admission into a list of doublets, but the editorial process is of the same general type that produced the 'cross-reference doublets'.

---

[1] An interesting examination of Matthew's doublets will be found in G. D. Kilpatrick, *The Origins of the Gospel according to St Matthew* (Clarendon Press, 1946), pp. 84 sqq. The author concludes that 'the documentary hypothesis', that is, derivation of the several members of a doublet from different sources, 'is quite inadequate as an explanation of this feature of the Gospel' (p. 92).

CHAPTER X

INCLUSIO, FORMULAE AND ARAMAISMS

The subject of the Aramaic background of the Greek of the New Testament authors is delicate and highly controversial. Approaching it, as I must, only from the Greek side, I am bound to rely on the experts. In what follows it is not my purpose to prove that Matthew is a translation of an Aramaic original. I limit myself to the attempt to show that the Aramaisms of Matthew are such, and so distributed, as to preclude the hypothesis that this Gospel contains a Greek writer's improvement upon the Greek style of Mark; and that they force us to conclude that Matthew is either a translation of an Aramaic original or an original composition (not a compilation from Greek sources) by one who habitually thought in Aramaic, though he had a good command of Greek.[1] I do not offer an exhaustive study of Matthew's Aramaisms; for such a study, the reader may be referred to Lagrange's introduction to his commentary on Matthew, on which, and on Chapman's *Matthew, Mark and Luke*, I depend throughout this chapter.

I

Matthew, alone of the New Testament writers,[2] uses the phrase βασιλεία τῶν οὐρανῶν. Οὐρανοί is a plural practically unknown to the Greek language except when it refers to a theory of several 'heavens' (very rare). Mark, except for passages paralleled in Matthew, has it only at xii. 25; Luke has it at x. 20 and xii. 33 but never takes it over from Matthew or Mark. Elsewhere in the New Testament it occurs twice in Acts, ten times in Epp. Paul, seven times in Ep. Hebrews, once in I Peter, six times in II Peter, once in Apocalypse. 'Heaven' in Hebrew and Aramaic is always plural. The Matthaean phrase βασιλεία τῶν οὐρανῶν represents the Aramaic מַלְכוּתָא דִשְׁמַיָּא, *reign of the heavens*, a rabbinic circum-

---

[1] Mark has Aramaisms that are not found in Matthew. On these, see the following chapter of this book.

[2] Assuming that the correct reading in John iii. 5 is 'of God'.

locution for *reign of God*, due to a reverential avoidance of the word 'God' itself. Matthew has the expression thirty-two times, and eleven of these occur in passages where Mark runs parallel; in every case Mark either has 'kingdom of God' or lacks the mention of 'kingdom' altogether. St Matthew had no absolute objection to 'kingdom of God'—why should he?—and in fact uses the expression three times himself (xii. 28, xxi. 31, 43) but on no occasion when Mark and Matthew are parallel. It is therefore hardly conceivable that he should have imported βασιλεία τῶν οὐρανῶν so frequently into his reproduction of Mark, but very natural that St Mark, in copying Matthew, should omit or change this quite un-Greek expression which no New Testament writer except St Matthew himself will tolerate. In Matthew the phrase will either (and much more probably) be a literal translation from the Aramaic, or a clear sign that the writer thinks in Aramaic and is not guided by Greek sources.[1]

The plural 'heavens' occurs also in Matthew in the phrase 'Father in (the) heavens', thirteen times. The only other example in the New Testament is Mark xi. 25, and we have given the strongest reasons for supposing that this is due to the influence of the 'Our Father' in Matt. vi. 9ff. Matthew further uses 'heavenly Father' seven times; it occurs nowhere else in the New Testament. Both these phrases are Jewish equivalents for 'God' and doubtless represent our Lord's own usage. But only one of these occurrences is in a passage paralleled in Mark, apart from Mark's use of the 'Our Father' at xi. 25.

II

Ἰδού occurs fifty-eight times in Matthew (apart from quotations), of which twenty-five are in narrative, not discourse. Such and so frequent a use of the word (meaning 'Lo') is certainly, says Lagrange, a sign of Semitism. Specially characteristic is ἰδού after a genitive absolute (eleven times, of which four are in Marcan passages, but Mark eschews the usage). No less than thirty-four of Matthew's instances of ἰδού are in passages which have parallels in Mark, but

---

[1] Norden's judgement, reported by Lagrange, was that Luke's Greek is far more classical than Matthew's. But St Matthew is, nevertheless, quite dexterous, for instance, in the use of μέν...δέ (which St Mark only uses when he can borrow it from Matthew).

Mark retains the word in only six of these cases, and it occurs nowhere else in that Gospel. Mark has ἴδε eight times, three of which are parallel to Matthew's ἰδού, one to ἴδε in Matthew, and the other four without parallel. It is hardly conceivable that St Matthew added ἰδού on all these occasions when engaged in improving Mark's Greek style; but it is entirely natural that St Mark should dislike and eschew the word whenever he meets it in Matthaean narrative, and in all except six occurrences in Matthaean discourse. St Luke is fonder of the word in speeches than is St Matthew, but much less fond of it in narrative; yet he adds it eight times to Matthew's narrative, perhaps because he deliberately imitated the style of the LXX.

III

Matthew's use of τότε is far more significant. The word in Greek means 'then', but with the simultaneous meaning ('at that time') stressed rather than the sequential ('after that'). Τότε would translate 'then' in the sentence, 'He came here last year; but I did not see him then.' But in the sentence, 'He came here yesterday and stayed for half an hour; then he went away again', the word 'then' would normally in Greek be ἔπειτα or εἶτα or μετὰ ταῦτα.

Matthew has τότε eighty-nine or ninety times, and in over fifty of these instances the meaning is definitely 'after this'.

St Luke uses the word only fourteen times, and of these instances six are borrowings from Matthew or Mark. Of the remainder, one has the meaning *eo tempore*, six mean *posthac*, and one is ἀπὸ τότε.

Mark has the word six times in all, of which five instances are also in the corresponding context of Matthew.

These facts practically compel us to conclude that in Matthew the word habitually represents the Aramaic אֱדַיִן or בֵּאדַיִן, for which the LXX has τότε thirty times.

Matthew has τότε in Marcan passages about fifty-one times, elsewhere about thirty-eight times. It is hardly conceivable that a Greek compiler, using Mark as one of his sources, should have added the Aramaic τότε forty-five times to Mark's text. But it is quite natural that St Mark should have ruthlessly rejected the word in copying Matthew, on all occasions of its occurrence except five.

The three probable Aramaisms so far discussed support one another and, together with the further evidence considered below, raise a very serious problem for the Marcan priorist. It is inadequate to reply that Matthew was written to commend Christianity to the Jews. For if, with that end in view, it had been desired to impart a strong Aramaic colouring to an enlarged edition of Mark, the aim could have been achieved by *translation into Aramaic.* If we wished to popularize the French Existentialists in England we should not rewrite their works in Anglicized French; we should translate them into English. The important point is that, if Matthew depends on Mark, we cannot explain these Aramaisms as accidental results of the Aramaic cast of St Matthew's mind; they will be deliberate. So, too, St Luke's Septuagintalisms must, on the whole, represent a deliberate purpose of writing the sacred history in a hieratic or liturgical style, a Greek style already consecrated for religious purposes. What deliberate aim can St Matthew have had for his Aramaisms, if he depends on Mark?

IV

St Matthew is fond of the Semitic stylistic device of *inclusio*, that is, the resumption at the end of a paragraph of a phrase or words which occurred at its beginning. Lagrange (p. lxxxi) has a list of thirteen examples, but two of these (xxii. 45, xxi. 41) are unimpressive; and for another (xix. 9) should be substituted xix. 8 (cf. xix. 4). This leaves eleven instances, of which seven occur in passages that have parallels in Mark. Mark, however, preserves the *inclusio* only once (Mark xi. 33). It is especially striking that at x. 31 Mark has the phrase ('Many shall be first', etc.) with which St Matthew introduces the parable of the Labourers in the Vineyard, to which an echo at the end of the parable affords a good example of *inclusio*. Marcan priorists must say that St Matthew, meeting these words in Mark, realized that the parable would aptly (?) illustrate them, inserted it, and then repeated the phrase at the end of the parable. Such a theory is a *tour de force*. The obvious explanation is that St Mark is copying Matthew, leaves out the parable (as he leaves out such large quantities of discourse), but retains the opening words, though they are poorly led up to by the preceding paragraph and have, of course (in Mark), no sequel.

As regards St Matthew's general use of *inclusio* in 'Marcan' sections, it would show a Semitism of *parti pris* that an editor, writing in Greek, should take Mark and deliberately insert these cases of a deliberate Semitic stylism.

V

Hawkins (*op. cit.* pp. 135–8) gives twenty-five examples of Matthaean 'formulae'—'short sentences, or collocations of two or more words, which recur mainly or exclusively' in Matthew, as compared with Mark and Luke, 'so that they appear to be favourite or habitual expressions' of the writer. Of these no less than seventeen (including καὶ ἐγένετο ὅτε ἐτέλεσεν, κτλ., as having a non-verbal parallel in Luke vii. 1) occur once or twice in Mark or Luke, but are also used elsewhere in Matthew without parallel in either of the other two Synoptic Gospels; twelve occur thus once or twice in Mark, the others in Luke. Hawkins comments: 'A careful examination of such cases certainly leaves the impression that the mind of [St Matthew] was so familiar with these collocations of words that he naturally reproduced them in other parts of his narrative, besides the places in which they occurred in his sources. It is to be observed that these apparent reproductions often occur earlier in the Gospel [that is, in Matthew] than do the apparently original occurrences of the formulae, which seems to argue that [St Matthew] drew them from his memory of the sources and not from documents before him. So far as it goes, then, the drift of this section is in favour of the oral theory.'

It is hardly necessary to point out that this interesting paragraph of Hawkins is pervaded by the presumption that if one of Matthew and Mark is dependent on the other, it must be Matthew who does the copying. Hence the admission that the 'drift of this section is in favour of the oral theory'. If the question is approached without prejudice a quite different inference is suggested. We are faced with two documents A and B, one of which is a source of the other, and we seek to determine which is the dependent document. We note that A is a highly stylized composition, and that it has a fondness for 'formulae', each repeated once or more often in the course of the document. We further observe that B, which does not cover the whole area of A, has one, or sometimes two, examples of several of these formulae (often, however, not that example which comes first in the course of A), but that regularly A has more occurrences of each than B, while some of A's formulae are not represented in B at all. The inference, of course, is that A (Matthew) is the original document and B (Mark) a series of extracts from it.

It might be urged that the force of this argument is somewhat attenuated by the fact that nineteen of the formulae are in discourse, not in narration,[1] and that therefore they show the repetitiveness of our Lord and other speakers, not of St Matthew. But the original speakers must be presumed to have used Aramaic, whereas we are faced with an identity of Greek renderings, so that the argument still has a certain validity.

VI

Some further instances of Matthew's pervasive Aramaic colouring may here be considered, and amongst them one striking piece of evidence that suggests strongly that Matthew is a translation of an Aramaic document, not a compilation of Greek sources.

(a) λέγει (λέγουσιν) used asyndetically to introduce direct speech is—in view of the Aramaic features of Matthew already observed—most probably a Semitism. For it occurs twenty-nine times in Matthew, the normal Greek usage being the verb φάναι inserted after the first word or words of the direct quotation. It occurs once in Mark and twice in Luke. Seventeen of Matthew's instances are in passages where Mark is running parallel, and the Marcan priorist is thus compelled to suppose that St Matthew inserted this Aramaism into his Greek improvement upon Mark.

(b) *Casus pendens* resumed by a pronoun, as in Gen. xxviii. 13 (LXX), is a probable Semitism. It occurs in Matthew three times (xii. 36, xiii. 19, xxv. 29); the second of these is in Marcan context, but Mark's parallel passage lacks the construction.

(c) εἶς (without accompanying genitive) for τις: Matt. ix. 18 (Mark adds a genitive), xxvi. 69 (Mark adds a genitive), xxi. 19 (om. Mark μίαν), xix. 16 (so also Mark), xviii. 24 (not a Marcan passage). An interesting set of data.

(d) ὁρᾶτε = ἰδού: Matt. xxiv. 6 (om. Mark); cf. Gen. xxxi. 50 (LXX), etc.

---

[1] ἤγγικεν ἡ βασιλεία, κτλ. is rather the summary of a message than a reported saying. The only other *narrative* formula of Matthew that appears also in Mark is ἐκτείνας τὴν χεῖρα.

(*e*) οὐκ (οὐδέποτε) ἀνέγνωτε; occurs three times in Mark, and in the parallel passages of Matthew. It also occurs in Matt. xii. 5, xix. 4 (om. Mark), xxi. 16. It seems to reflect the Jewish atmosphere of appeal to Scripture.

(*f*) ἀργύρια = pieces of money, a curiously un-Greek usage. It occurs eight times in Matthew (being parallel in xxvi. 15 to Mark's ἀργύριον) and nowhere else in the New Testament.

(*g*) γενηθήτω = *fiat*. Five times in Matthew (note xv. 28; om. Mark), and nowhere else in the New Testament except in quotations.

(*h*) δῶρον (of religious offerings), eight times in Matthew (note viii. 4; om. Mark), Mark once, Luke twice, nowhere else in the New Testament except Hebrews.

(*i*) λεγόμενος or ὁ λεγόμενος, especially where it introduces a surname or soubriquet (cf. Aramaic אִתְקְרִי):

iv. 18 surname (om. Mark);
ix. 9 Μαθθαῖον λεγόμενον (om. Mark);
x. 2 surname (om. Mark);
xxvi. 14 ὁ λεγόμενος Ἰούδας Ἰσκαριώτης (om. Mark);
xxvi. 36 λεγόμενον Γεθσημανεί (Mark changes);
xxvii. 16 λεγόμενον Βαραββᾶν (also Mark);[1]
xxvii. 17 and 22 surname (om. Mark);
xxvii. 33 καὶ ἐλθόντες εἰς τόπον λεγόμενον Γολγοθᾶ, ὃ ἔστιν κρανίου τόπος λεγόμενος.

This is a passage that deserves a moment's thought. 'That is' is expressed in the New Testament in several ways:

Matt. i. 23   Ἐμμανουὴλ ὃ ἔστιν μεθερμηνευόμενον Μεθ᾽ ἡμῶν ὁ θεός.
'Emmanuel, *which is* (being interpreted) God with us.'

Mark iii. 17   Βοανηργὲς ὃ ἔστιν υἱοὶ βροντῆς.
'Boanerges, *that is* Sons of thunder.'

John i. 38   Ῥαββεὶ ὃ λέγεται μεθερμηνευόμενον Διδάσκαλε.
'Rabbi, *which is expressed, when translated*, as Master.'

---

[1] If Ἰησοῦν Βαραββᾶν is read in Matthew, the absence of Ἰησοῦν in Mark would suggest that Matthew is original.

John i. 43   σὺ κληθήσει Κηφᾶς ὃ ἑρμηνεύεται Πέτρος.
              'Thou shalt be named Cephas, *which is translated
              as Peter.*'
John xx. 16   Ῥαββουνεὶ ὃ λέγεται Διδάσκαλε.
              'Rabboni, *which is expressed* as Master.'

It will be noticed that the neuter singular ὃ has as its antecedent the word or words to be translated,[1] not the meaning of those words. The antecedent can be masculine singular, masculine plural, neuter plural (Mark xii. 42), feminine singular (Mark xv. 16), or not a noun at all (Mark vii. 34). But as ὃ is itself a neuter singular, a participle qualifying it in the relative clause is of course put into the *neuter* singular.

In Matt. xxvii. 33 the participle λεγόμενος in the relative clause is masculine (contrast Matt. i. 23 *supra*). It does not agree with ὃ but with τόπος. And the English of the whole passage (καὶ ἐλθόντες... λεγόμενος) is therefore: 'And coming to a place called Golgotha, which means to say "a place called of a skull".' In other words, St Matthew appears, in the relative clause, to be translating into Greek not Γολγοθᾶ, nor τόπον Γολγοθᾶ, but τόπον λεγόμενον Γολγοθᾶ. But why should he do this? St Mark, in the parallel passage (xv. 22), writes fairly naturally τὸν Γολγοθᾶ τόπον ὃ ἔστιν μεθερμηνευόμενον κρανίου τόπος—'The place of Golgotha, which is, being translated, "place of a skull"'.

The explanation of St Matthew's unique phraseology is surely that he is *translating a non-Greek document* which read, 'And coming to a place called Golgotha'. He realizes that merely to translate this into Greek leaves the meaning of 'Golgotha' obscure; so after translating it he proceeds to explain 'a place called Golgotha' by the fully Greek phrase 'a place called of a skull'. Λεγόμενος here is not equivalent to μεθερμηνευόμενον, but has the same meaning as in the other examples listed above.

Had St Matthew been copying not a non-Greek document but Mark, he would either have kept Mark's turn of phrase in the relative clause (cf. Matt. i. 23 *supra*); or, if he preferred a Johannine usage, he could have written εἰς τόπον λεγόμενον Γολγοθᾶ, ὃ λέγεται κρανίου τόπος; or again he could have used the concise

---
[1] The Greek for 'the word "man"' is τὸ ἄνθρωπος.

form ὅ ἐστιν Κρανίου τόπος. His actual wording, awkward in any view, is quite gratuitously awkward on the theory of Marcan priority.

(I was glad to find that Lagrange (*ad loc.*) agrees with my verdict on the passage. He writes: 'The substance is the same as in Mark and John...but Matthew's rendering, as is not usually the case, is the most clumsy, with a double λεγόμενος, instead of μεθερμηνευό-μενος (Mark).[1] The Aramaic text[2] must, like Syrˢ, have had simply "the place named Golgotha";[3] the rest is revealed by its very awkwardness as the translator's work.' Quite so. But holding this view of the passage Lagrange ought not to have translated it as he does: 'Au lieu nommé Golgotha—c'est le lieu nommé "du Crâne".' An accurate French rendering would be: 'Au lieu nommé Golgotha —ce qui signifie "le lieu nommé *du Crâne*".')

(*j*) πληροῦσθαι, of the fulfilment of prophecy, is a characteristic Matthaean usage (twelve times). It occurs three times in Luke, six times in John. Its only occurrence in Mark is in xiv. 49, parallel to Matt. xxvi. 56.

(*k*) σκανδαλίζεσθαι ἐν. Once in Mark (vi. 3), parallel to Matt. xiii. 57. There are three other instances in Matthew, and of them two are paralleled in Mark by σκανδαλίζεσθαι without the Semitic ἐν.

(*l*) σφόδρα intensifying a *verb*. Not found in Mark, but six times in Matthew, four of which are in Marcan passages.

This chapter has been largely devoted to the compilation of evidence suggesting that Matthew has, in its Marcan passages, Aramaisms not taken over from Mark, in such quantity and of such quality as to make it difficult to suppose that the author was a writer of Greek composing a Gospel by combining the Greek Mark with other sources and materials. The force of the evidence is of course cumulative, and is not greatly weakened if a few of the exmples given are thought to be unconvincing. It is not weakened but

---

[1] Mark actually writes, and so would St Matthew have had to write, μεθερμηνευό-μενον. [B.C.B.]

[2] Lagrange thinks that Matthew was originally written in Aramaic. [B.C.B.]

[3] Syrˢ's translation is an interesting confirmation of the view we have taken of this passage. [B.C.B.]

rather strengthened by any adducible evidence that St Matthew could write good Greek. For a good Greek writer, working on a Greek source, is less likely than a bad one to introduce Aramaisms on a large scale. But working on an Aramaic document—or composing directly without sources in Greek from an Aramaic mental background—he may be expected to reflect in his composition the Aramaic of his sources or his mind.

I would again emphasize the fact that the existence in Mark of Aramaisms which are not found in the parallel passages of Matthew is not denied. The problem they present is examined in the following chapter. But if Matthew depends on Mark, the Aramaisms in Matthew's Marcan passages which are not derived from Mark are so numerous and regular that, *in that case*, they must be deliberate and intended. The question for the Marcan priorist is: Can a reasonable explanation of such a deliberate policy be conceived?

CHAPTER XI

ST MARK'S GOSPEL

In preceding chapters an attempt has been made to show that Mark's discourses depend on a source indistinguishable from Matthew, and that a similar dependence can be discovered in many sections of Mark that are not purely discourse. It has been pointed out that Streeter (in 1911) and Burney, approaching the subject from very different angles, both held that Mark was dependent on Q (a document whose reality we have seen grave reasons to doubt), and that Bishop Rawlinson falls back on the hypothesis that Mark depends on a Roman parallel to Q. Further, a direct examination of Matthew suggests that the true explanation of several of the doublets in that Gospel is incompatible with Marcan independence, while the pervasive Aramaic colour of Matthew's Greek has seemed to make the theory of its author's dependence on Mark peculiarly difficult to maintain. But if such considerations combine to undermine any simple theory of Marcan priority, it may still be asked whether we are compelled to adopt the reverse hypothesis, a simple theory of Mark's dependence on Matthew. And if such a theory would appear to be suggested by the evidence hitherto considered, what are we to make of the arguments (other than the faulty inference exposed in chapter v) that have been the mainstay of the theory of Marcan priority? To these two questions we now address ourselves.

I

Since a large part of the evidence which we have examined in the preceding chapters is taken from the discourses and teaching of our Lord as found in Matthew and Mark, it might be suggested that the discourses now found in Matthew were originally composed separately (in Aramaic?) by St Matthew, and circulated separately in Greek before either Matthew as a whole or Mark was written; that these (Greek) discourses were utilized by St Mark; and that they were also taken up again by St Matthew and by him combined with Mark to produce our present Matthew. It might further be argued that this hypothesis gives a good meaning to the former half of Papias's famous statement: 'Matthew composed the *Logia* in Hebraic speech, and each man interpreted them as he could.'

Such a suggestion has the *a priori* disadvantage that it is more complicated than a simple theory of the originality of Matthew as a whole, and the *onus probandi* would therefore be upon its supporters. We may again appeal to Turner's dictum: 'I have an incurable preference for simple solutions of literary problems.'

It would mean that St Matthew, when he came to write his complete Gospel, had before him his own discourses, previously 'unpublished', and Mark, and began by working through Mark and indicating for omission every discourse and every scrap of teaching that Mark had derived from the Matthaean discourse-document. He would then have had to fit in some of the discourses at the exact spots chosen by St Mark for some of his excerpts, and to invent places for the Sermon on the Mount and the Mission Charge. I think this makes of St Matthew too acute a documentary scholar and at the same time too ingenious a compiler.

But secondly, though the bulk of our evidence against Mark's priority has been drawn from the Marcan version of our Lord's teaching as compared with Matthew's, it would be extremely difficult to concede Mark's dependence on Matthew's discourses and yet to deny its dependence in other respects. We have seen that the Marcan version of the preaching of St John the Baptist and of our Lord's temptation probably depended on Matthew's. We have seen that the concluding comment after the Sermon on the Mount ('they were amazed at His teaching', etc.) appears to have been borrowed by St Mark in i. 22, and that in the same context he seems to have been influenced by Matthew's story of the Gadarene incidents. Sometimes, again, the Matthaean discourse on which Mark depends is part and parcel of a conversation between our Lord and His disciples, or our Lord and opponents or enquirers (Matt. xii. 22–32 and presumably to *v.* 37; xiii. 3–32; xv. 1–20; xvi. 1–4;[1] xvi. 13–23; xviii. 1–10;[1] xix. 3–9; xix. 27–xx. 16; xxii. 34–40). And then there are passages which are even more typically narrative, in which we seem driven to conclude that the dependence is on

[1] Two passages which probably show St Matthew's final editorial work, since they have 'cross-references' causing doublets.

Mark's side rather than on Matthew's: ix. 18–26; xv. 21–8; xxvi. 6–13; xxvii. 3–10, 33. Furthermore, if we were right in regarding ὀψίας γενομένης as a typical Matthaean phrase (see p. 141 *supra*), then we have to explain St Mark's use of this phrase, every time probably in parallel with Matthew;[1] if he owes the phrase to Matthew, then that by itself settles the case.

On the whole, it must be agreed that the suggested hypothesis of a separate edition of the Matthaean discourses, used by St Mark, and then again along with Mark in the compilation of Matthew, is an unworkable compromise.

II

Vosté advocated a different and very interesting solution of the problem. He suggested that Matthew is the translation of an Aramaic original; that this Aramaic original was a source for Mark; and that its translator into Greek subsequently used Mark as a guide in his work. Thus there would be reciprocal dependence of Matthew and Mark:

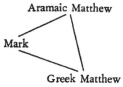

Aramaic Matthew

Mark

Greek Matthew

In discussing this theory, of which the attraction in Vosté's eyes may have been that it preserved the traditional priority of (the Aramaic) Matthew, left room for the traditional Petrine influence on Mark, and went some way to meet the upholders of the priority of Mark *vis-à-vis* the Greek Matthew, we again insist that the *onus probandi* is on the theory that substitutes a complicated for a simple scheme of literary relationships. One argument in its favour is that Mark has Aramaisms which are absent from the parallel passages of Matthew. We admit that this is a point to which justice must be done, and it is discussed in the next section of this chapter. Here it is proposed to put together some considerations which, taken in combination, seem to be decisive against Vosté's hypothesis:

(*a*) It is psychologically most improbable that the translator of Matthew, with a good Aramaic text to work from, and a perfectly

---

[1] For at Mark iv. 35 it is probably derived from Matt. viii. 16.

159

adequate command of Greek, if we may judge from his performance in the non-Marcan sections of the Gospel, should nevertheless deliberately adapt, in his rendering of the Aramaic Matthew, the poor Greek of Mark. Respect for the prestige of Mark, or of St Peter as its oral source, cannot be invoked, for the compliment of imitation would be too subtle and recondite.

(b) Some of the Aramaisms which Matthew has over and above Mark in the Marcan passages are particularly hard to explain on this hypothesis. Why, for instance, while dealing so rigorously with Mark's εὐθύς (Mark 42 times; Matthew once separately, six times with Mark, but never in Mark's otiose usage; Matthew also has εὐθέως seven times parallel to Mark's εὐθύς), should St Matthew have inserted τότε all over the place?[1] Why should he deliberately and frequently substitute βασιλεία τῶν οὐρανῶν for βασιλεία τοῦ θεοῦ, although he will use the latter phrase when Mark does not? Why so faithful to ἰδού when Mark has shown him how to get rid of it? It is worth while to meditate the list of deliberate and repeated Aramaisms in Matthew (cf. the previous chapter) and then ask whether it is probable that a writer would or could follow his Aramaic original as closely as these indicate that this one did, and at the same time follow Mark's Greek as closely as Vosté's hypothesis implies that he did; note especially the facts concerning λέγει (λέγουσιν) introducing direct quotation, ἀργύρια, ὁ λεγόμενος.

(c) It is also particularly difficult to suppose that a competent translator of an Aramaic original would frequently turn to Mark for guidance when the Marcan parallel is not in the context of Mark which at any given moment he was following. This, on Vosté's hypothesis, Matthew would have done at v. 13?; vii. 28f.; ix. 36?; x. 17-22; xi. 10; xiii. 12 (though Mark iv. 25, it is true, is not far from the context); xviii. 3 (?).

(d) Nor is it easy to believe that where Mark has spoilt the Aramaic rhythm of the original sayings of our Lord, St Matthew, while utilizing Mark's Greek, has been able to restore the rhythm, or would have tried to do so.

[1] It may be replied: Why should Mark omit Matthew's ἰδού and sprinkle εὐθύς freely into a text derived from Matthew? But Mark's Greek is immeasurably poorer than Matthew's, and I believe that St Mark's εὐθύς is the mannerism of an oral narrator. See further the next section.

(e) Vosté's hypothesis involves, in several cases, improbable coincidence or most improbable subservience, on Matthew's part, to Mark's Greek: (i) συντέλεια τοῦ αἰῶνος being a favourite expression of St Matthew (συντέλεια occurs elsewhere in the New Testament only in Heb. ix. 26), it is an improbable coincidence that Mark should present him with συντελεῖσθαι (not found elsewhere in Mark) at Mark xiii. 4, as a basis for his use of that phrase in Matt. xxiv. 3.

(ii) Mark iv. 24 is an improbably lucky source for Matt. vi. 33*b*, καὶ προστεθήσεται ὑμῖν.

(iii) Mark xi. 25, as was pointed out p. 136 *supra*, has, in the phrase ἔχειν τι κατά τινος, a usage which is unique in the New Testament except for Matt. v. 23. We have shown that this verse of Mark appears to be borrowed from Matt. vi. 14, with reminiscences of vi. 5 and v. 23. If Mark is based on the Aramaic Matthew, and the Greek Matthew on Mark, the use of the same phrase (ἔχειν τι κατά τινος) in the two Greek Gospels is unexplained, since it would be absurd to suppose that Matthew looked ahead to Mark xi. 25 and borrowed it thence.

(f) It is more probable that St Mark borrowed ὀψίας γενομένης from the Greek Matthew than that St Matthew's use of the phrase (in Marcan and also non-Marcan contexts) developed out of St Mark's.

On the whole it seems true to say that Vosté's theory, though satisfying far more of the evidence than the hypothesis of Marcan priority does, is itself so inherently improbable, and so hard to reconcile with some of the evidence, that it should not be admitted unless the theory of Mark's dependence on the Greek Matthew be found to be at least improbable.

III

Thus we turn to the final question: Can the theory of Mark's dependence on the Greek Matthew overcome the difficulties with which it is faced? For instance: (a) St Mark's version of an incident is often notably fuller and longer than Matthew's, and he often supplies details lacking in the other Gospel. Moreover he frequently conveys the impression of giving the vivid, picturesque account of an actual eyewitness. (b) St Mark, though lacking many of Matthew's Aramaisms, has a number of his own that are not derived from the

Greek Matthew.[1] (c) Matthew's Greek, in grammar and style, is better than Mark's, and, as Streeter says, the difference is not merely that Matthew writes better Greek: ⸢It is the difference which always exists between the spoken and the written language. ⸢Mark reads like a shorthand account of a story by an impromptu speaker—with all the repetitions, redundancies, and digressions which are characteristic of living speech. And it seems to me most probable that his Gospel, like Paul's Epistles, was taken down from rapid dictation by word of mouth.'[2] ⸢(d) In seven instances Mark preserves, though he also translates, the original Aramaic words used by our Lord (om. Matthew). (e) It may appear that Matthew has sometimes introduced changes for reasons of reverence or decorum: our Lord is addressed as κύριε; at Nazareth 'He *did not many* mighty works' (whereas Mark says 'He *could* do there no mighty work, except that He laid His hands on and healed a few sick persons'); for 'Why callest thou Me good?' (Mark x. 18) we read in Matthew 'Why askest thou Me concerning the good?'. (f) Matthew may seem to have heightened the miraculous element, and some of the miracles narrated by him have been thought to be legendary.

Take it for all in all, it is an impressive case. Streeter can only suppose that persons who have worked through the details collected by Hawkins and still think that Mark depends on Matthew 'have eccentric views of what constitutes evidence'.

Our own views on what constitutes evidence in the field of com-

---

[1] As before, in dealing with Aramaisms, I follow Lagrange (*S. Marc*, 1st ed., pp. lxxix–xcvii). I suggest that the following may be regarded as significant: Interrogation at the start of a parable. Pleonastic style. Εἶναι with present participle for finite verb. iv. 21 ἔρχεται ὁ λύχνος (a mistranslation from the Aramaic?). xiv. 45 ἐλθὼν εὐθὺς προσελθών (cf. xvi. 1). vii. 24 and x. 1 ἀναστάς. Ἀποκριθείς (with no previous remark to reply to), several times without Matthew. Verb preceding subject, often where Matthew lacks this phenomenon. i. 7 οὗ...αὐτοῦ (cf. also vii. 25; xiii. 19). vi. 7 δύο δύο (cf. also vi. 39, 40). ix. 8 ἀλλά (Matthew εἰ μή). vi. 2 διὰ τῶν χειρῶν. v. 34 ὕπαγε εἰς εἰρήνην. ii. 6 and 8 διαλογίζεσθαι ἐν καρδίᾳ. εὐθύς (?). vi. 9 ἀλλά (suggesting אֶלָּא, where Matthew's text suggests וְלֹא)? i. 15 πιστεύειν ἐν. i. 23 ἐν πνεύματι ἀκαθάρτῳ. viii. 17 ὅτι=why?. xi. 29 καὶ ἀποκρίθητέ μοι. xii. 28 πρώτη πάντων (bad Greek). xiv. 8 προέλαβεν μυρίσαι. Frequency of καί and rarity of other particles. The list could probably be extended, but it shows the kind of evidence that has to be met. Such evidence cannot be dismissed, but it in no way diminishes the force of the evidence from Matthew's special Aramaisms in Marcan passages.

[2] For reasons that will appear below I welcome this clearly stated judgement.

parative documentary criticism in part coincide with Streeter's and in part diverge. We believe that the most formally relevant evidence is not that which appeals to any *a priori* theory of the evolution of the Christian attitude towards Christ, or of the relatively late intrusion or magnification of the miraculous element in the Christian tradition,[1] but that which consists of the results of a direct comparison of parallel passages in their respective contexts and a determination on the basis of such comparison of the document which shows signs of the displacements, incoherences and so forth that are liable to be caused by the rearrangement and more or less loose reproduction of a written source. This is the kind of criticism exemplified by Streeter's able essay in *Oxford Studies*, 'Mark's knowledge and use of Q'. And we have, in preceding chapters, accumulated a good deal of such evidence to show that the theory of Marcan priority is completely untenable, so far as concerns the relations between Mark and Matthew. But are we bound to leave the two sets of evidence—that indicated by Streeter and that accumulated in these chapters, of which only too much was completely neglected by him—in unreconciled conflict?

To the remainder of this section may be applied some words borrowed from Newman's defence of his theory of the development of doctrine: 'It is undoubtedly an hypothesis to account for a difficulty; but such too are the various explanations given by astronomers from Ptolemy to Newton of the apparent motion of the heavenly bodies, and it is as unphilosophical on that account to object to the one as to object to the other.' I would point out that the hypothesis offered below is on a different footing from the critical studies that have forced the problem upon us. The facts disclosed by those studies do not depend on this hypothesis; the hypothesis depends on them. They cannot be evaded by rejecting the hypothesis. All that would remain would be to supply another more satisfactory hypothesis consistent with those facts.

[1] 'Prétendre que des récits miraculeux ne peuvent émaner des contemporains et des témoins des faits, c'est nier par exemple que le journal *La Croix* ait raconté des miracles comme s'étant passés à Lourdes devant ses correspondants dans la semaine de la publication' (Lagrange, *S. Marc*, p. 1). I received a letter from an English businessman a few years ago, telling me that on a recent visit to Fatima, the place of pilgrimage in Portugal, he had seen the 'miraculous' cure of a sick person by whose side he was when the cure occurred.

And along with the results of the examination conducted in the previous chapters, which may be summarized as the proof that Q did not exist and that Mark is in a relation of dependence on Matthew, we accept also, as data to be met by our hypothesis, the facts listed under headings (a), (b), (c) and (d) at the beginning of this section. As regards (e) we accept the fact of an apparent greater decorum and reverence in Matthew, but we deny Streeter's inference that this shows that that Gospel came into existence later than Mark. And as regards (f) we again admit that Matthew has some alleged wonders that are not in Mark, but we deny that they are legendary accretions of a period subsequent to Mark's composition.

Once it is agreed to suppose, if only for the sake of argument, that Matthew is not dependent either on Mark or on the conjectural document Q, its Aramaisms and Semitic mode of composition can be given their full value, and it immediately becomes a reasonable suggestion that this Gospel is the translation of an Aramaic original. We may in fact say with some confidence that this suggestion would have been accepted long ago, but for the supposed relation of the Gospel to Greek sources. It harmonizes perfectly with the impression created on the mind by the book's contents. We may be permitted to quote from the attractive lectures, *The Synoptic Gospels* by J. H. Ropes,[1] the distinguished American scholar and contributor to F. J. Foakes-Jackson and K. Lake's *Beginnings of Christianity*:

There is abundant reason to believe that the author of our First Gospel was a born Jew. His whole Gospel is pervaded by Jewish color...and he is strongly interested in the relation of Jesus, both positively and negatively, to the Jews and to Jewish ideas. What a gentile author would be likely to do with the Jewish allusions in the narratives and the sayings of Jesus can be seen by observing what Luke has actually done. The author of Matthew has a profound knowledge of Hebrew prophecy applicable to Jesus as Messiah, and perhaps shows an acquaintance with the original Hebrew of some of the prophecies he adduces. Moreover his characteristic use of the term 'Kingdom of Heaven'...is distinctively Jewish, and he uses 'the Son of David' to mean the Messiah with special fondness, as he does 'the heavenly Father', 'the Holy City', meaning Jerusalem, and the expression 'the God of Israel' —all of them characteristic of the Jews. And it is probable that he shows signs of

---

[1] Harvard University Press, 1934. The author believed in the priority of Mark, which he considers the only assured result 'of the vast amount of incessant labor which has been expended on the so-called Synoptic Problem in the whole of the past hundred years and more'. He doubts the Q hypothesis. It is precisely the acceptance of the theory of Mark's priority which has rendered sterile the efforts of criticism in this field.

rabbinical knowledge.... The sayings [in the Sermon on the Mount] are almost everywhere conspicuously related to the conditions of Jesus' life and times in Palestine.... No one can doubt that the roots of the Gospel of Matthew strike deep into the knowledge and tradition and thought of the primitive Jewish believers of the church of Jerusalem (pp. 39–58).

Ropes adds that Matthew, 'as we have it', gives unmistakable indications that it was written at some time after the year A.D. 70. These indications are presumably only obvious to those who accept the priority of Mark. What is really striking about Matthew is that, despite the author's awareness that the Christian message, rejected by the Jews, is to be carried to 'all nations', the Gospel betrays no consciousness of the special problems and needs of the Gentile mission. We have seen, for instance, that St Mark had to make considerable changes in the story of the Chanaanite woman for the sake of the Gentile Christians, and that Matthew does not use 'the Gospel' as a description of Christianity. One receives the impression that the controversy between Gentile and Jew had not yet broken out in the Church when this Gospel was composed.

It will also be apparent that, if Matthew was a source for Mark and Luke, both of which works address themselves primarily to the needs of Gentile churches, it probably originated before the Church bifurcated into Jewish and Gentile parallel streams. In other words, it is not likely that the Jewish-Palestinian colouring of Matthew is due to reaction; it is probably a sign of early date.

And if, behind our Greek Matthew, there lies an Aramaic original, the date of the latter's composition must of course be pushed back behind the date of the Greek version used by Luke and implied by Mark. In fact, *once it is admitted that Matthew is not based on Mark or on Q,* there is a great deal to be said for, and virtually nothing against, the view that it emanated in its Aramaic form from the body of our Lord's own companions before they dispersed beyond the borders of Palestine.[1]

Let us then suppose, for a moment, that St Matthew—whose authorship is usually denied because of the alleged dependence of the

[1] The most recent published study in English of the date and provenance of Matthew is *The Origins of the Gospel according to St Matthew,* by G. D. Kilpatrick (Clarendon Press, 1946). Professor Kilpatrick seeks these origins in a Phoenician Christian community between A.D. 90 and 100, a community that was Greek-speaking and not bi-lingual, yet profoundly Jewish in character, untouched by Paulinism, and

Gospel on Mark—did write the Aramaic version of the Gospel that carries his name. Who would be more likely to clamour for copies of such an invaluable aid to the Christian missioner and preacher than his fellows among 'the Twelve' and other 'ministers of the word'? Each of the original eyewitnesses had his own recollections of those few months of earthly intercourse with our Lord, but experience would soon teach them that memories fade and that discrepancies are to be feared in the accounts given, even by eye-witnesses, of a long and rich series of historical events, particularly when the series includes a wealth of sayings and discourses of a creative Teacher, who taught 'not as the scribes'. We can therefore well imagine the early Christian missionaries, as they went forth from Jerusalem to the rest of Judaea, to Samaria and then farther afield, carrying each his copy of the precious volume, and learning to rely upon it more and more for his repertory of teaching.

Then, in a very few years, the Christian mission and movement begins to take root in Greek-speaking towns and regions. At first the missionaries will be constrained to translate their borrowings from the Aramaic volume impromptu and as occasion dictates, 'as each was able'—to borrow a phrase from a famous fragment of Papias. But here again, how eagerly would they welcome, as soon as it appeared, a complete and authentic translation of the work. Forthwith it would be reproduced in numerous copies, and in the next stage it would be this Greek translation of the Gospel that would give substance to their oral teaching, though (except when they were literally reading from the text) their reproduction would be coloured by their memories of the Aramaic original and of their own previous halting attempts to translate *en courant*. They would not, of course, confine their versions of the incidents of our Lord's life to the meagre mnemonic details preserved in Matthew. St Matthew's brief account, shall we say of the healing of the 'epileptic' boy, would

in close relation (of antagonism) to contemporary Rabbinical Judaism. The book was, he suggests, 'deliberately produced as a pseudonymous work with the approval of the authorities in the community' (p. 140). It will be observed that there is a difference of half a century in the dates assigned by Professor Kilpatrick and myself to Matthew. But it will also be observed that his theory abounds in paradox. He has been driven to it because he accepts without question or criticism the Two-Document hypothesis—of which his conclusions, elaborated with patient thoroughness, may be regarded as a *reductio ad absurdum*.

This is where John 8 comes from

be for them (assuming them to have been eyewitnesses) the Open
Sesame to their own dormant recollections of an event that had
thrilled them to the core. So his short version will be expanded on
their lips, will gain colour and life, will develop like a Japanese
flower in a bowl of water.

At this point it will be noticed that we join forces with Dibelius.
It was once the fashion to maintain that Mark's version of incidents
in our Lord's life was more likely to be original than Matthew's,
because it was fuller and more vivid. But Dibelius would seem to
regard the short 'paradigm' as an earlier type of Christian narrative
than the 'Novellen' with their more secular tone. If so, it is at once
apparent that Matthew with his short and businesslike accounts is
closer to the primitive form of the stories than are many of Mark's
masterpieces of the preaching art.

One thing, however, the preacher will not do. In face of an
audience that is hungry for stories of the great Wonder-worker of
Galilee, he will not put the attention of his hearers to the strain of
listening to long reported sermons, which at best he could only
read, more or less *verbatim*, from his document—since he would
not pretend to be able to remember the sequence and details of
a sermon with the accuracy with which he could recall his own life
being saved by the miraculous stilling of a tempest at sea.

Now, as Streeter says, Mark reads 'like a shorthand account of
a story by an impromptu speaker'. The Christian tradition is that
Mark has preserved for us in written form 'the things preached by
Peter'.

Peter? The suggestion was taken up by Turner,[1] who made
a study of the features of Mark which, in his view, suggest that
St Peter was Mark's source. He goes so far as to say—but it must
be remembered that he writes on the hypothesis of Marcan priority—
that 'while Matthew and Luke write a biography of Christ, Mark
writes down the autobiography, or at least a story based on the
autobiographical reminiscences, of a disciple'. He observes that,
at xi. 21, 'Peter remembered and said...', and asks: 'Who but
Peter would have noted that "Peter *remembered* and said"?' He
further observes that, though of course Mark shows St Peter as
the leader and spokesman of the disciples, it contains also all that

[1] *Catholic and Apostolic*, pp. 183 ff.

the Gospels tell us in disparagement of him;[1] that he rebuked our Lord at Caesarea Philippi and was rebuked by Him; that he presumed to promise loyalty, though all others should fail, and yet alone in set terms denied Him.

The latter point is made much more impressive if we believe that St Peter was using Matthew as his *aide-mémoire*. For in telling the Caesarea Philippi incident he has, in that case, torn out of the story the high praise of himself and the promise of his peculiar status *vis-à-vis* the Church, while leaving the stinging rebuke. And again, he has omitted the incident of the Temple-tribute, which seems to put him into a peculiarly close relation with his Master, and that of his walking on the waters. We can therefore fully accept Turner's 'explanation of this unique feature' of Mark: 'It is St Peter himself, who wished to put on record, side by side with his prerogative, the occasions of his failure'. . . Ought we to wonder that the Prince of the Apostles had learnt the lesson of Christian humility well enough to lay bare not only his strength but his weakness?' He points out that the principal section of ethical teaching in Mark (ix. 33–x. 45) is 'specially concerned with the inculcation of the type of greatness at which the disciples of Christ were to aim. Not riches, not rule and authority. . .but ministry, and reverence for the little ones that believe, and to be not only a servant but the slave of all. Peter had learnt that to be *princeps apostolorum* was not so high a thing as to be *servus servorum Dei*' (*op. cit.* p. 187). And we have learnt that this special admonition to the 'Prince of the Apostles' has been inserted, at Mark ix. 35, into a context which in Matthew is only concerned to give a general lesson on childlikeness to the disciples as a body.

We can further understand that if St Mark 'writes down the autobiography' of St Peter, he must inevitably omit the birth and infancy of our Lord, and begin, as he does, with the ministry of St John the Baptist. Everything fits in, and our hypothesis does justice to both the two sets of evidence. St Peter made use of Matthew as the source-book for his own 'instructions', he selected passages which his own memory could confirm and enlarge upon, he omitted incidents that occurred before he met our Lord, and most of Matthew's discourse-material, as not suitable for his purpose and not such as he could reinforce with a personal and independent

[1] He does not think that John xviii. 10 is meant to be disparaging.

recollection.[1] He altered his Palestinian-Jewish source in various ways to make it more palatable to his Gentile audience, and added one or two brief pieces of teaching or conversation, and one or two incidents independently remembered. And he told the whole story in his inimitable discursive way, in a Greek which is partly Matthew's, partly a reflexion of his own Aramaic mind. He liked to insert the remembered Aramaic word or phrase that worked a cure. He is not literary enough, he is too much aware of the remembered familiarity of Galilee, and he is on too easy colloquial terms with his audience to be over-careful about reverence in expression. It was presumably for the benefit of a Roman audience that he mentions (om. Matthew) that St Simon of Cyrene was the father of Rufus (cf. Rom. xvi. 13) and Alexander.

St Mark, for his part, it would seem, 'made it his one care to omit nothing of what he heard' in these Petrine instructions, 'and to reproduce them faithfully'. But it may well be that he had Matthew in front of him when he came to write out his Gospel, and was thus in a position to check his notes of St Peter's reminiscences.

I have pointed out that the above hypothesis is on a different footing from the results established by the objective documentary criticism on which it is, in part, based. Those results can only be impugned by demolishing the critical arguments on which they rest. As regards the hypothesis itself, I would at least be inclined to adapt some words of the Platonic Socrates in reference to the myth in the *Phaedo*. It might ill beseem a sensible man to affirm definitely that things were so as we have described them; but to affirm that either this or something like this is true may be deemed neither unsuitable nor rash. Ταῦτα ἢ τοιαῦτα. For myself, I suspect, and rather more than suspect, that we have in Mark St Peter's counter-signature to the witness of his fellow-apostle in Matthew.

[1] In relating a dramatic cure he was willing to omit the less interesting of two demoniacs altogether, in order to concentrate on one vivid personality.

EPILOGUE

A clear distinction is needed between the Higher Criticism, which seeks to discover the historical evolution of primitive Christianity, and documentary criticism, which seeks to determine the date, provenance, authorship and sources of a primitive Christian document. And within the field of documentary criticism, it is again necessary to distinguish between the relations linking document to document, as discovered by objective comparison, and the theories of composition built upon those discovered relations. Higher Criticism depends on documentary criticism, and it is an error of method to control the latter by the former—except, indeed, in the last, synthetic, stage of our critico-historical studies. Similarly, the relations discovered between documents by objective comparison of their contents cannot be affected by the improbability of a theory built upon them. It is important to realize that there is nothing so improbable as the actual.

In the first chapters of this study it has been, we maintain, demonstrated that Q is an unnecessary and vicious hypothesis, the comparison of Matthew and Luke in the Q passages and their contexts having disclosed that Luke's direct dependence on Matthew is not only an adequate, but the only adequate, explanation of the data. In the succeeding chapters, still at the same level of documentary comparison, it was sought to show that Matthew is a source of Mark. The theory of composition based upon the latter relationship will seem to many scholars most improbable. But the rejection of the theory will leave the relationship intact, and we venture to suggest that no satisfactory case can be made out against it on its own level of documentary criticism.

It will further be objected that the historical order of theological development is inverted by a solution of the Synoptic Problem that makes Matthew a source of Mark. To this there is a double reply: (a) we must deduce the historical order of theological development from a critical determination of literary sequence, not *vice versa*; (b) many scholars hold that the Epistle to the Galatians is of earlier date than those to the Thessalonians; yet the theological

170

development of the former is far more advanced. The truth is that a speaker or a writer may have far more in his mind than he expresses in word. The parish magazine is not necessarily of earlier date than the *Summa Theologica* of St Thomas.

Finally we may point out that, revolutionary (or reactionary) as the position adopted in this study may appear, adumbrations of various aspects of it may be found in Harnack, Streeter (in the *Oxford Studies*), Burney, Bishop Rawlinson and the Form Critics. It solves the surds left over by the Two-Document hypothesis; while it does justice to what is accurately observed in the analyses of the Form Critics (as opposed to the fantastic deductions drawn by them). It cannot but appear remarkable that so many scholars should have come so near the truth, and yet failed to stumble upon it. It would seem that the priority of Ur-Markus was first propounded as a direct retort to the absurd theory that Mark depends on both Matthew and Luke. Ur-Markus was later discovered to be as illusory a conjecture as we have tried to show its partner, Q (Weisse's *Logian* source), to be; but it was not noticed that when Mark took its place the conditions of the problem of the 'triple tradition' were essentially altered. This inadvertence was assisted by accurate observation of the crude conversational style of Mark, and the theory of Mark's (as opposed to Ur-Markus's) priority was therefore never subjected, in the Classical period of Synoptic criticism, to the test of real documentary comparison, the only decisive criterion in these matters. Once that criterion is loyally and thoroughly applied to the two elements of the Two-Document hypothesis the whole structure crumbles.

INDEX OF
NEW TESTAMENT PASSAGES

INDEX

INDEX

Made in the USA
Lexington, KY
01 October 2014